Foreign Investment and Privatization in Eastern Europe

Also by Patrick Artisien-Maksimenko

MULTINATIONALS IN EASTERN EUROPE

FOREIGN INVESTMENT IN RUSSIA AND OTHER SOVIET SUCCESSOR STATES
(*with Yuri Adjubei*)

FOREIGN INVESTMENT IN CENTRAL AND EASTERN EUROPE
(*with Matija Rojec and Marjan Svetličič*)

NORTH–SOUTH DIRECT INVESTMENT IN THE EUROPEAN COMMUNITIES
(*with Peter J. Buckley*)

MULTINATIONALS AND EMPLOYMENT (*with Peter J. Buckley*)

DIE MULTINATIONALEN UNTERNEHMEN UND DER ARBEITSMARKT
(*with Peter J. Buckley*)

YUGOSLAV MULTINATIONALS ABROAD (*with Carl H. McMillan
and Matija Rojec*)

YUGOSLAVIA TO 1993: Back From the Brink?

JOINT VENTURES IN YUGOSLAV INDUSTRY

Also by Matija Rojec

FOREIGN INVESTMENT IN CENTRAL AND EASTERN EUROPE
(*with Patrick Artisien-Maksimenko and Marjan Svetličič*)

FOREIGN PRIVATISATION IN CENTRAL AND EASTERN EUROPE
(*with John H. Dunning*)

INVESTMENT AMONG DEVELOPING COUNTRIES AND TRANSNATIONAL
CORPORATIONS (*with Marjan Svetličič*)

SLOVENIA'S STRATEGY FOR ACCESSION TO THE EUROPEAN UNION
(*with M. Mrak and J. Potočnik*)

YUGOSLAV MULTINATIONALS ABROAD (*with Patrick Artisien-Maksimenko
and Carl H. McMillan*)

Foreign Investment and Privatization in Eastern Europe

Edited by

Patrick Artisien-Maksimenko
Consultant in International Business

and

Matija Rojec
Senior Research Fellow
Slovene Institute of Macroeconomic Analysis
Ljubljana

This book is dedicated to
Carl (Professor Carl H. McMillan)
our friend and mentor

First published 2001 by
PALGRAVE
Houndmills, Basingstoke, Hampshire RG21 6XS and
175 Fifth Avenue, New York, N. Y. 10010
Companies and representatives throughout the world

PALGRAVE is the new global academic imprint of
St. Martin's Press LLC Scholarly and Reference Division and
Palgrave Publishers Ltd (formerly Macmillan Press Ltd).

ISBN 0–333–64795–5

This book is printed on paper suitable for recycling and made from fully managed and sustained forest sources.

A catalogue record for this book is available from the British Library.

Library of Congress Cataloging-in-Publication Data
Foreign investment and privatization in Eastern Europe / edited by Patrick Artisien-Maksimenko and Matija Rojec.
    p. cm.
Includes bibliographical references and index.
ISBN 0–333–64795–5 (cloth) ✓
    1. Investments, Foreign—Europe, Eastern. 2. Privatization—
—Europe, Eastern. I. Artisien-Maksimenko, Patrick, 1951–
II. Rojec, Matija.
HG5430.7.A3 F666 2001
332.67'3'0947—dc21
                                                        00–046874

10 9 8 7 6 5 4 3 2 1
10 09 08 07 06 05 04 03 02 01

Printed and bound in Great Britain by
Antony Rowe Ltd, Chippenham, Wiltshire

Contents

v

List of Tables

List of Figures

Preface

This book is the fourth in a series of manuscripts on foreign investment in Central and Eastern Europe, published by Palgrave (Macmillan).[1]

PATRICK ARTISIEN-MAKSIMENKO
MATIJA ROJEC

---

1. Previous books in this series included *Multinationals in Eastern Europe*, edited by Patrick Artisien-Maksimenko, 2000; *Foreign Investment in Russia and Other Soviet Successor States*, edited by Patrick Artisien-Maksimenko and Yuri Adjubei, 1996; and *Foreign Investment in Central and Eastern Europe*, edited by Patrick Artisien-Maksimenko, Matija Rojec and Marjan Svetličič, 1993.

Notes on the Editors and the Contributors

The Editors

Patrick Artisien-Maksimenko is a Partner in the Consultancy Firm P.A. & G.M. Investments, specializing in economic and political risk analysis in Central and Eastern Europe.

Dr Artisien-Maksimenko has worked in the field of East European Business for twenty-five years. During this period he has acted as Consultant to the International Finance Corporation, the Organization for Economic Cooperation and Development, *The Economist*, the Soros Foundation, Oxford Analytica and a number of multinational corporations.

He has authored and edited ten books on International Business and taught at undergraduate, postgraduate and post-experience levels in Europe, North America, South-East Asia and Southern Africa.

Dr Artisien-Maksimenko also teaches International Business at the University of Cardiff, UK.

Matija Rojec is Assistant Professor in the Economics Faculty at Ljubljana University. He also acts as Adviser to the Slovene Government's Institute for Macroeconomic Analysis.

Dr Rojec has taken part in some twenty research projects funded by the United Nations, the European Union, the Organization for Economic Cooperation and Development and *The Economist*.

He has authored numerous journal articles and research papers. His recent books include *Foreign Investment in Central and Eastern Europe* (with Patrick Artisien-Maksimenko and Marjan Svetličič), *Foreign Privatization in Central and Eastern Europe* (with John H. Dunning) and *Slovenia's Strategy for Accession to the European Union* (with M. Mrak and J. Potočnik).

The Contributors

Yuri Adjubei is a member of the Trade Division of the United Nations Economic Commission for Europe in Geneva.

John H. Dunning is Emeritus Professor of International Business at the University of Reading, and State of New Jersey Professor of International Business at Rutgers University.

Vitalija Gaucaite is a member of the Economic Analysis Division of the United Nations Economic Commission for Europe in Geneva.

Philip Hanson is Professor of Economics at the Centre for Russian and East European Studies at the University of Birmingham.

Gabor Hunya is a Research Economist at the Institute for Comparative Economic Studies in Vienna.

Maria Illes is Professor of Applied Economics at the University of Budapest.

Wladyslaw Jermakowicz is Professor of Business at the University of Southern Indiana in Evansville.

Klaus Meyer is Associate Professor in the Centre for East European Studies at the Copenhagen Business School.

Alena Zemplinerova is Professor of Economics at the Centre for Economic Research and Graduate Education at Charles University, Prague.

Part I
Contextual Aspects

1
Foreign Investment and Privatization in Eastern Europe: An Overview

Patrick Artisien-Maksimenko and Matija Rojec

Introduction

Privatization, with its ultimate objective of raising economic efficiency, is a process central to the transformation of the economies of Central and Eastern Europe (CEE). It represents more than just a transfer of ownership from the state/social to the private sector; it also forms the basis for the transformation of the former socialist economies. In the first phase, the emphasis was on nationwide privatisation schemes where noncommercial methods of privatization of state/social assets by indigenous private owners prevailed – free distribution, preferential financial schemes and buy-outs. In phase two the emphasis has shifted towards increasing the efficiency of the CEE economies: here, the objective has been to consolidate the ownership structure set up in phase one. The major actors in this phase consist of small shareholders and investment funds operating as sellers and of financial and strategic investors acting as buyers. The first phase of the privatization process was not expected to contribute much to economic efficiency. Only in the second phase would privatisation bring about 'responsible' owners with the objectives of improving company profits, efficiency and long-term development. A specific advantage of foreign direct investment (FDI) as an instrument of privatisation in CEE is that it provides active and 'responsible' owners, who can make an immediate input to the host's economic efficiency, internationalization and integration in the world economy. FDI is intended to bring in foreign entrepreneurs with higher levels of motivation prompted by new opportunities for company expansion and diversification. By bringing in a package of machinery, equipment, technology, managerial and marketing techniques, foreign investors can facilitate the transition of the former socialist economies and their reintegration into the world economy.[1]

The perception of FDI in CEE and more precisely that of foreign privatiz-ation has been shrouded in emotional prejudice and daily political needs and is often remote from rational economic considerations. This makes official

3

(government, parliament) and public attitudes towards FDI rather divergent: illusions, on the one hand, that FDI can solve major economic shortcomings at a stroke, and fears, on the other, that national interests – particularly in the public sector utilities – may be sold out to foreign interests.[2]

The aim of this introductory chapter is to examine the role of FDI in privatization in CEE, with particular reference to the Czech Republic, Hungary, Poland and Slovenia. The four 'sample' countries are the most developed of the transition economies: they have gone farthest in opening up their domestic markets to foreign competition and have been the most successful in attracting foreign investors.

Methodology

Data on FDI in CEE are mostly limited to a sectoral, industrial and investing country distribution. Reliable and systematic official data on privatization through FDI are also lacking. Therefore, we opted for the direct approach to CEE companies privatized by strategic foreign investors. The survey in this chapter is based on questionnaires addressed mainly to large companies in the Czech Republic, Hungary, Poland and Slovenia. Of the 370 companies targeted, 75 either responded to the questionnaire or agreed to be interviewed, thus providing a response rate of 19.4 per cent.

The questionnaire and the interviews

The questionnaire was designed to obtain an in-depth insight of all aspects of foreign privatization operations, both from the host country/target company and foreign investor (parent company) viewpoints. The questionnaire consists of four major parts. The first deals with general information on acquired CEE and foreign parent companies. Part II examines the pre-acquisition stage, namely company motivation, entry strategy and pre-acquisition strategies. Part III addresses the acquisition stage (bidding and major elements of the acquisition). Part IV considers the post-acquisition stage, including the changes introduced by the foreign parent, the operational aspects of the acquired company, the balance of payments, the technological and research and development (R&D) implications as well as the restructuring and development impact of foreign acquisitions on the host country.

An examination of the questionnaire reveals the use of both open-ended and selective questions. The open-ended approach was used to minimize the level of constraint on respondents and give them the opportunity to answer all relevant issues at length. The selective method consisted of multiple-choice questions and Yes/No answers and was used to ensure the comparability and completeness of responses.

Profile of sample target companies

The 75 sample companies privatized through foreign acquisitions had combined annual sales of $2019.9 million (mn) in 1993 (ranging from $1.5 mn for a Czech company to $229.4 mn in a Hungarian company), total equity of $1420.8 mn (ranging from $80 000 in a Czech company to $220.6 mn in a Hungarian firm) and total foreign equity of $943.3 mn. The latter makes up a representative proportion of FDI in the four countries: foreign equity ranges from $10 000 in a Polish company to $68.4 mn in a Hungarian company, with an average of $12.7 mn per company. Employment in the sample companies totals 49 433: the smallest company is Polish and employs 3; the largest workforce of 6500 is employed by a Hungarian company (see Table 1.1). Forty-six per cent of sample companies employ more than 500 people, while those employing less than 10 people represent only 6.8 per cent of our sample. The smallest companies overall are Polish[3] and the largest Slovene.[4]

This is mostly the consequence of different sampling techniques: Slovene and Hungarian samples are concentrated in larger foreign privatizations than their Czech and Polish counterparts. The below average size of Polish sample companies indicates the spontaneity of Poland's development: the majority of Polish firms are small businesses, restructured and downsized during the last few years preceding acquisitions. The above average size of Slovene foreign privatizations is due mostly to that country's privatization concept: almost all small and medium sized companies have opted to privatize through internal buy-outs and stay beyond the reach of foreign investors.

The majority of sample companies are engaged in multi-business operations, with the manufacturing sector taking the dominant position. More

Table 1.1 Basic characteristics of sample companies in the Czech Republic, Hungary, Slovenia and Poland

Country		Annual sales ($mn)	Total equity ($mn)	Foreign equity ($mn)	Foreign share (%)	Employment
Czech Rep.	Total	512.9	351.7	255.2	72.5	15 306
(23 companies)	Mean	23.3	16.0	11.6	–	695
Hungary	Total	644.8	434.2	205.1	47.2	18 400
(14 companies)	Mean	46.1	31.0	14.7	–	1 314
Slovenia	Total	373.0	473.4	364.9	77.1	9 314
(10 companies)	Mean	62.7	47.3	36.5	–	931
Poland	Total	489.2	161.5	118.1	73.1	6 413
(28 companies)	Mean	17.5	5.7	4.2	–	229
Total	Total	2 019.9	1 420.8	943.3	66.4	49 433
(75 companies)	Mean	27.3	19.2	12.7	–	668

[1] Not all companies provided data on all variables in the table. The mean for each variable is calculated only for companies which gave the appropriate data.
Source: Authors' survey.

than 80 per cent of acquired sample companies are engaged in manufacturing: 13 companies are in chemicals, petrochemicals, rubber and plastics, eight in non-metallic mineral products, six in food, beverages and tobacco, six in fabricated metal products and six in transport equipment (see Table 1.2). The sample's sectoral distribution closely reflects the general sectoral distribution of FDI in CEE.

Profile of sample foreign parents

Sample foreign investors originate from 13 countries: Germany is the main source (21), followed by Austria (11), the USA (8) and France (6) (see Table 1.3), This country distribution also reflects the overall geographical distribution of foreign investors in CEE. Thirty-eight foreign parent companies (see Table 1.4) have total annual sales of $484.1 bn (billion), ranging between $25 mn and $125 bn. The average sales of sample foreign parent companies are the highest in Poland ($21.3 bn) and the lowest in Slovenia and Hungary ($1.1 bn and $2.1 bn respectively).

The majority of sample foreign parent companies are engaged in multi-country activities: the number of foreign subsidiaries per parent company ranges from 2 to 150. The largest number of subsidiaries are based in Poland; the lowest in Hungary. Inter-country comparisons also indicate that sample foreign parent companies with the largest experience of CEE are based in Slovenia and Hungary, whose economies have had the longest exposure to market reforms.

The data on employment are available for 49 foreign sample companies. The lowest number of employees is 41 and the highest 373 000. Employment in the sample CEE companies ranges from 0.3 per cent to 57.1 per cent of the foreign parent companies' total employment; on average it amounts to 4.0 per cent, the highest being in the Czech Republic, followed by Hungary, Poland and Slovenia.

In sum, the sample foreign parent companies tend to be large multinational enterprises (MNEs), which is not typical of foreign investors in CEE. The advantage of such a sample is that our interviews of larger foreign investors provide insights into more relevant categories of foreign investors in CEE. It is also likely that, on average, foreign investors are larger in the case of the acquisitions, which form the basis of this survey, than in greenfield investments.

Foreign privatization in Central and Eastern Europe

Foreign privatization as an FDI structure

Once a foreign company has decided in favour of FDI, its next step is to select the most appropriate FDI structure. The selection, to a large degree, depends on the investor's motive and on the industry's characteristics. In

Table 1.2 Sectoral distribution of sample target companies(%)

ISIC* code	Description	Czech Republic	Hungary	Slovenia	Poland	Total
1	Agriculture	–	–	–	5.7	2.5
31	Food, beverages & tobacco	4.5	23.1	10.0	2.8	7.5
32	Textile, wearing apparel & leather	–	7.7	–	8.5	5.0
33	Wood products	–	–	–	8.5	3.8
34	Paper products	4.5	–	20.0	2.8	5.0
35	Chemicals, rubber & plastics	18.2	–	30.0	17.1	16.3
36	Non-metal products	4.5	15.4	20.0	8.5	10.0
37	Basic metal industries	9.1	15.4	–	2.8	6.3
381	Fabricated metal products	13.6	–	–	8.5	7.5
382	Machinery, except electrical	18.2	–	–	2.8	6.3
383	Electrical machinery	–	7.7	20.0	5.7	6.3
384	Transport equipment	9.1	7.7	–	8.5	7.5
385	Professional equipment	4.5	7.7	–	2.8	3.8
5	Construction	4.5	7.7	–	2.8	3.8
6	Trade & Tourism	9.1	–	–	5.7	5.0
7	Transport	–	7.7	–	2.8	2.5
8	Finance & Insurance	–	–	–	2.8	1.3
Total	(%)	100	100	100	100	100
		= 22	= 14	= 10	= 28	= 74
		companies	companies	companies	companies	companies

* International standard industrial classification

†The sum total is higher than 100 because some sample companies reported more than one activity

Source: Authors' survey.

Table 1.3   Countries of origin of foreign parents in sample (%)

Country	Czech Republic	Hungary	Slovenia	Poland	Total
Germany	31.8	7.1	50.0	28.6	28.4
United States	18.2	–	–	14.3	10.8
Great Britain	4.5	7.1	–	10.7	6.8
Switzerland	4.5	–	10.0	10.7	6.8
Austria	9.1	28.6	30.0	7.1	14.9
France	13.6	7.1	–	7.1	8.1
Netherlands	9.1	–	–	7.1	5.4
Sweden	4.5	7.1	–	7.1	5.4
Denmark	–	–	–	3.6	1.4
Japan	–	–	–	3.6	1.4
Italy	4.5	14.3	10.0	–	5.4
Russia	–	14.3	–	–	2.7
Belgium	–	14.3	–	–	2.7
Total (%)	100	100	100	100	100
	= 22 companies	= 14 companies	= 10 companies	= 28 companies	= 74 companies

Source: Authors' survey.

principle, no mode is better or worse than any other: the final decision often depends on individual intentions and circumstances.

The first issue in this respect is the choice between a greenfield investment and the acquisition of an existing local company. In the case of the CEE countries the choice is between 'privatization and greenfield' ventures. FDI implies privatization where the acquisition or the partnership involves a local company (directly or indirectly) in state ownership, that is (a) the partial or full acquisition of a state-owned company, (b) additional investment (recapitalization) in a state-owned company, and (c) a joint venture with a state-owned company. The first method could be labelled a direct foreign acquisition/privatization; the second and third indirect foreign acquisitions or privatization. In the CEE countries, FDI will be closely linked to privatization until such time as the privatization process has substantially changed the ownership structure of the economies. FDI in CEE does not imply privatization only if FDI is in the form of a newly established wholly foreign-owned subsidiary or if a privately owned company acts as a local partner/target company. Major factors affecting the foreign investor's choice between 'privatization and greenfield' include:

- *Labour versus capital-intensive factors*: The more capital-intensive the industry, the higher the cost of a greenfield venture as opposed to

Table 1.4 Basic characteristics of sample foreign companies

Country	Annual sales ($mn)	Number of foreign subsidiaries	Years of activity in CEE	Years of activity in host country	Employment
Czech rep. (12 companies)					
Total	164 490	255	36	30	41 809
Mean[1]	13 708	13.4	3.3	2.5	3 484
% of acquired company in foreign parent company[2]	0.17	–	–	–	19.9
Hungary (7 companies)					
Total	15 098	54	68	67	84 800
Mean	2 156	6.0	5.2	5.1	12 114
% of acquired company in foreign parent company	2.1	–	–	–	10.8
Slovenia (6 companies)					
Total	6 604.7	130	77	77	383 964
Mean	1 100.8	14.4	8.5	8.5	95 856
% of acquired company in foreign parent company	5.7	–	–	–	1.0

Table 1.4 Basic characteristics of sample foreign companies (continued)

Country	Annual sales ($mn)	Number of foreign subsidiaries	Years of activity in CEE	Years of activity in host country	Employment
Poland (13 companies)					
Total	297 871	771	53	47	125 475
Mean	21 276	40.6	4.2	3.6	9 652
% of acquired company in foreign parent company	0.01	–	–	–	4.2
Total (38 companies)					
Total	484 071.7	1 210	234	221	636 048
Mean	12 738	31.8	6.2	5.8	16 738
% of acquired company in foreign parent company	0.21	–	–	–	4.0

[1] Not all companies provided data on all variables in the table. The mean for each variable is calculated only for companies that gave the appropriate data.

[2] Share of acquired sample CEE companies' mean in their foreign parent companies' mean.

Source: Authors' survey.

privatization. The more labour intensive the industry, the higher the cost of privatization due to the over-employment problem.

- *Market share*: If the foreign investor's product is already widely known, a greenfield may be as viable as privatization; if the local producer has a strong market share and local brand recognition, the foreign investor may opt to tap into this strength via privatization.

- *Local supply and distribution networks*: The well-developed supply and distribution network of a local producer could be a strong argument for the 'privatization route'.

- *Potential restructuring costs*: The costs of restructuring the target company could prove to be higher than the establishment of new capacity.

- *Ownership status and restitution*: Unresolved ownership status due to a restitution process could be an important argument against the 'privatization route' (Gatling and Reed 1992).

Foreign privatization (acquisitions) in FDI inflows in CEE

A sample of 294 privatizations in CEE collected by Sader (1993) shows that the CEE countries have generated some 85 per cent of total FDI inflows through foreign privatizations. The figure includes not only direct but also indirect acquisitions in the form of joint ventures. Host country data, which generally only include direct sales to foreign investors, offer much lower estimates:

- In the Czech Republic over a third of foreign investments were made in companies privatized within the large-scale privatization scheme.
- In Hungary, between 50 and 60 per cent of FDI stock at end 1992 was accounted for by foreign privatizations (Böhm and Simoneti 1993, p. 147; Facts about Hungarian Privatization, 1990 to 1992, 1993). A more recent estimate reduced the share of FDI used for the purchase of companies via privatization to 40 per cent and increased the share of greenfield FDI to 60 per cent.
- Of $2150 mn of total foreign investment in Poland at end 1992, $1350 mn (62.8 per cent) was used as a privatization vehicle for Polish state-owned enterprises, mostly ($1 bn) indirectly via joint venture acquisitions (Jermakowicz 1993).
- In Slovenia a third of existing FDI stock came into the country via the direct sales of non-privatized companies to strategic foreign investors. The remainder is accounted for by joint venture acquisitions, that is joint ventures between parts of non-privatized local companies and foreign investors.

Table 1.5 illustrates major changes in individual forms of FDI in CEE: while the ratio of FDI stock in direct acquisitions and greenfield investments has increased, that of joint ventures (mostly joint venture acquisitions) has

Table 1.5   Distribution of FDI entities in CEE according to the form of FDI (1988–92)

Year	Greenfield FDIs (%)	Joint ventures (%)	Direct acquisitions (%)	Total $mn	%
1988	2.5	93.3	4.1	808	100.0
1989	9.4	64.6	25.8	2 507	100.0
1990	22.2	53.8	24.0	5 150	100.0
1991	22.3	46.5	31.3	10 120	100.0
1992	31.2	30.0	38.7	15 155	100.0

Source: Authors' survey.

decreased. In 1988–89, the joint venture was the most attractive way of improving the financial condition of state-owned enterprises. By 1992, direct privatization and greenfield opportunities had become more plentiful and attractive.

When analysing foreign acquisitions (privatization) as an entry mode into CEE, we should also distinguish between the number of FDI entities and the value of FDI inflows. The prevalence of direct and indirect acquisitions (privatizations) in value terms is in sharp contrast to the dominance of greenfield FDI in terms of numbers of FDI entities. In Poland, for example, in 1993 there were 10 738 (92.9 per cent) greenfield investments but only 815 (7.1 per cent) acquisitions. However, total FDI inflows in greenfield investments was lower ($840.2 mn) than in acquisitions ($969.7 mn). Clearly, the average investment in acquisitions is much higher than in greenfield investments. But, even in the case of acquisitions, we found a high concentration of invested foreign capital in a small number of large acquisitions. The Czech Republic, Poland and Slovenia have a large number of small, even marginal, greenfield FDI entities established 'just in case' or on a 'wait and see' basis. Therefore, the foreign investor's size and commitments to the host country do seem to affect the choice between privatization and greenfield. If the investor is a large company with strong commitments to the local market, the tendency will be to acquire local firms. By contrast, foreign investors unwilling to commit large funds prefer the greenfield strategy. Thus a greenfield investment allows the uncommitted investor to start a venture in CEE with minimal capital and risk requirements.

A pattern emerges in Poland: in the case of FDI from the European Union (EU), two-thirds of all investment are made through the acquisition of existing businesses and only one-third via greenfield allocations. With FDI from the rest of the world, the proportions are reversed: two-thirds of FDI are in the form of greenfield investments. Geographical proximity also seems to favour acquisitions.

Foreign investors' reasons for preferring acquisitions (privatization) to greenfields

The most common reasons for choosing privatization in preference to the greenfield route in CEE normally include 'purchasing a market share' and 'tapping existing distribution channels'. In some cases 'purchasing specific technology' was also mentioned. On the other hand, foreign investors who opted for greenfield investment listed among their priorities a clear assessment of the results of business activity arising from joint investments; influence over the new company's strategy; reductions in costs; the introduction of a new production programme; modernization and technological innovation. In short, foreign investors who were significantly concerned about potential restructuring costs preferred greenfield investments (Business International and Creditanstalt 1993).

In order to assess the most important factors in the choice of entry, we asked the sample companies to list the reasons for such a choice. The motives are dominated by the acquisition of specific advantages in the target company. These included market considerations, strategic factors, previous cooperation between the target and foreign parent companies and good opportunities. The relative importance of those factors is shown in Table 1.6.

Foreign privatization through direct sales and joint venture acquisitions

Foreign privatizations mostly take the form of direct sales of companies to strategic foreign investors. Direct sales have, from a host country viewpoint, some distinct advantages as a privatization method:

1 It can have a significant and rapid impact on the restructuring and efficiency of the acquired company. Other issues of importance include job preservation and the additional inflow of FDI following foreign privatization.
2 A direct sale can also be applied in conditions of undeveloped capital markets, which still prevail in CEE.
3 A direct sale does not require extensive and costly governmental administration specialized in surveying the privatization process.
4 The lack of adequate and reliable accountancy information (financial audits) does not prevent direct sale transactions from being completed, although it does, to a certain extent, have a restraining impact by delaying their completion.
5 A direct sale can act as a relatively uncomplicated way of attracting strategic investors (buyers), who usually are traditional partners of the target company seeking to acquire a controlling share in the company. From this perspective, a direct sale may be viewed as an effective means of acquiring a fresh infusion of capital, technology and managerial expertise.

Table 1.6   Factors determining the choice of market entry: survey results

| Factors | Level of importance (max. 3; min:1)[1] | | | | |
	Czech Rep.	Hungary	Slovenia	Poland	Total
(1) Acquired company's local market share	2.0	2.2	2.1	2.0	2.1
(2) Acquired company's export markets' share	1.4	1.7	1.9	1.3	1.5
(3) Acquired company's distribution network	1.6	1.8	1.6	1.9	1.7
(4) Acquired company's trademark/brand name	1.6	1.9	1.1	1.6	1.6
(5) Acquired company's supply network	1.5	1.4	1.1	1.1	1.3
(6) Advantage of acquired company's integration into the local economy	1.9	1.8	1.1	2.0	1.9
(7) Suitability of acquired company	2.2	2.4	2.9	2.3	2.4
(8) Favourable price of the acquired company	1.8	1.8	1.8	1.8	1.8
(9) Acquisition price plus restructuring costs lower than greenfield investment	2.4	2.2	2.5	2.5	2.4
(10) Capital intensity of the activity	1.5	2.0	1.4	1.6	1.6
(11) Simple privatization procedure	1.3	1.7	1.0	1.4	1.3

[1] Average scores were derived as follows: (3) very important, (2) important (1) unimportant.
Source: Authors' survey.

6   The direct sale type of privatization generates revenue for the seller (the state), although this is not the key objective of privatization in CEE.

The direct sale seems to be an appropriate technique of privatization in CEE. However, the direct sale of companies to strategic (foreign) investors cannot be used on a broad scale as a method of speedy privatization of the entire economy. Direct sale arrangements tend to be complex and involve price, financial and commercial acquisition arrangements, further investment and development, adequate guarantees, employment issues, a marketing strategy, preserving the company's identity and ensuring minority shareholders' rights. Individual direct sale transactions have their own specificities with regard to the conditions and needs of the company as well as investors' aspirations.

The direct sale to a strategic foreign investor is particularly suitable where new technology, new markets, know-how and input supplies are required for the company's survival and further development. Of particular significance is the impact of the strategic investor's capital infusion on the target company's operations. Direct sales in the privatization process are most relevant to large and medium-sized companies (see Jašovic 1993; Korze and Simoneti 1992 and K. Szabo 1992).

Direct sales can be implemented through share deals or asset deals. With the former, the strategic investor acquires the majority (controlling) equity share. A similar goal can be achieved through an asset deal, that is by buying the target company's assets, which are then used by the strategic investor to continue operations in the new wholly foreign-owned or joint company. The asset deal has a number of advantages for a foreign investor:

- The object of the purchase is to gain those assets that are necessary for a particular activity; the outstanding assets remain in the existing company.
- The employees stay on with the old company; hence, the new owner does not encounter over-employment problems (the investor hires only as many workers as necessary).
- The transaction bypasses the possibility of taking on hidden responsibilities and losses, especially in the absence of a proper financial audit or of the revision of the company's legal status.
- The assets purchased are newly evaluated, which results in higher depreciation and has tax implications.
- In the case of a joint venture acquisition, where local assets act as the host partner's equity contribution to a joint venture, newly invested foreign capital does not go to the appropriate state agency (as in an acquisition) but remains within the newly formed company.

From the foreign investor's viewpoint, the joint venture acquisition realizes the same objectives as the asset deal. The joint venture acquisition has the status of a new legal entity and is formed by part of the existing local company (its assets) and the new capital invested by the strategic foreign investor. In an asset deal, the foreign investor only buys the assets necessary for a given activity, while in the case of a joint venture acquisition, the local partner contributes only that part of total assets that are necessary for the required activity.

One of the foreign investor's main concerns in a joint venture acquisition is to prevent the non-privatized local partner in the joint venture from being taken over by a competitor. This concern is usually resolved by a contractual clause giving the foreign investor a pre-emptive right to the local partner's share in the joint venture.

From the target company's viewpoint, the major concern in an asset deal and joint venture acquisition is the possibility that only the best parts of the company are privatized by the strategic (foreign) investor, while problems of over-employment and unsettled claims remain, to a large extent, with the non-privatized part.

Table 1.7, which shows the distribution of sample acquired companies by type of acquisition, confirms that joint venture acquisitions are the most frequent mode of market penetration in CEE (56.6 per cent), followed by share acquisitions (28.9 per cent). The exception is Hungary, where equity increasing was used in just under half of the sample companies.[5]

Asset acquisitions are almost absent from our sample (only 2 cases). The preference for joint venture acquisitions stems partly from legal reasons: prior to the transition, joint venture acquisitions were frequently the only legally permissible type of foreign capital engagement in CEE.

The reasons listed in Table 1.8 for choosing a joint venture acquisition confirm the general trends in the literature. The two most important reasons are that joint venture acquisitions were the only form of market entry at the time (average score 2.2) and provided the advantages of setting up a new company (2.3). The latter was stressed by smaller companies, which seemed more concerned about starting up new businesses and establishing themselves on the market than larger firms. In addition, foreign parents mentioned the advantages of having a local partner that reduces risk and has local expertise, and the potential for gaining control of a company with a smaller investment (2.0). Both foreign parents and acquired firms stressed the importance of purchasing money staying in the acquired company (2.0). Conversely, interviewees gave a low ranking to acquiring the interesting parts of a target company (1.5) and avoiding hidden liabilities and debts (1.5). These two factors are positively correlated with company size (the first measured by foreign equity: $r = .415$ and the second by total equity: $r = .469$). Larger companies seemed to have a better understanding of the advantages of joint venture acquisitions.

Foreign privatization in the overall privatization process of CEE countries

Data on the share of foreign privatization in total privatization are mostly restricted to the ratio of revenues from foreign privatization to total privatization. This raises several drawbacks: (*a*) the revenue generated is not the most important objective of mass privatization schemes in CEE; and (*b*) a large segment of privatization in most CEE countries consists of free distribution or buy-outs with considerable discounts and limited revenue generation from which foreigners are generally excluded. Therefore, the data on revenue overestimate the actual share of foreign privatization in total privatization.

A sample of 294 privatization transactions in CEE for the period 1988–92 with a sales value of $5.7 bn (Hungary: 141 transactions worth $2.5 bn; the

Table 1.7 Types of acquisitions: survey results (%)

Types of acquisition	Czech Rep.	Hungary	Slovenia	Poland	Total
(1) Joint venture acquisition	54.5	37.5	60.0	67.9	56.6
(2) Share acquisition	36.4	12.5	40.0	28.6	28.9
(3) Asset acquisition	–	6.3	–	3.6	2.6
(4) Equity increasing	9.1	43.8	–	–	11.8
Total (%)	100	100	100	100	100
(number)	=22	=14	=10	=28	=74
	companies	companies	companies	companies	companies

Source: Authors' survey.

Table 1.8　Factors leading to joint venture acquisition: survey results

Factors	Level of importance (max: 3; min: 1)[1]				
	Czech Rep.	*Hungary*	*Slovenia*	*Poland*	*Total*
(1) The only type allowed	2.0	1.4	2.8	2.7	2.2
(2) Advantages of having a local partner[2]	1.9	1.4	2.3	2.1	2.0
(3) Acquisition of only interesting parts of the acquired company*	1.5	1.4	1.8	1.2	1.5
(4) Avoiding risk of hidden liabilities and debt**	1.4	1.3	1.5	1.4	1.5
(5) Purchasing money stays in the acquired company	2.3	1.6	1.3	2.0	2.0
(6) Avoiding legal and administrative problems	1.6	1.1	1.2	1.4	1.5
(7) Advantages of being a new company***	2.5	1.5	1.0	2.8	2.3

Correlations:
* with sales (r = .419 Sig. 005); with equity (r = .415 Sig. 020)
** with total equity (r = .469 Sig. 001); with employment (r = .383 Sig. 007)
*** with sales (r = −.343 Sig. 023); with total equity (r = −.405 Sig. 004); with foreign equity (r = −.644 Sig. 000); with employment (r = −.330 Sig. 021)
[1] Average scores were derived as follows: (3) very important; (2) important; (1) unimportant.
[2] Risk sharing, lower capital exposure, 'local' expertise, connection and image.
Source: Authors' survey.

former Czechoslavakia: 55 transactions worth $1.9 bn; Poland: 67 transactions worth $0.7 bn) shows that foreign investors were instrumental in the privatization of 194 companies, for which they paid $5.3 bn, or over 90 per cent of total privatization revenues generated by the privatization of sample companies (Sader 1993). According to this source the major reason for such a high level of foreign participation is the fundamental lack of domestic savings. Sader's database, however, includes only 'pay-out' privatization and larger privatization projects, where foreign investors are over-represented. This explains why individual countries' data do not support his high estimates of foreign privatizations in total privatization revenues.

In the Czech Republic the privatization process was divided into 'small-scale' and 'large-scale' schemes. In order to expedite the transfer of ownership to the private sector, the authorities used voucher privatization to encourage private individuals to bid for state enterprise assets. About one-third of national assets have been distributed through voucher privatisations.[6]

Foreign participation in the Czech privatization process was, in principle, confined to large-scale privatization covering some 4000 of the Czech

Republic's largest state-owned enterprises, including financial institutions, insurance companies, state farms, industrial enterprises and foreign trade organizations. Projects with foreign participation were subject to particular scrutiny and could be highly controversial, as they generally involved the best enterprises. In evaluating projects with foreign investment, specific attention was devoted to both the deal structure (debt versus equity, plans to increase equity) and employment and environmental issues.

As of 1993 a total of 315 privatization projects with proposed foreign participation had been negotiated in the Czech Republic. Of these, 146 were approved with a total asset value to be sold to foreign investors of 25 bn Crowns. Up to the end of 1992, privatization projects with foreign participation represented only 1.2 per cent of all large-scale privatization projects submitted; however, foreign participation was the source of 52 per cent (21 658 m Crowns or $754.6 m at 1992 exchange rates) of all the Property Fund's proceeds from large-scale privatization. Clearly, foreign investors are, on average, engaged in much larger privatizations than their domestic counterparts. Future foreign investment flows are likely to become an increasingly important factor in company restructuring.

Unlike the Czech Republic, Poland and Slovenia, Hungary has not introduced a preferential scheme for residents and domestic investors in privatization. Foreign investors fall under the same regulations as all other participants in privatization. Only in cases of equal offers will priority be given to certain categories of resident investors.[7]

Hungary's 1990 privatization strategy put the accent on speeding up privatization on a business basis and on the prompt settlement of sales. As there were few significant domestic savings, openings had to be made to foreign investors. By the end of 1994, some 50 per cent of all state property was targeted for privatization, with foreign participation reaching 30–35 per cent (Ministry of Foreign Affairs 1991). Thus, Hungary is the only CEE country with a really significant share of foreign capital in total privatization. In 1990, 1991 and to a lesser extent in 1992, foreign investors dominated Hungarian privatization.

The Polish privatization concept is based on a multi-track approach and includes (*a*) commercialization followed by privatization; (*b*) privatization through liquidation; (*c*) FDI through joint ventures with state-owned companies; (*d*) reprivatization (restitution) and (*e*) small-scale privatization. Foreign investors can participate in the first three methods. The implementation of Poland's privatization programme and the participation of foreign capital, although impressive in quantitative terms, fell behind original forecasts. Most foreign capital came in via joint ventures with state-owned enterprises (SOEs), which could only broadly be treated as a privatization method.[8]

Commercialized companies[9] in Poland can be privatized along one of four methods: by direct sale, initial public offering, mass privatization and privatization through restructuring. The direct sale method, in which buyers take a majority holding at a price negotiated with the Ministry of Privatization, is ideally suited for foreign investors; companies privatized in this manner fall into the most attractive sectors of Poland's manufacturing industry. The average firm sold to foreign investors in the framework of a direct sale was seven times as large as that sold to Polish citizens.

Initial Public Offerings (IPOs)[10] have not been as attractive to foreign investors. Of $213.2 m of shares distributed through IPOs by mid-1993, foreign investors accounted for a mere 8.9 per cent.

Foreign participation in the Mass Privatization Programme was initially in the form of foreign management groups hired by National Investment Funds – which were set up to manage the shares of some 600 State Treasury corporations. Subsequently, foreign investors took over companies to be privatized under the Mass Privatization Programme.

Privatization through restructuring started as late as September 1993. By the end of 1993 eleven firms had entered the programme, and five management groups were established exclusively by foreigners or with foreign partners (Jermakowicz, Jermakowicz and Konska 1993).

Slovenia's privatization concept has consisted of the free distribution of shares (each Slovene citizen received an ownership certificate with a nominal value of between 4000 and 6000 DM, depending on age, which could be exchanged for the shares of privatized companies) and commercial privatization. The Law on Ownership Transformation of Enterprises provides for several methods of privatization: (*a*) the free transfer of ordinary shares to the Compensation/Restitution Fund (10 per cent), the Pension Fund (10 per cent) and the Development Fund (20 per cent); (*b*) the internal distribution of shares to employees in exchange for ownership certificates; (*c*) the internal buy-out of shares; (*d*) the sale of company shares at public offerings, public auctions or tenders. The total value of 2157 Slovene enterprises to be privatized under the Law on Ownership Transformation of Enterprises was approximately $8.4 bn (Agency for Restructuring and Privatization of the Republic of Slovenia data). The total foreign stock of enterprises privatized by foreign acquisitions at the end of 1993 was approximately $250 m, or less than 3 per cent of the value of enterprises to be privatized. If joint venture acquisitions are added, the share still does not surpass 6.0 per cent.

All major foreign acquisitions in Slovenia were carried out before the current privatization law was adopted. Although the law does not prevent foreign participation in the privatization process of any Slovene company, the free distribution of 'ownership certificates' to residents and discounts to employees in internal buy-outs did not encourage Slovene companies to include foreign investors in the privatization process.

Two sets of conclusions seem appropriate at this stage: first, in spite of the relatively high foreign involvement in the large-scale privatization of

CEE companies, foreign privatizations have not played a major role in mass privatization schemes. Foreign investors have restricted their purchases of companies to a narrow range of industries such as consumer goods, including tobacco products, automobile production, the paper industry and power generating and telecommunications equipment (UNECE 1993a).

Second, in countries with mass privatization schemes – where the objective is to compensate for the lack of domestic savings and give preferential treatment to residents – foreign strategic investors have played a lesser role. This explains the low participation of foreign investors in small-scale privatization in the Czech Republic and Poland.

Pre-acquisition stage of privatization strategies

Motivation of foreign investors

FDI can be divided into four types: market seeking, resource seeking, efficiency seeking and strategic asset seeking. These four types of FDI are 'pushed' or 'pulled' abroad by different factors and are attracted by different host countries. Market-seeking FDI is attracted by countries with large and prosperous markets; resource-seeking FDI is determined by the availability and quality of natural resources in the host economy; efficiency-seeking FDI follows the national competitive advantages of host countries (thus, labour intensive FDI is directed at countries with low wages, while technology intensive FDI favours advanced industrial countries with good supporting infrastructure). Strategic-asset-seeking FDI is partly firm-specific, but normally takes place in countries with similar economic structures and living standards.

In assessing the major factors determining the foreign parent's decision to take over a CEE company, the respondents stressed that market-seeking and strategic motives were dominant in the foreign investors' decision to invest. Table 1.9 confirms the prevalence of a market-seeking strategy in the Czech Republic, Hungary, Poland and Slovenia. The size of Poland's market of 40 million consumers is clearly a significant factor. A second important factor was the setting up of an export base for the CEE region. The Russian, Ukrainian and Belarus combined markets of 220 million consumers have a clear appeal to potential investors. Here again, Poland, as an export platform, has a distinct advantage, given its proximity to the CIS. The foreign parent's strategic reasons are a major motive for investing in Hungary and Slovenia. Our survey confirms other recent studies[11] which no longer see CEE's cheap labour force as a major motive for foreign investors.

A relatively small sample limits the relevance and reliability of the correlation analysis. Nevertheless, it is worth noting that the correlation between the size of the acquired CEE company – measured by annual sales, foreign equity and employment – and the foreign investor's motives for the acquisition draws out some interesting distinctions between larger and

Table 1.9   Factors determining foreign investors' decisions to acquire a CEE company: survey results

Factors	Level of importance (max: 3; min: 1)[1]				
	Czech Rep.	Hungary	Slovenia	Poland	Total
(1) To gain access to the local market*	2.7	2.3	2.3	2.7	2.6
(2) To reduce costs	1.7	2.1	2.4	2.0	2.0
(3) To reduce labour costs**	1.7	2.3	2.0	1.4	1.7
(4) To secure inputs	1.4	1.1	1.1	1.3	1.3
(5) To increase profit levels***	1.6	1.9	2.0	1.6	1.7
(6) To create an export base:****					
– in general	1.6	2.1	2.2	1.9	1.9
– for CEE	2.0	2.2	2.1	2.5	2.3
(7) Strategic reasons	1.9	2.6	2.4	2.1	2.1

Correlations:
*   with total equity (r = –.369 Sig. 029)
**   with sales (r = .414 Sig. 002); with total equity (r = .280 Sig. 025); with employment (r = .377 Sig. 002)
***   with sales (r = .507 Sig. 000); with employment (r = .256 Sig. 039)
****   with total equity (r = .587 Sig. 000)
[1] Average scores were derived as follows: (3) very important, (2) important, (1) unimportant.
Source: Authors' survey.

smaller host companies. In the case of larger host companies, foreign investors are more attracted to the possibility of reducing labour costs (r = .414, for annual sales), increasing profit levels (r = .507, for annual sales), and creating an export base for CEE (r = .587, for the value of foreign equity). On the other hand, they seem less interested in gaining access to the local market (r = –.369, for the value of foreign equity).

Motivation of target companies

The most frequently quoted host company motives are listed in Table 1.10. Our survey shows that the most important motive was to secure the target company's long-term development; this was followed by the need to obtain new sources of development financing, management and marketing skills, new technology and foreign markets. Our correlation analysis indicates that the acquisition of new technology (r = .246) and access to foreign markets (r = .345) were more important to the management of larger rather than smaller target companies (measured by the size of sales and the number of employees).

Previous cooperation between foreign parent and target company

The existing literature on FDI in CEE countries suggests that a number of FDI projects have grown from previous cooperation between the foreign parent and the acquired company. This is in part due to the fact that under-

Table 1.10   Target companies' motives in seeking strategic foreign investors: survey results

Motives	Level of importance (max: 3; min: 1)[1]				
	Czech Rep.	*Hungary*	*Slovenia*	*Poland*	*Total*
(1) To save the company from bankruptcy	1.5	1.7	1.6	2.0	1.7
(2) To obtain new sources of development financing	2.2	2.3	2.1	2.3	2.3
(3) To acquire new technology*	2.2	2.2	2.3	2.1	2.2
(4) To preserve employment	1.5	1.8	1.3	1.4	1.5
(5) To enter foreign markets**	2.1	1.9	2.2	1.8	2.1
(6) To get management/ marketing skills	2.0	1.9	2.0	2.3	2.2
(7) To gain access to raw materials, components, inputs	1.3	1.2	1.3	1.5	1.3
(8) To secure the company's long-term development***	2.4	2.7	2.7	2.9	2.7

Correlations:
*   with sales (r = .246 Sig. 056); employment (r = .242 Sig. 045)
**   with sales (r = .345 Sig. 007); employment (r = .318 Sig. 009)
*** with total equity (r = .293 Sig. 014)
[1] Average scores were derived as follows: (3) very important, (2) important, (1) unimportant.
Source: Authors' survey.

developed capital markets and information systems in CEE are obstacles to finding a suitable partner or target company (see Business International and Creditanstalt 1993). Our sample does not fully confirm this view. More than half (56.8 per cent) of sample foreign parent companies had no previous contacts with the target company. Either they were invited by a government agency to take part in a tender or a direct sale, or they were targeted by the representatives of a host country management group. The route of previous cooperation was most popular in Slovenia (79 per cent) and the Czech republic (54.5 per cent), but less so in Hungary (28.6 per cent) and Poland (32.1 per cent). These differences seem to be correlated to methods of company sales. Both Slovenia and the Czech Republic undertook a more selective search of foreign investors, whilst Poland and Hungary had a higher propensity to put companies up for tender (see Table 1.11).

Acquisition stage

Bidding process

The bidding process assumes transparency, the participation of consultants and the discussion of key elements in the acquisition transaction. Bidding is usually a lengthy process where buyers and sellers try to set a

Table 1.11 Previous cooperation between foreign parent and target company*: results

		Czech Rep.	Hungary	Slovenia	Poland	Total
(1)	Exports/imports	33.3	50.0	71.4	77.8	56.3
(2)	Licensing agreements	25.0	–	28.6	44.4	28.1
(3)	Subcontracting	25.0	–	14.3	11.1	15.6
(4)	Other types of contractual cooperation	33.3	50.0	14.3	11.1	25.0
Total (%)		100[1]	100[2]	100[1]	100[1]	100[1]
No. of companies with previous cooperation		=12	=4	=7	=9	=32
Share in total no. of companies		54.4	28.6	70.0	32.1	43.2

Correlations:
* with sales (r = .915 Sig. 000); with total equity (r = .387 Sig. 022); with foreign equity (r = .349 Sig. 040); with employment (r = .466 Sig. 005)
[1] The sum total is higher than 100% because some companies reported several forms of previous cooperation.
Source: Authors' survey.

price and establish acceptable sales and purchasing conditions. The analysis of the bidding procedure and negotiations in Table 1.12 indicates that the target company's management plays a key role in the negotiation process (87.8 per cent). The target company's management chooses the foreign investor, sets the price and discusses the basic features of the acquisition transaction. The role of the government agency (assessed as important in 56.8 per cent of sample cases) is clearly less important than that of the management. Paradoxically, the role of legal and financial consultants hired by the government agency (assessed as important in 52.7 per cent of sample cases) is only marginally less important than that of the government agency itself.

The correlation analysis shows two significant tendencies: first, the role of hired consultants is greater in smaller target companies (measured by foreign equity), as they tend to rely more on external assistance. Second, the role of government agencies in negotiating and concluding the contract grows along with the size of the target company. Large companies still seem to be under the close supervision of government institutions because of their broader impact on the local economy.

Table 1.12   Major characteristics of the bidding procedure: survey results

		Czech Rep.	*Hungary*	*Slovenia*	*Poland*	*Total*
(1)	Transparent bidding procedure	63.6	35.7	30.0	39.3	44.6
(2)	Competitive bidding	63.6	35.7	30.0	39.3	44.6
(3)	Management of the target company was important in negotiations	86.4	78.6	100.0	89.3	87.8
(4)	Hired consultants were important in negotiations*	68.2	14.3	–	78.6	52.7
(5)	Government agency was important in deciding on key elements of the acquisition**	63.6	42.9	40.0	64.3	56.8
(6)	Management of the target company was important in deciding on key elements of the acquisition	86.4	57.1	100.0	75.0	78.4
Total (%)		100[1]	100[1]	100[1]	100[1]	100[1]
Total no. of companies		= 22	= 14	= 10	= 28	= 74

Correlations:
* with foreign equity (r = –.562 Sig. 000)
** with sales (r = .276 Sig. 050) and with employment (r = .248 Sig. 039)
[1] The sum total is higher than 100% because most companies reported several characteristics.
Source: Authors' survey.

Incentives and guarantees

Government incentives and guarantees to foreign strategic investors are major elements of the acquisition process as they can influence the price of the target company.

The impression gained from Table 1.13 is that, with the exception of tax incentives (present in 40.5 per cent of sample cases), government agencies prefer to give guarantees on profit repatriation (36.5 per cent), indemnification for hidden liabilities (36.5 per cent) and hidden ecological damage (25.7 per cent). The inter-country comparison points out that the Hungarian agency above offers attractive incentives such as reductions in the purchasing price, loans, subsidies from government funds and the provision of infrastructure facilities. The Polish authorities are more generous with tax incentives and profit repatriation guarantees, while in Slovenia guarantees of indemnification for hidden liabilities and ecological damage seem to be favoured.

Table 1.14 does not support the view that incentives, as one of the cost determinants of FDI, are only of marginal importance to foreign investors. In our sample, government guarantees to foreign parent companies were rated as important or very important in over half of sample cases (51.4 per cent). The incentives and guarantees appear to be more important for larger acquired companies sold by government agencies, but insignificant in the case of smaller companies sold by their management (r = .352 for sales and r = .461 for total equity).

The guarantees and promises of a foreign buyer are also an integral element of his offer and of the final acquisition agreement. In the criteria developed by the Slovene Privatization Agency and Development Fund, investment and employment guarantees have jointly more weight (40 out of 100 points) than the price offered (30 out of 100 points). Our sample foreign parent companies more or less accepted the guarantees and promises required by the host country (see Table 1.15).

Post-acquisition stage

Foreign acquisitions of non-privatized companies not only change the formal status of the acquired company but also start a process of company restructuring and adaptation to market conditions. Bringing in a strategic foreign investor is closely related to expectations of new technology, management techniques, accounting standards and organizational culture. In this section we discuss whether pre-acquisition expectations have been fulfilled and what changes have been brought about by the strategic investor.

Post-acquisition changes introduced by the foreign company

Table 1.16 summarizes the changes and restructuring undertaken by foreign parent companies in our sample in the post-acquisition period. It

Table 1.13 Government incentives and guarantees to foreign parent companies: survey results

Incentives/guarantees	Czech Rep.	Hungary	Slovenia	Poland	Total
(1) Tax incentives*	13.6	42.9	30.0	64.3	40.5
(2) Reduction in purchasing price	–	14.3	–	–	2.7
(3) Loans/subsidies from govt. funds**	–	7.1	–	–	1.4
(4) Provision of infrastructure facilities	–	14.3	–	–	2.7
(5) Subsidies for the resolution of overstaffing problems	13.6	7.1	–	25.0	14.0
(6) Guarantees to introduce tariffs on competitive imports	–	–	–	–	–
(7) Profit repatriation guarantees	22.7	28.6	30.0	53.6	36.5
(8) Guarantees of indemnification for hidden liabilities***	13.6	14.3	100.0	42.9	36.5
(9) Guarantees of indemnification for hidden ecological damage****	40.9	–	100.0	–	25.7
Total (%)	100¹	100¹	100¹	100¹	100¹
Total companies	= 22	= 14	= 10	= 28	= 74

Correlations:
*   with sales (r = .636 Sig. 000); with total equity (r = .265 Sig. 034); with employment (r = .292)
**   with total equity (r = .783 Sig. 000); with employment (r = .728 Sig. 000)
***   with foreign equity (r = .435 Sig. 018)
****   with total equity (r = .342 Sig. 0006); with foreign equity (r = .930 Sig. 000)
¹ The sum total is higher than 100% because some companies reported several incentives/guarantees
Source: Authors' survey.

Table 1.14   Ratings of government incentives and guarantees in foreign firms' decisions to invest: survey results

	Incentives/guarantees	Czech Rep.	Hungary	Slovenia	Poland	Total
(1)	Insignificant	63.6	40.0	40.0	42.9	48.6
(2)	Important	22.7	60.0	60.0	10.7	28.6
(3)	Very important	13.6	–	–	46.4	22.9
Total (%)		100	100	100	100	100
Total no. of answers		= 22	= 10	= 10	= 28	= 70

Correlations:
* with sales (r = .352 Sig. 003); with total equity (r = .461 Sig. 005)
Source: Authors' survey.

Table 1.15   Guarantees and promises of foreign parent companies: survey results

	Guarantees/promises	Czech Rep.	Hungary	Slovenia	Poland	Total
(1)	Employment guarantee*	31.8	21.4	30.0	28.6	28.4
(2)	Best effort employment promise	36.4	28.6	20.0	28.6	29.7
(3)	Future investment guarantee**	50.0	42.9	30.0	78.6	56.8
(4)	Best effort investment promise	22.7	28.6	50.0	57.1	40.5
(5)	Employment promise to the existing management of the target company***	50.0	28.6	70.0	53.6	50.0
Total (%)		100[1]	100[1]	100[1]	100[1]	100[1]
Total no. of companies		= 22	= 14	= 10	= 28	= 74

Correlations:
*   with sales (r = .269 Sig. 035); with total equity (r = .352 Sig. 003); with foreign equity (r = .461 Sig. 005); with employment (r = .312 Sig. 008)
**   with sales (r = .338 Sig. 007); with total equity (r = .265 Sig. 033); with employment (r = .320 Sig. 007)
***   with employment (r = –.260 Sig. 030)
[1] The sum total is higher than 100% because some companies reported several guarantees/promises
Source: Authors' survey.

shows that new foreign parent companies tend to introduce new production programmes (70.3 per cent of sample cases), reorganize marketing activities (70.3 per cent), undertake training (63.5 per cent) and reorganization (48.6 per cent) of management and consolidate financially

Table 1.16   Post-acquisition changes and restructuring in the acquired companies: survey results

	Changes/restructuring	Czech Rep.	Hungary	Slovenia	Poland	Total
(1)	Financial consolidation*	27.3	42.9	30.0	53.8	40.5
(2)	Selling of non-business or non-core-business assets**	27.3	7.1	–	14.3	14.9
(3)	Reduction in overstaffing	59.1	–	20.0	21.4	28.4
(4)	Reorganization of management***	31.8	57.1	80.0	46.4	48.6
(5)	Replacing members of management****	18.2	21.4	30.0	21.4	21.6
(6)	Training of management*****	54.5	57.1	80.0	67.9	63.5
(7)	Introduction of new programmes	68.2	28.6	90.0	85.7	70.3
(8)	Reorganization of marketing activities	54.5	50.0	60.0	96.4	70.3
(9)	Reorganization of supply activities******	27.3	21.4	40.0	35.7	31.1
Total (%)		100[1]	100[1]	100[1]	100[1]	100[1]
Total no. of companies		= 22	= 14	= 10	= 28	= 74

Correlations

*   with sales (r = .426 Sig. 001); with total equity (r = .271 Sig. 025); with employment (r = .262 Sig. 031)

**   with sales (r = .295 Sig. 020); with total equity (r = .250 Sig. 037); with employment (r = .362 Sig. 002)

***   with sales (r = .383 Sig. 002); with total equity (r = .299 Sig. 012); with employment (r = .240 Sig. 045)

****   with sales (r = .412 Sig. 001)

***** with employment (r = – .332 Sig. 008)

****** with sales (r = .273 Sig. 032); with employment (r = .244 Sig. 042)

[1] The sum total is greater than 100% because most companies reported several post-acquisition changes and restructuring operations.

Source: Authors' survey.

(40.5 per cent). The non-business and non-core-business assets of target companies were sold in only 4.9 per cent of sample cases.

Management training and reorganization has been prevalent in all four transition economies and falls in line with the employment promises given to management during negotiations.

Post-acquisition operational aspects, objectives and expectations

Most sample companies (65.8 per cent in the Czech Republic; 71.4 per cent in Hungary; 80 per cent in Slovenia and 64.3 per cent in Poland) produce the same goods as the foreign parents. This indicates the major intention of foreign investors in CEE: to supply the local market through local production.

In Table 1.17, host companies, government agencies and foreign parents were asked if the results of the post-acquisition operations had met their pre-acquisition objectives and expectations. The target companies' management was the most satisfied with the acquisitions (47.3 per cent fully and 36.5 per cent partially); among foreign parent companies, 38.4 per cent were fully satisfied and 41.1 per cent partially satisfied, while government agencies thought it premature to make an assessment. According to the East European Investment Survey conducted by Business International and Creditanstalt in 1993, 'after all the problems one faces when making an East European investment, the best measure of satisfaction of those doing business in the region is whether they are increasing or decreasing their planned investment'. In 74 per cent of sample cases, foreign parent companies expressed an interest in further expanding their investment.

Table 1.17 Realization of objectives and expectations of foreign and host country partners: survey results

	Czech Rep.	Hungary	Slovenia	Poland	Total
Results of the acquisition met the objectives/expectations of:					
(1) Government agency*					
(a) Fully	27.3	75.0	100	14.3	38.2
(b) Only partially	31.8	12.5	–	7.1	14.7
(c) Not at all	–	–	–	–	–
(d) Too early to evaluate	40.0	12.5	–	78.6	47.1
Total (%)	100.0	100.0	100.0	100.0	100.0
No. of answers	= 22	= 8	= 10	= 28	= 68
(2) Acquired company/its management					
(a) Fully	36.4	71.4	40.0	46.4	47.3
(b) Only partially	40.1	21.4	60.0	32.1	36.5
(c) Not at all	–	–	–	–	–
(d) Too early to evaluate	22.7	7.1	–	21.4	16.2
Total (%)	100.0	100.0	100.0	100.0	100.0
No. of answers	= 22	= 14	= 10	= 28	= 74
(3) Foreign parent company					
(a) Fully	42.9	50.0	50.0	25.0	38.4
(b) Only partially	28.6	35.7	50.0	50.0	41.1
(c) Not at all	–	–	–	–	–
(d) Too early to evaluate	28.6	14.3	–	25.0	20.5
Total (%)	100.0	100.0	100.0	100.0	100.0
No. of answers	= 21	= 14	= 10	= 28	= 73

Correlations:
* with total equity ($r = -.373$ Sig. 004); with foreign equity ($r = -.554$ Sig. 002); with employment ($r = -.316$ Sig. 016)
Source: Authors' survey.

Technology and research and development

FDI can promote technological change in a host country in a number of ways. The direct impact may occur through its contribution to higher factor productivity, changes in product and export composition, research and development (R&D) undertaken by foreign subsidiaries, the introduction of organizational innovation and improved management practices, employment and training. The indirect impact occurs through collaboration with local R&D institutions, technology transfer to local downstream and upstream producers, the effects of the presence of foreign affiliates on competition and on the efficiency of local producers and the turn-over of trained personnel. It comes, therefore, as no surprise that the technological and R&D aspects of foreign privatizations are among the objectives of CEE governments and target companies.

In as much as 79.9 per cent of sample cases (57.1 per cent in Hungary, 72.7 per cent in the Czech Republic, 89.3 per cent in Poland and in all sample cases in Slovenia, the foreign parents transferred new technology/know-how/products to the host subsidiary. In 54 per cent of cases, the transfer was in the form of machinery and equipment; in 53 per cent of cases, it took the form of industrial property rights, manufacturing, marketing, organizational and managerial know-how, computerization of production and the training of management and employees. Most technologies and products transferred (68.6 per cent of all transfers) to the newly acquired subsidiaries (50.0 per cent in the case of Slovenia, 63.6 per cent in the Czech Republic, 75.0 per cent in Poland and 85.7 per cent in Hungary) had to be adapted to the needs of the acquired companies.

Suggestions for the post-privatization period

The legal framework and recent experience of the CEE countries highlight two favoured methods of foreign privatization: either foreign investors enter through 'the front door', that is via direct sales organized by the state. Alternatively, they enter through 'the back door' by buying shares from investment funds, the general public or new issues. To date, the first option has prevailed. In the longer term, however, the CEE countries will be faced with the second set of options.

As a result of mass privatization, foreign strategic investors will face a rather dispersed ownership structure, which could be problematic for potential company buyers until efficient secondary capital markets become operational. Further, as the privatization agencies and ministries forgo the authority to approve and monitor foreign acquisitions, domestic sellers will become the new owners (employees, management, institutional investors) with limited knowledge and experience of engaging in direct sale transactions with foreign investors.

This new *modus operandi* calls for new approaches. First, a concentration of dispersed ownership is required to implement foreign strategic acquisitions. Besides Stock Exchanges, additional mechanisms need to be set up for shares not eligible for trading on Stock Exchanges.

Second, the regulatory mechanism governing foreign acquisitions will need to focus on anti-monopoly legislation. Here, greater transparency will be required to define the regulatory framework for the acquisition of shares, thresholds for domestic and foreign acquisitions and company disclosure.

Finally, given the lack of expertise, experience and adequate staffing, it is likely that most privatized target companies will not be able to execute direct sale transactions adequately. Hence, the CEE governments will need to address the question of how to optimize the expertise gained to date for future company sales to strategic foreign investors.

Notes

1 We are referring here to the transformation process in the broadest possible sense, that is the internal and external liberalization of the economies under consideration, their reintegration into the international division of labour, their sectoral restructuring and the introduction of a managerial and entrepreneurial class.

2 Even Hungary, which is the CEE country with the most determined and clear-cut policy towards FDI, could not avoid polarized discussions on FDI. 'Concerning foreign capital, some believe that accusations and uncertainty prevail, and it is harmful. Others speak of the selling out of markets and selling the national property at a low price and step up with the charge of 'betraying the nation'. Some would transfer the management of the property to foreigners as fast as possible amid the widest range of preferences. Others would introduce restrictions against foreigners' (T. Szabo, 1993, p. 8)

3 In terms of sales, the average Polish sample company is one-third smaller than the average sample company, and 3.6 times smaller than the average Slovene sample company. The average Polish sample company is even smaller in terms of total equity (29.7 per cent of average sample company), foreign equity (33.2 per cent) and employment (34.3 per cent).

4 With annual sales 2.3 times, total equity 2.5 times and foreign equity 2.9 times higher than the sample average.

5 Both foreign parent companies and target companies mentioned contributions in kind (new machinery and equipment) as major reasons.

6 Every citizen over 18 years was allowed to buy a voucher book worth 1000 investment points for a symbolic price of 1000 Crowns ($35). About 77 per cent of eligible citizens participated in voucher privatization and bid for the shares of 2000 enterprises with an estimated value of 350 bn Crowns ($12.2 bn).

7 First, to the business association or cooperative operating with the participation of its employees (if at least 25 per cent of the employees take part); second, to the employee share programme with the participation of the company's employees; third, to the company's employee as a private entrepreneur; and fourth, to the existing or former property manager.

8 Establishing a joint venture partnership does not mean that the SOE has already been privatized. It implies that part of the SOE's assets are invested in a new type of partnership with a foreign investor and that part of the assets are under the joint venture's management control.

9 Commercialization means the transformation of state-owned enterprises into single-person treasury-owned joint stock companies.

10 The initial public offering (of shares at the Warsaw Stock Exchange), sometimes known as the British style case by case method, has played an essential role in the development of Poland's capital market and is the second main source (after direct sales) of budget revenues from privatization.

11 See the EBRD (1994) for a review of FDI country studies in CEE.

2
Assessing the Costs and Benefits of Foreign Direct Investment: Some Theoretical Considerations

John H. Dunning

Introduction

Any assessment of the impact of foreign direct investment (FDI), or the activities of transnational corporations (TNCs), on the economic welfare of host countries requires some understanding of the reasons why TNCs undertake FDI in the first place, and also the policies pursued by the host countries which, directly or indirectly, may affect the level and composition of that investment.

This is because the consequences of FDI on a particular host country are a function of the interaction between the competitiveness of its location-bound resources and the competitive advantages of the investing firms. Neither of these sets of advantages is immutable; they are constantly changing over time: *inter alia*, in response to new demands by consumers, technological progress and political and economic developments.

The last decade has witnessed more of these changes than, perhaps, any other comparable decade of the twentieth century. We shall identify some of these later in this chapter, but one which particularly affects the structure of the interface between the competitive advantages of firms (particularly TNCs) and those of countries is the paradigmatic shift now taking place in the structure of the capitalist system, and in the micro-organization of economic activity (Perez 1983, Best 1990 and Gerlach 1992). This change is best described as the movement from *hierarchical* to *cooperative* or *alliance* capitalism, and is occurring as a result of a series of systemic technological and institutional developments which, taken together, are heralding a new paradigm of production – known variously as 'flexible production', 'Toyotism' and the 'new competition'.[1] While, as yet, it is too early to pronounce the demise of the mass, or Fordist, system of production, in several of the industrial sectors, e.g. autos and consumer electronics, in which scale value adding activity was once lauded as the 'best practice' system, this new techno-economic paradigm has already been widely adopted – not only by Japanese firms, where it was first introduced, but by US and European producers as well.

This chapter proceeds in the following way. In the next sections we shall examine some of the changes which have taken place in the thinking of scholars about the determinants of FDI and TNC activity. We believe such thinking should be of interest to governments of Central and East European economies as they seek to improve the attractiveness of their own location-bound resources and capabilities to foreign investors, and to evaluate the consequences of such investment for the welfare of their citizens.

The major part of the chapter is, however, devoted to examining the main consequences of inbound FDI for the competitiveness of host countries. We have taken the upgrading of national competitiveness (at the minimum possible cost) as the main criterion by which inbound FDI is judged; and we shall discuss the ways in which different kinds of TNC activity are likely to affect which components of competitiveness. We shall also argue that the economic consequences of inbound FDI are likely to depend critically on specific characteristics of host countries, and particularly on the legal and institutional infrastructure, and on the macro-organizational policies pursued by governments.

Following this discussion, we shall identify some of the actions that national governments might take to ensure that, in this emerging age of alliance capitalism, FDI can best fulfil its intended purpose. The final section will consider some alternatives to inbound TNC activity as a means of securing the resources, capabilities and markets for upgrading competitiveness.

From the perspective of individual firms: what determines FDI?

It is worth emphasizing that all the received theories and paradigms of FDI and TNC activity essentially view the TNC as an independent hierarchy of horizontally or vertically integrated value adding activities. While the existence of collaborative arrangements are recognized, these are usually perceived as *alternative* forms of economic organization, rather than an *extension of the boundaries* of the firm, and/or as *part and parcel of a system, or network*, of TNC-related *activities*. Moreover, the boundaries of the firm are assumed to be well defined, and to be coincident with its ownership of, or control over, a particular set of resources and capabilities. This means that, while accepting that firms may interact with each other in a variety of ways, the extant literature views the key unit of analysis as the independent firm, rather than the firm as part and parcel of a network of interrelated activities, or indeed the network itself.[2]

In such conditions, the theory of the TNC is a *theory of the firm whose boundaries are determined by its ownership*; and the theory of TNC activity is *a theory of the activities of firms of a particular industry, country or region.*

Of the various theories and paradigms of TNC activity[3] which have emerged over the past thirty years, the most comprehensive is the *eclectic paradigm*, which provides a framework within which a number of specific propositions about the determinants of FDI and international production can be accommodated. The paradigm avers that the extent and pattern of TNC activity will be determined by the interaction between the competitive advantages embedded in firms and those embedded in countries; and the way in which firms choose to combine and coordinate these two sets of advantages across national boundaries.[4]

The paradigm essentially considers two main forms of economic organization: namely, *arm's-length transactions and hierarchies*. It assumes (as does its near neighbour – the internalization paradigm) that these two modalities represent the extremes of a continuum, which ranges from perfect competition, with zero transaction and coordination costs, to a perfect hierarchy with zero internally administered costs.[5] In between, there is a series of intermediate stages, which involve some kind of time-related cooperative agreement between two or more independent firms. As one moves along the continuum, it is assumed the transaction and coordination costs of using markets increase relative to those of, first, quasi and, later, full hierarchical control. However, for the most part, each of these alternative forms is assumed to be a *substitute* for, and not a *complement* to, each other; and, even in the case of a cooperative arrangement, the unit of analysis is the individual firm, rather than the two or more firms involved in the arrangement.

Turning now to the eclectic paradigm of TNC activity, this paradigm suggests that firms will engage in FDI in a particular country when:

- They possess a portfolio of resources and capabilities, including organizational and innovatory competencies, which gives them a unique set of advantages – so-called ownership (O) specific advantages[6] – over their competitors, or potential competitors, serving, or seeking to serve, the same markets. The necessary conditions for such O advantages to be sustainable over time have recently been set out by Peteraf (1993) in her analysis of the resource-based theory of the firm.[7]
- They find it beneficial to internalize the market for these advantages, rather than to sell the right to use them to other, i.e. separately owned, firms. This they will do whenever they perceive they can coordinate these advantages with other value added activities more beneficially than by using markets as an exchange mechanism. These advantages are called internalization advantages (I) and it is these which essentially are the *raison d'être* of hierarchies.[8]
- Their global goals are best met by adding value to these advantages from a production site(s) in a foreign country, i.e. that the chosen country offers location-bound resources and capabilities superior to those of the home country of the investing firm.

The eclectic paradigm accepts that the precise configuration of OLI advantages will depend on three main contextual variables. These are:

1 The type and range of products produced by TNCs or potential TNCs.[9]
2 Their country of origin, and the country(ies) in which they are contemplating investment and
3 A variety of firm-specific factors, including the past strategies pursued by the investing companies.

Until the mid-1980s, the literature distinguished between three motives for foreign-owned value added activity: namely, to acquire natural resources, to seek markets and to restructure (i.e. rationalize) an existing portfolio of market-seeking or resource-seeking investments. Most of the operational theories, or models of TNC activity seek to explain one or other of these three kinds of FDI, or a particular aspect of all of these.[10]

More recently (see Dunning 1993a), the eclectic paradigm has been widened to embrace two other kinds of TNC activity:

1 The first is where a firm (usually an established TNC) makes an investment to acquire assets which, it perceives, will protect or strengthen its global competitive advantages, *vis-à-vis* those of its competitors. Such FDI is called *strategic asset seeking investment*. Rather than exploiting existing O-specific advantages, this kind of TNC activity is directed to gaining new advantages. It is particularly noticeable in the high technology sectors serving global markets, and is primarily concentrated within the advanced industrial nations. Much of the cross-border merger and acquisition (M&A) and strategic alliance activity of the last decade falls into this category. Some examples of this kind of FDI are given in chapter 3 of Dunning (1993a).
2 A feature of the modern, large, integrated TNC is that its portfolio of assets consists of a variety of organizational arrangements, each of which it treats as an integral part of a network of activities. While, taken separately, these arrangements are similar to those set out in Table 2.1, collectively they represent an *organizational system* in which each component is not *substitutable* but *complementary* to the other; and each benefits from being associated with the others. One example of such activity is the Japanese *keiretsu*, or network of firms, in which each firm is fused with, or linked to, the others by ownership or by a less formal, but no less committed, mode of bonding. Frequently, and especially in vertical *keiretsus*,[11] there is a core, or lead, firm – usually a large industrial customer–that determines the structure and composition of the network. In horizontal networks (e.g. clusters of firms engaged in similar activities) there may be no such flagship firm. In the 1990s, there is evidence to suggest that network relationships are becoming increasingly

Table 2.1 A reconfiguration of the eclectic paradigm of international production

1. Ownership-specific advantages
(of enterprise of one nationality (or affiliates of same) over those of another)

Hierarchical-related advantages

(a) Property right and/or intangible asset advantages (Oa).
Product innovations, production management, organizational and marketing systems, innovatory capacity, non-codifiable knowledge: 'bank' of human capital experience; marketing, finance, know-how, etc.

(b) Advantages of common governance, i.e. of organizing Oa with complementary assets (Ot).

(i) Those that branch plants of established enterprises may enjoy over *de novo* firms. Those due mainly to size, product diversity and learning experiences of enterprise, e.g. economies of scope and specialization. Exclusive or favoured access to inputs, e.g. labour, natural resources, finance, information. Ability to obtain inputs on favoured terms (due, e.g. to size or monopsonistic influence). Ability of parent

Alliance or network-related advantages

(a) *Vertical alliances*

(i) Backward access to R&D, design engineering and training facilities of suppliers; regular advice by them on product innovation and improvement and implications of projected new production processes for component design and manufacturing. New insights into, and monitoring of, developments in materials and how they might affect existing products and production processes.

(ii) Forward access to industrial customers, new markets, marketing techniques and distribution channels, particularly in unfamiliar locations or where products need to be adapted to meet local supply capabilities and markets.

(b) *Horizontal alliances*
Access to complementary technologies and innovatory capacity. Access to additional capabilities to identify new uses for related technologies Encapsulation of development time. Such inter-firm interaction often generates its own knowledge feedback mechanisms and path dependencies.

(c) *Networks*
(i) Similar firms
Reduced transaction and coordination costs arising from better dissemination and interpretation of knowledge and information, and from mutual support and cooperation between members of network. Improved knowledge about process and product development and

Table 2.1   A reconfiguration of the eclectic paradigm of international production (*continued*)

1. Ownership-specific advantages
(of enterprise of one nationality (or affiliates of same) over those of another)

Hierarchical-related advantages	*Alliance or network-related advantages*
company to conclude productive and cooperative inter-firm relationships e.g. as between Japanese auto assemblers and their suppliers. Exclusive or favoured access to product markets. Access to resources of parent company at marginal cost. Synergistic economies (not only in production, but in purchasing, marketing, finance, etc., arrangements)	markets. Multiple, yet complementary, inputs into innovatory developments and explanation of new markets. Opportunities to develop 'niche' R&D strategies; shared learning and training experiences, e.g. as in the case of cooperative research associations. Networks may also help promote uniform product standards and other collective advantages.
ii) Which specifically arise because of multinationality. Multinationality enhances operational flexibility by offering wider opportunities for arbitraging, production shifting and global sourcing of inputs. More favoured access to and/or better knowledge about international markets, e.g., for information, finance, labour, etc. Ability to take advantage of geographic differences in factor endowments, government intervention, markets, etc. Ability to diversify or reduce risks, e.g. in different currency areas and creation of options and/or political and cultural scenarios. Ability to learn from societal differences in organizational and managerial processes and systems. Balancing economies of integration with ability to respond to differences in country-specific needs and advantages.	(ii) Business districts As per (i) plus spatial agglomerative economies, e.g. labour market pooling. Access to clusters of specialized intermediate inputs, and linkages with knowledge-based institutions, e.g. universities, technological spill-overs.

40

Table 2.1 A reconfiguration of the eclectic paradigm of international production *(continued)*

2. Internalization incentive advantages (i.e. to circumvent or exploit market failure)	
Hierarchical-related advantages	*Alliance or network-related advantages*
Avoidance of search and negotiating costs. Avoidance of costs of moral hazard, information asymmetries and adverse selection; protection of reputation of internalizing firm. Avoidance of cost of broken contracts and ensuing litigation. Buyer uncertainty (about nature and value of inputs (e.g. technology) being sold). When market does not permit price discrimination. Need of seller to protect quality of intermediate or final products. Capture of economies of interdependent activities (see (*b*) above). Compensation for absence of future markets. Avoidance or exploitation of government intervention (e.g. quotas, tariffs, price controls, tax differences, etc.) Control of supplies and conditions of sale of inputs (including technology). Control of market outlets (including those which might be used by competitors). Potential to engage in practices, e.g. cross-subsidization, predatory pricing, leads and lags, transfer pricing, etc., as a competitive (or anti-competitive) strategy.	While, in some cases, time limited inter-firm cooperative relationships may be a substitute for FDI, in others, they may add to the I incentive advantages of the participating hierarchies, i.e. R&D alliances and networking (which, for example, when preferred to M&As, may help strengthen the overall hierarchical advantages of the participating firms). Moreover, the growing structural integration of the world economy is requiring firms to go outside their immediate boundaries to capture the complex realities of know-how trading and knowledge exchange in innovation, particularly where such assets are tacit and need to speedily adapt to structural change. Alliance or network-related advantages are those which prompt a 'voice' rather than an 'exit' response to market failure; they also allow many of the advantages of internalization without the inflexibility of bureaucratic or risk-related costs associated with it. Such quasi-internalization is likely to be most successful in cultures in which trust, forbearances, reciprocity and consensus politics are at a premium. It suggests that firms are more appropriately likened to archipelagos linked by causeways rather than self-contained 'islands' or conscious powers.

Table 2.1 A reconfiguration of the eclectic paradigm of international production *(continued)*

3. Location-specific variables
(these may favour home or host countries)

Hierarchical-related advantages	*Alliance or network-related advantages*
Spatial distribution of natural and created resource endowments and markets.	The L-specific advantages of alliances arise essentially from the presence of local complementary assets, organized within a framework of alliances and networks. The extent and type of business districts, industrial or science parks and the external economies they offer participating firms are examples of these advantages which, over time, the presence of foreign-owned firms might expect. Cross-border alliance or network relationships may also allow foreign firms to better tap into, and exploit, the comparative technological and organizational advantages of host countries. Networks may also help reduce the information asymmetries and likelihood of opportunism in imperfect markets.
Input prices, quality and productivity, e.g. labour, energy, materials, components, semi-finished goods.	
International transport and communication costs.	
Investment incentives and disincentives (including performance requirements, etc.)	
Artificial barriers (e.g. import controls) to trade in goods and services.	
Societal and infrastructure provisions (commercial, legal, educational, transport and communication).	
Cross-country ideological, language, cultural, business, political, etc, differences.	
Economies of centralization of R&D production and marketing	
Economic system and policies of government: the institutional framework for resource allocation.	

Source: These variables are culled from a variety of sources, but see especially Dunning (1993a), Kobrin (1993) and Teece (1994).

widespread, *and that TNCs and other firms regard the membership of a network as a competitive or O advantage in its own right.*

Because of these two developments of the last decade, which we will take up below, it may be appropriate to widen the *de facto* boundaries of the individual firm to include other firms which, as a result of the ongoing relationships it has with them, substantially affect its own O-specific advantages. In practice, this may be an exceedingly difficult thing to do, not only because the precise boundaries of each firm are different, but because each activity of a multi-activity firm might involve a different set of collaborative relationships. At the same time, it makes little sense to argue that, because a firm sheds some of its activities, e.g. disinternalizes part of its value chain, yet immediately enters into a cooperative production or marketing agreement with the firm(s) now undertaking these activities, it surrenders all the advantages which stemmed from its internal governance.

Since the 1990s, due to technological advances and competitive pressures, large TNCs have been increasingly disaggregating activities which they perceive do not directly contribute to their core O-specific advantages. Partly, this reflects the growing preference for innovation-led *flexible production* systems, as compared with cost-reducing *mass production* systems; and partly because some of the overhead costs of production, e.g. research and development (R&D), are becoming so astronomical that firms are being forced to limit their product range and innovatory activities. At the same time, the growing interdependence between different technologies,[12] and the need of firms to continue to exert some influence over the disaggregated activities, mean that the form and pattern of their inter-firm relationships are becoming more critical influences on their core competencies. Hence, hierarchical-related transactions are being replaced by alliance-related transactions of one kind or another. And hence, too, when firms go overseas, or increase their foreign value activities, they now pay especial attention to the availability and quality of these complementary activities, which, in TNC hierarchies, would have been internalized to minimize the costs associated with their coordination and transaction.

The switch of emphasis from *independent* to *relational firms* or *enterprise networks*, and from *hierarchical* to *alliance capitalism*, partly reflects the growing production and coordinating costs of undertaking multiple activities within a single ownership; and partly the increasing perception that inter-firm collaborative arrangements are a viable – and sometimes a preferable – alternative to full vertical or horizontal integration. This change in perception is partly a reflection of technical forces, e.g. the increasing costs (and the risks associated with such costs) of innovatory activities and the truncated product life cycles; and partly a demonstration by Japanese firms that, in the right business culture, informal inter-firm alliances or networks based on trust, mutual support, forbearance and reciprocity *can* adequately protect the proprietary assets of the cooperating parties, while allowing each to exploit the economies of synergy and co-specialization associated with the techno-economic system of innovatory-led production.

In the 1990s, the lessening of such market imperfections as opportunism, information incompleteness and asymmetry, uncertainty, and bounded rationality by the establishment of mutually beneficial inter-firm relationships, rather than by the replacement of imperfections by single hierarchies, seems to be an increasingly preferred route of economic organization. It is, indeed, an extension of Albert Hirschman's 'voice' response to the problem of market failure (Hirschman 1970). It is particularly relevant to problems of customer–supplier relationships (e.g. high rejection rate, unreliable delivery dates, opportunistic behaviour), where such a response would involve the two parties working together until the problems are corrected; and it contrasts with Hirschman's concept of an 'exit' strategy where, for example, the response of a customer to problems with a supplier is to find a new supplier or internalize the market for the product being supplied.[13]

It may be useful to consider how the traditional configuration of the competitive advantages of firms, and their interpretation of the locational activities of countries, are affected by extending the concept of the individual firm to embrace those activities over which it has some influence, and which, it perceives, affect its own competitive position in a significant way. We do this in Table 2.1. Whereas the left-hand side of the table sets out the OLI advantages traditionally identified (e.g. Dunning 1993a, ch. 4, p. 81), the right-hand side suggests how these advantages may be affected, for good or bad, by the cooperative relationships that firms enjoy with other firms – be the relationship that of a dyadic alliance or part of an industrial or spatial network of activities.

Why should host countries seek to attract FDI? What are the specific advantages of FDI?

To the extent that host countries want FDI primarily for the O-specific advantages that are unique to the investing firms, and which the former believe they need to promote their long-term economic goals, it might be reasonably supposed that its impact will be most pronounced where these O advantages are the most distinctive. This is, in fact, generally the case, although it is possible that, at the same time, the price which the TNC extracts for the provision of these advantages is unacceptable to the host country. To that country, it is the net *benefit* it expects to receive from FDI, i.e. the domestic value added, which is the relevant variable to assess.

The domestic value added by inbound FDI is of various kinds. In particular, we might identify:

1 The value added created and retained in the host country by the foreign investment, *less* the value added which could have been generated by obtaining the assets in other ways (including producing them within the country).

2 The 'spill-over' effects on the value added of other firms, e.g. suppliers, customers and competitors,[14] as a direct result of the investment.

3 The impact which the investment has on the allocation and reallocation of indigenous economic activity; and, in particular, the extent to which it assists an efficient inter-sectoral or intra-country distribution of resources and capabilities (e.g. by promoting increasing returns to scale and fostering industrial districts), it advances a country's dynamic competitive advantage.

Each of these consequences may be due to:

• Assets (and especially technology and information) transferred by the foreign firm to the host country;
• The organizational control exercised over the use of these assets and the location-bound assets of the host country used in conjunction with them.

It is, indeed, the way TNCs organize their global resources and capabilities, which often results in a different international division of labour than would have occurred had the assets been organized by indigenous firms, that is one of the most distinctive features of TNC activity.

From an investing firm's perspective, it will view a foreign location in terms of its contribution towards its regional or global economic and strategic objectives. Of course, much depends on the motivation for the investment, and whether it is an 'initial' or 'sequential' investment; and whether it is a 'stand-alone' investment or one which is part and parcel of a globally integrated strategy (Dunning 1993a). The response of firms to a set of locational 'pulls' and 'pushes' will also depend on firm-specific characteristics other than the nationality of their ownership. Thus, small, non-diversified investors may view a particular locational opportunity differently from large diversified firms. An oligopolistic firm which takes the initiative of investing abroad may value a given set of locational variables differently from those who follow it; a leading innovating firm may respond differently from a following imitating firm; a *de novo* foreign direct investor may judge the opportunities offered by a particular host country differently from a TNC with many foreign subsidiaries.[15] At the same time, the contribution of each of these different types of firms to the objectives of a host country's goals is also likely to be distinctive.

The need to understand what attracts firms to locate their activities in a particular country

The second reason for a government of a country to understand about the determinants of FDI is to guide it in its own actions in so far as these may affect FDI and its consequences. At the same time, national governments may also wish to know what actions are being pursued by other governments that might affect the locational choice of TNCs. They finally may wish to assess the extent to which they can get the benefits expected of FDI by alternative routes (i.e. licensing, the encouragement of indigenous industries).

We shall deal with each of these issues as our chapter proceeds. But here we would make the point that governments may affect both the extent to which they attract inbound FDI, and the benefits flowing from it in two main ways. The first is by the actions they take to affect the level and structure of FDI. These include the conditions of entry[16] for, and the ownership or financial limitations placed on, FDI; the performance or operating requirements expected of foreign affiliates;[17] and any restrictions on the remission of earnings or the repatriation of capital. Clearly, any action which decreases the total revenue, increases the total costs or lowers the net profits of a particular FDI is going to reduce its locational attractiveness to the investing company.

Exactly how much it will affect this attractiveness will depend on the economic rent the TNC is earning and its alternative investment opportunities. These will clearly vary according to firm-, industry- and country-specific considerations. But the evidence does suggest that TNCs are becoming more sensitive to differences in foreign investment policies pursued by governments – particularly where the FDI is in export-oriented manufacturing and service sectors.

The second type of policies are more general, but are becoming more important with the growing integration of the world economy. These embrace actions which are not directed specifically to foreign investors, but which, nevertheless, impinge on their global competitiveness. Moreover, it is important to consider not only the competitiveness of the affiliates, but of the TNCs of which they are a part.

Of the more important of these, taxation rates, political stability, competition policy and general macroeconomic policies are usually put at the top of the list. But, as capital, technology and other intangible 'created' assets become more mobile across national boundaries, the role of government in affecting the availability and efficiency of location-bound resources which support these assets, e.g. transport and communications infrastructure, industrial and/or regional clusters, and some kinds of human capital, has become more important. Also, governments, by some of their non-economic programmes, e.g. environmental regulations, affect the competitiveness of their own firms and their ability to offer complementary resources and capabilities to investors.

At the turn of the century, it would appear that the extent of the complementarity between O-specific resources and capabilities of foreign investors and the L-specific resources and capabilities offered by countries, together with the macro-organizational framework which determines the way these two sets of assets are coordinated, has become the critical explanatory factor of the form and composition of TNC-related activity. *Inter alia*, as has already been suggested, this is because of the changes now taking place in the socio-institutional framework of market economies which we have described as alliance capitalism. The critical feature of alliance capitalism is that firms need to cooperate actively with each other to produce a given product or engage in a set of value adding activities. This cooperation is tending to replace the internal markets of multi-activity firms, which was a central characteristic of hierarchical capitalism. Such internalization of markets is proving increasingly costly, as firms find they need to devote their attention to building up their core competences and combining these with those of other firms.

Alliance capitalism may take various forms. It may be inter- or intra-firm. Inter-firm cooperation may be between firms producing at different phases of the value chain, as in the case of Japanese *keiretsu* of assemblers and suppliers in the automobile industry. Alternatively, it may be between firms producing similar products or processes, as in the case of many strategic alliances in the biotechnology, computer and aircraft industries – particularly in the higher echelons of the value chain – or it may be between firms related in interests, grouped in networks or federations, e.g. cooperative research associations.[18] Another form of cooperation is exemplified by the business or industrial district in which the participating firms reap a variety of agglomerative economies, i.e. economies external to themselves but internal to the district or region in which they operate. In each form of cooperation, the participating firms retain their financial independence. The alliance is mainly formed to exploit the benefits of information sharing, technological complementarity, the availability of specialized inputs and labour pools, the spreading of risks and costs and the speeding up of the production process. The belief is that, by being members of the alliance (which might be between two firms or very many), the value of a firm's core competencies is protected or increased.

To be successful, alliance capitalism also requires a closer cooperation between the different stake-holders of a firm – and in particular between labour and management – than in the case of Fordism where workers were servile to the routinizing tasks and the conveyor belt. It is, indeed, a feature of innovatory-led production that it relies on shop-floor workers to play a more constructive and critical role in the organization of production. Without their active support for such practices as job rotation, total quality management, continuous product improvement, and just-in-time deliveries, the flexible production system, which is now increasingly replacing the Fordist or scale production system,[19] could not operate efficiently. It follows then that inward investors who believe that their competitive advantages rest on such a system will prefer a location where the local workers are sympathetic to it – or can be trained to be so.[20]

A final aspect of alliance capitalism concerns the relationship between governments and firms. Again, it is instructive to look at the symbiosis between the objectives and strategies of Japanese firms and the Japanese government, as both have striven to improve the former's competitiveness in world markets.[21] Too often, in the past, the relations between governments in Western countries have been adversarial; and too often policy has been limited to advancing the *static* efficiency of domestic resource allocation. Yet, in these days of global and innovation-led competition, governments and firms need to give at least equal weight to upgrading the competitiveness of indigenous resources and promoting *dynamic* comparative advantages. For their part, firms need to be as efficient as possible in the use of their O-specific resources and capabilities. But, to achieve this goal, they need to access the right kind of physical and human inputs, cutting-edge transport and communications facilities, and an efficient legal and commercial infrastructure, each of which are location-bound resources which governments either provide directly, or strongly influence their conditions of supply.

We have discussed the political and economic environment for FDI (and for that matter domestic investment as well) at some length, because we believe that the availability and quality of complementary assets, which are essential to the efficient use of the core assets possessed by foreign investors, are becoming a more important determinant of the locational decisions of firms. While this is most obviously the case with FDI in advanced industrial countries, the concept of alliance capitalism is not confined to these countries.

The division of labour forged by the new production system affects developing and transition economies as well – and affects them increasingly as they move up their development paths. Certainly, any attempt by (e.g.) Central European governments to attract FDI *purely* on the basis of favourable wage rates, raw material and component prices or fiscal incentives is unlikely to succeed in the long run – for these advantages may only be temporary and do not attract high value FDI. For host countries to attract inbound investment of the right kind and on the right terms, they need to assign a high priority to (*a*) upgrading the availability and quality of their location-bound created assets and (*b*) encouraging a mentality of, and institutional framework for, alliance capitalism, by which both foreign and domestic firms can draw upon resources and capabilities external to their own assets but internal to those of the alliances.

The changing world of FDI

The changing attitudes of countries

In the early 1990s, most countries – or more particularly governments of host countries – welcomed FDI as 'good news', after a period of being highly critical – if not downright hostile – to it in the 1970s and early 1980s.[22] There are several reasons for this change of heart. Some of these are set out in Table 2.2. The first is the renewed faith of most countries in the workings of the market economy, as demonstrated, for example, by the wholesale privatization of state-owned assets, and the deregulation and liberalization of markets over the last 8 to 10 years. While these events are being most vividly played out in Central and Eastern Europe and in China, the need to remove structural market distortions has also been acknowledged by national or regional governments in many other parts of the world – notably in the European Community, India, Mexico and Vietnam.

Table 2.2   The changing world of foreign direct investment

(a)   *From a country's perspective*
- Renaissance of the market system
- Globalization of economic activity
- Enhanced mobility of wealth-creating assets
- Increasing number of countries approaching 'take off' stage in development
- Convergence of economic structures among advanced countries, and some industrializing countries
- Changing criteria by which governments evaluate FDI
- Better appreciation by governments of the costs and benefits of FDI

(b)   *From a firm's perspective*
- Increasing need to exploit global markets (e.g. to cover escalating R&D costs)
- Competitive pressures to procure inputs (raw materials, components, etc.) from cheapest possible source
- Regional integration has prompted more efficiency-seeking investment
- Growing ease of trans-border communications and reduced transport costs
- Heightened oligopolistic competition among leading firms
- Opening up new territorial opportunities for FDI
- Need to tap into, and/or monitor, foreign sources of technology and organizational capabilities; and to exploit economies of agglomeration
- New incentives to conclude alliances with foreign firms
- Changes in significance of particular locational costs and benefits
- Need to better balance the advantages of globalization with those of localization

The second explanation is the increasing globalization of economic activity and the integration of international production and of international financial markets (UNCTAD 1993). Among other things, as will be described later in this chapter, globalization is bringing structural transformation and a new division of labour in the world economy. It is also going hand in hand with alliance capitalism; and it is compelling both governments and firms to pay more attention to the dynamic competitiveness of the resources and capabilities under their jurisdiction. The third reason is that the key ingredients, namely, contemporary economic growth of created assets, such as technology, intellectual capital, learning experience and organizational competence, are not only becoming more mobile across national boundaries, but are becoming increasingly housed in TNC systems.[23]

The fourth reason why governments are modifying their attitudes towards FDI is that a growing number of economies – especially in East Asia – are now approaching the 'take-off' stage in their economic development; and that, as a result, the competition for the world's scarce resources of capital, technology and organizational skills is becoming increasingly intensive. The fifth is that the economic structures of the major industrialized nations are converging, one result of which is that intra-Triad competition is becoming both more intra-industry and more 'created'-asset intensive.

The sixth explanation is that the criteria for judging the success of FDI by host governments have changed over the years, and changed in a way which has made for a less confrontational and a more cooperative stance between themselves and foreign investors. More particularly, the emphasis of evaluating inbound TNCs over the past two decades has switched from the direct contribution of foreign affiliates to its wider impact on the upgrading of the competitiveness of a host country's indigenous capabilities and the promotion of its dynamic comparative advantage. And the last reason is that the learning experience of countries about what TNCs can and cannot do for host countries has enabled their governments to better understand and assess its consequences, and to take action to ensure that it more efficiently promotes their economic and social goals.

The world economy in the mid-1990s is, indeed, a very different place from that of even a decade ago, and the changes that have occurred have had implications both for the responses of individual nation states to FDI and for the very character of FDI itself.

The changing behaviour of firms

The events we have just outlined have also affected the attitudes, organizational structures and behaviour of business corporations. Such enterprises, for example, have found it increasingly necessary to capture new markets to finance the escalating costs of their research and development and marketing activities, both of which are considered essential to preserve or advance their competitiveness.[24] Cross-border strategic alliances and networks have been prompted for similar reasons, and to encapsulate the time it takes to innovate and learn about new products, processes and management cultures.

Firms have been no less pressured to reduce the cost and improve the quality of their raw materials and components; while, as a growing number of countries are building their own arsenals of skilled labour and technological capacity, foreign investors are finding it more and more desirable to diversify geographically their information gathering and learning capabilities. Competition in internationally oriented industries is becoming increasingly oligopolistic, while – as we shall describe in more detail later – the nature of the competitive advantages of firms, and the factors influencing their locational choices, are very different in the early 1990s to those only a decade or so ago.

Finally, in the more complex global environment of the 1990s, TNCs are being forced to pay more attention to achieving the right balance between the forces making for the global integration of their activities, and those requiring them to be more oriented towards, and sensitive to localized supply capabilities and consumer tastes and needs – what Akio Morita of Sony has referred to as 'glocalization'. For, alongside the acknowledged benefits of globalization, there is a growing awareness, particularly among the citizens of smaller countries, of the need to preserve – and indeed promote, as a comparative advantage – their distinctive cultures, institutional structures, lifestyles, working relationships and consumption preferences. TNCs ignore these country-specific differences – which many observers, e.g. Naisbitt (1994), believe will become important in the future – at their peril.[25]

The changing modality of international commerce

At one time, firms used to engage in international transactions primarily through arm's-length exporting and importing. Today, the main vehicles are FDI and cooperative alliances. As an earlier section of this chapter has shown, alliance capitalism is challenging hierarchical capitalism as the dominant characteristic of market-based capitalism. Initially, the foreign-based activities of TNCs were driven by trade; today, they are inextricably fused with trade. Outside the primary sector, upwards of two-thirds of the world's exports of goods and services are accounted for by TNCs; and 30–40 per cent of these take place within these same institutions – 60–70 per cent in the case of intangible assets such as technology and organizational skills (Dunning 1993a; UN *World Investment Report* 1993).

Today, TNCs are the main producers and organizers of knowledge-based assets; and they are the principal cross-border disseminators of the fruits of these assets. It is true that the ambience of innovatory activities, the availability of risk capital and the educational infrastructure is strongly influenced by the actions of governments. It is also the case that a myriad of small firms and individual entrepreneurs are significant seed-beds of new ideas and inventions.

However, increasingly, economic progress is being shaped by the way new knowledge and organizational techniques are created, systematized and disseminated. Sometimes, the market system is able to perform this task satisfactorily by itself; but, because many emerging innovations are both generic and multipurpose, and have to be coordinated with other assets to be fully productive, firms frequently find it beneficial to supplement or supplant external markets by their own governance systems. Sometimes – as we have already suggested – and increasingly, the efficient production and use of created assets requires firms to cooperate with each other, and even to be located in close proximity to each other.[26]

To some extent, this has always been the case. One of the earliest definitions of a business enterprise was that it was a 'coordinated unit of decision taking';[27] but, today, the firm is better described as 'a coordinator of a network of interrelated value-added activities' (Dunning 1993b) or a 'nexus of treaties'. At one time, the boundaries of the firm were firmly determined by its ownership. Now, *de facto*, they are much fuzzier; as their capability to control the allocation of resources may be exercised through a variety of cooperative arrangements, or networking agreements.[28] The more activities a firm pursues, the more it engages in coalitions with other firms, and the more countries it produces in, or trades with, then the more its competitiveness is likely to be determined by its ability to integrate these activities systemically.

The 'systemic' view of the TNCs[29] implies very different governance structures than those implemented by traditional foreign investors. Rather than acting as an owner of a number of fairly autonomous or 'stand-alone' foreign affiliates, each of which is expected to earn the maximum economic rent on the resources invested in it, the systemic TNC aims to manage its portfolio of spatially diffused human and physical assets – including those owned by other firms in which it has some proprietary interest – as a holistic production, financial and marketing system. Of course, there are costs of coordinating intra- and inter-firm cross-border activities; and these will ultimately determine the extent and pattern of a firm's territorial expansion. But, recent advances in international transport and telecommunication technology have pushed out these limits. In cases where corporations have shed some of their foreign assets, this has mainly been to reduce the scope or diversity of their activities and the form of their networking, rather than that of the geography of their international transactions.

A final feature of the FDI of the 1980s and 1990s, which accords with the systemic view of TNC activity, is that probably as much as 90 per cent of it is currently undertaken by already established TNCs; i.e. it is *sequential* rather than *initial* investment. This is not to deny that new TNCs are emerging all the time – probably at the rate of 4000 to 5000 a year,[30] and increasingly form developing countries, notably China; but, as yet, the total foreign capital stake of these companies is thought to be quite small. Now, research has established that *sequential* FDI – which, as far as a particular country is concerned, might be a first-time investment – is not only likely to be more geared to the interests of the rest of the investing company's value activities, but is likely to generate its own unique costs and benefits, i.e. over and above those generated by an initial investment (Kogut 1983; Buckley and Casson 1985). These essentially arise from the consequences of multinationality *per se*. They include such gains as those arising from the diversification of exchange risk and economic uncertainty, the spreading of environmental volatility, and the opportunity to better exploit the economies of geographical scope and specialization. They also include the costs of coordinating the activities and markets of foreign affiliates in widely different business cultures and political regimes (Kogut and Kulatihala 1988), and those associated with the setting up and sustaining of a cross-border network of intra- and inter-firm relationships.

The criteria for evaluating FDI

Global economic events of the last decade or so, and particularly those driven by technological advances, regional integration and the realignment of economic systems and policies, have, then, fundamentally altered the perception by governments of host countries of how FDI may contribute towards their economic and social goals. These same events have also caused a reappraisal by firms of *why* and *how* – and, indeed, *where* – they need to engage in international transactions. It is for these reasons that the current generation of scholars – not to mention governments and firms – continue to want to know more about the benefits (and costs!) of FDI. To what extent and in what way is the global economy causing these to change; and what should national and regional administrations do to ensure that inward TNC activity contributes the most benefits it possibly can to their economic and social needs and aspirations?[31]

While host nations have a multiplicity of economic and social goals they wish to achieve, the priority of which may vary over time, the principal economic criterion by which national administrations appear to be evaluating inbound FDI in the 1990s is by

> its perceived contribution to the improvement of the competitiveness and productivity of the resources and asset creating capabilities located within their areas of jurisdiction.[32]

This, indeed, is probably the single most important medium- to long-term economic objective of the great majority of nations, and particularly of those which are most dependent on foreign sources of supply and foreign markets for their prosperity.

How, then, might the competitiveness or productivity of a country be advanced? Table 2.3 identifies five main ways. The first is for a country's firms to produce more efficiently whatever they are currently producing, e.g. by reducing organizational costs and/or raising labour or capital productivity. The second is by the innovation of new, or the improvement of the quality of existing products, production processes and organization structures. The third is by the reallocation of resources and capabilities to produce goods and services which are in better accord with the country's comparative dynamic advantage. The fourth is by capturing new foreign markets – providing this is cost effective. And the fifth is by reducing the costs, or speeding up the process, of structural adjustment to changes in global demand and supply conditions.

Up to fairly recently, most Western economists – especially those of a neo-classical persuasion – have treated competitiveness as a *static* phenomenon, and have mainly been concerned with upgrading the productivity of firms or countries through improving the usage of *existing* resources and capabilities. However, as the focus of raising economic welfare has been increasingly directed to product improvement and innovation, so the

Table 2.3   The five ways for a nation to upgrade its competitiveness and comparative advantage

1   Increase the efficiency of its existing asset deployment by more effective quality control procedures: e.g. by networking with other firms; by more cost-effective sourcing; by reducing lead times; by raising labour and capital productivity.

2   Improve the allocation of its existing resources and capabilities: e.g. from less productive to more productive activities; and towards those in which its perceived dynamic comparative advantage is increasing.

3   Innovate new products, processes and organizational structures: e.g. by improving national innovatory systems; by better exploiting the economies of the spatial clustering of related activities; by ensuring risk capital is available for start-up firms.

4   Capture new markets: e.g. by improving knowledge about foreign markets and about customer needs; and by better marketing and distribution techniques.

5   Reduce the costs and/or increase the speed of structural adjustment: e.g. by encouraging flexible labour markets; by enhancing the quality of retraining programmes; by minimizing bureaucratic inefficiencies; by appropriate fiscal and other incentives for industrial restructuring; by a greater willingness to accept, and adjust to, change.

concept of *dynamic* competitiveness has gained attention. Such competitiveness refers to the relative capabilities of firms to market new products or production processes and/or to react speedily and appropriately to exogenous changes in demand and/or supply. Global competitive pressures, together with the new techno-economic paradigm of flexible production, are, then, impelling policy-makers to increasingly evaluate the merits of different organizational modes by their contribution to upgrading the medium- to long-term productivity to their location-bound assets.

The potential contribution of inbound FDI to each of these ways or vectors of upgrading competitiveness is fairly self-evident. It may provide resources or capabilities otherwise unattainable or only attainable at a higher cost. It may steer economic activity towards the production of goods and services deemed most appropriate by domestic and international markets. It may boost R&D, and introduce new organizational techniques. It may accelerate the learning process of indigenous firms. It may stimulate the efficiency of suppliers and competitors, raise quality standards, introduce new working practices, and open up new and cheaper sources of procurement. It may provide additional markets. It may better enable a host country to tap into, or monitor, the competitive advantages of other nations. It may inject new management talent and entrepreneurial initiatives and work cultures. It may encourage the formation of cross-border cooperative alliances, technological systems and inter-firm networking. It may foster the geographical clustering of related activities which generate their own agglomerative economies. In short, it may interact with the *existing* competitive advantages of host nations and affect their *future* competitive advantages in a variety of ways.

Some of these ways are summarized in a schema set out in Figure 2.1. This figure is an adaptation and extension of Michael Porter's diamond of competitive advantage (Porter 1990).[33] It suggests that inbound FDI may affect not only the four facets of the diamond, but the actions of host governments, and the mentality of competitiveness of the constituents in the host country. This it may do, for example, by injecting more market-oriented philosophies and practices, by encouraging more harmonious labour relations, and by raising the quality standards expected by consumers.

It is worth noting that the significance of the individual attributes of the 'diamond' of competitive advantage may not only vary between countries, but within a particular country over time. Thus, for example, the relative importance of the production and efficient deployment of created assets, and the means by which these are transmitted over space, has increased as the world economy has become more globalized. Similarly, there are suggestions that the ways in which complementary activities are organized along the value added chain, and the agglomerative economies to be derived from a spatial clustering of these, and other related activities, are becoming more significant. By contrast, the optimum number of

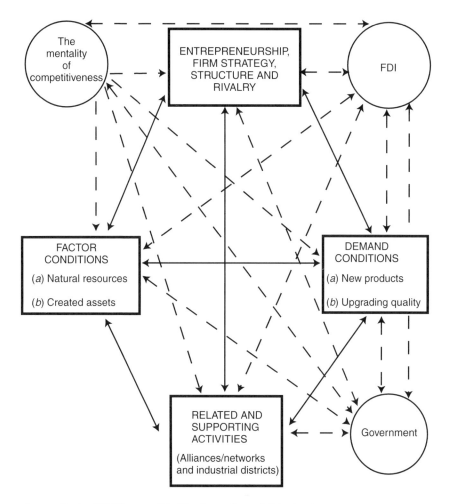

Source: Porter (1990) as modified by the author of this chapter.

Figure 2.1 The diamond of competitive advantage

domestic firms competing in their home market is probably falling as the geographical focus of competition becomes more regional or global, while the domestic availability of natural resources is generally becoming a less critical competitive advantage than once it was.

It is to be accepted that most of the competitive advantages just described are also available to domestic firms; but, it is our contention that the unique attributes of FDI – and especially those which arise from the multinationality of the investing firms, and their ability to engage in cross-border alliances and networks – offer financial, production, marketing and organizational benefits over and above those which indigenous firms may posses or can acquire.

At the same time, there are costs to a host country of inbound TNC activity. These may be divided into two groups. The first comprise various payments (e.g. profits, interest, dividends, royalties, management fees) which have to be made to attract the foreign investor or maintain the FDI. These will vary along a continuum. At one extreme, there are the payments below which a non-resident firm is unwilling to invest; and at the other, the payments above which a country is not prepared to accept the investment. The payments actually made will rest on the relative bargaining skills and negotiating power of the TNCs and the recipient governments. These, in turn, will depend on the price which a host country would have to pay to acquire the benefits of FDI in alternative ways and the options open to the investing companies to locate their activities in other countries. In the 1960s and 1970s, the main anxiety of host governments was that the monopoly power of foreign TNCs would enable them – the TNCs – to extract an unacceptably high share of the value added by their affiliates. Today, the greater concern is that, without the inbound investment, host countries may be deprived of the advantages of being part of an internationally integrated production and marketing system (UN *World Investment Report* 1993).

The second type of cost of FDI arises whenever the behaviour of the investing firms, which is geared to advance their global objectives, is perceived to produce unwelcome consequences for the host country. These include the restrictions which a parent company may impose on the sourcing of raw materials and components by its affiliates, and the markets they may serve. The affiliates may also be limited in the range of products they produce, the production processes they employ, the amount and kind of research and development (R&D) they undertake, and the pattern of their networking with indigenous firms. By transfer pricing manipulation, too, it is possible that income earned in the host country might be siphoned off to the home (or some tax haven) country.

Some determinants of the net benefits of FDI

To what extent is it possible to theorize about the net benefits of inbound FDI? Under what conditions will it be of most value to host governments? What can governments do to ensure that such investment best contributes to the upgrading of its indigenous resources and capabilities? The short – but hardly satisfactory – answer is that it all depends on the kind of FDI, the conditions which prompted it, the existing competitive advantages of the host country, and the economic policies pursued by host and other governments. But, fortunately, the economist can go a little further than this by identifying the situations in which a specific host country is likely to gain the most from FDI, and, in sub-optimal situations, what that country might do to increase this gain. In particular, we will argue that the benefits to be reaped from FDI critically depend on, first, the types and age of the investment; second, on the economic characteristics of the host countries; and third, on the macroeconomic and organizational strategies pursued by host governments.

Types of FDI

Table 2.4 sets out the main types of FDI identified by the literature.[34] The classification is mainly based on the *raison d'être* for the investment. The first two types of FDI, namely '*resource seeking*' and '*market seeking*', investment represent the two main motives for an initial foreign entry by a firm – be it in the primary, secondary or tertiary sectors. The latter two embrace the two main modes of expansion by established foreign investors. These 'sequential' investments are frequently aimed at increasing the efficiency of the TNCs' regional, or global, activities by the integration of its assets, production and

Table 2.4   Four main types of foreign direct investment

● *[Natural] resource seeking*
   (a)   Physical resources
   (b)   Human resources
 	
● *Market seeking*
   (a)   Domestic markets
   (b)   Adjacent (e.g. regional) markets
	Mainly motives for
	initial FDI

● *Efficiency seeking*
   Rationalization of production to exploit
   economies of specialization and scope
   (a)   Across value chains
         (i.e. product specialization)
   (b)   Along value chains
         (i.e. process specialization)
 	
● *Strategic (created) asset seeking*
   To advance regional or global strategy by
   acquiring foreign:
   (a)   Information and technology
   (b)   Organizational capabilities
   (c)   Markets, and
   (d)   To tap into the agglomerative and other
         economies of business networks
	Mainly motives
	for *sequential* FDI

markets; these are called *efficiency-seeking* investments. However, sequential, and occasionally first time, investments are increasingly taking the form of *strategic-asset-seeking* investments, the main purpose of which is to acquire resources and capabilities which the investing firm believes will sustain or advance its core competences in regional or global markets. These assets may range from innovatory capability and organizational structures to accessing foreign distribution channels and a better appreciation of the needs of consumers in unfamiliar markets.[35] Strategic-asset-seeking investment is frequently the most expeditious way of acquiring these kinds of competitive advantages (Wendt 1993).

In the 1960s and 1970s, most FDI was of the first or second types, although regional integration in Europe and Latin America was beginning to lead to some efficiency seeking (or rationalized) FDI, particularly by large US TNCs in sectors like autos, consumer electronics and office equipment. There was also a small amount of strategic-asset-seeking investment – usually by US firms which had not been among the first of their industry to invest in Europe, but now, encouraged by the prospects of market growth, were seeking a speedy means of catching up with their rivals.

In the 1980s and early 1990s, FDI has been increasingly of types 3 and 4. Exceptions include first-time investments by TNCs from developing countries and a new generation of first world TNCs. But, upwards of 75 per cent of all intra-Triad TNC activity since the mid-1980s has been by established European or US TNCs, and by Japanese companies, who, from the start of their internationalizing programmes, have sought to coordinate the deployment of their domestic and foreign assets, and have viewed each of their foreign affiliates, and frequently their associated suppliers and industrial customers, not as self-contained entities, but as part of a regional or global network of activities.

This last point is an important one. We have suggested that, in an age of flexible production systems and alliance capitalism, TNCs are increasingly engaging in a variety of modes of cross-border activity. These should be considered less as substitutes for each other and more as the components of a holistic and integrated network of activities. Sometimes, FDI is the appropriate modality; and, sometimes, some kind of non-equity relationship. But, increasingly, each is being viewed as a complementary means of gaining entry into foreign networks of related activities and into foreign markets. Increasingly, too, the competitive advantage of TNCs is being viewed in terms of their ability to coordinate their core competences with those of other firms – and sometimes of the public sector – located outside their home countries. Moreover, host countries, too, are increasingly viewing inbound FDI and cooperative agreements involving foreign firms as a means of advancing the economic interests of their indigenous firms – including those in the same networks as the foreign affiliates.

One very recent phenomenon is the export of vertically integrated networks by Japanese firms to the US and Europe. As yet, this is largely confined to the auto industry, in which sector, between 1980 and 1988, some 109 Tier 1 Japanese component suppliers – which were members of the same *keiretsu* as one or more of the six main Japanese auto assemblers[36] – established manufacturing facilities in the USA (Banerji and Sambharya 1994). However, as Japanese direct investment continues to increase, and as alliance formation becomes a more important part of the strategies of TNCs, one may expect networking FDI to be a feature of the global economy. The extent to which the phenomenon is primarily an intra-Triad one remains to be seen. But, a case could be made out that, in transition economies, in order to speed up the full integration of FDI with the rest of the local economy, foreign TNCs might encourage their home-based suppliers either to invest with them, or to conclude non-equity agreements with suppliers in the host country.[37] What is certain, however, is that in making their locational choices, foreign TNCs are now giving more attention to the quality of the supply capability of potential host countries, including that which arises out of being part of a network of related activities.

While FDI in developing countries – which in the period 1988–1992 accounted for about one-third of all new FDI (UNCTAD 1994) – remains primarily of a market- or resource-seeking kind, this, too, is changing. Increasingly, the liberalization of markets and regional integration in Asia and Latin America is enabling foreign investors to view their production and sourcing portfolios from a regional, rather than a national, perspective. The sub-region comprising the Eastern coastline of China, Hong Kong, Taiwan and Indo-China, is a case in point. Increasingly, too, many developing countries are being drawn into the hinterland of the globalizing firms from first world countries, as, in their bid to remain competitive, these firms are continually seeking new markets and cheaper, better quality and more stable sources of supply. Moreover, there is some suggestion that, *within* both developed and developing countries, foreign firms are increasingly locating their activities in either well established industrial districts (e.g. Silicon Valley and Route 28 in the USA), or in places with the potential to become new business districts (e.g. the new automobile complex now developing in north-east England around the Nissan plant.[38]

However, unlike the 1960s and 1970s, most investments now taking place in developing and transition countries by first world TNCs are not autonomous investments. Rather, they are part of an integrated production system (UN *World Investment Report* 1993). This means that the decisions of TNCs of *what to* produce in a particular country, *where to* source its inputs from and *who to* sell its output to, are based not only on the locational attractions of that country, *vis-à-vis* other countries, but what is perceived to best advance the global interests of the corporations, rather than the interests of one of its foreign affiliates, or group of affiliates. Among other things, and we shall return to this point later, this requires governments of host countries, in the formulation and implementation of their domestic macroeconomic and industrial strategies – and especially those which affect the decisions of foreign direct investors – to be cognizant of the strategies of governments of other countries whose firms are competing for the same resources and markets (Dunning 1992).

Table 2.5 we identify some of the attributes of each type of inbound direct investment which are most likely to enhance the competitive advantages of recipient countries. In practice, the precise contribution of each type of investment will be both activity- and firm-specific. It is also likely to vary according to age of the investment – generally speaking,

Table 2.5 Some likely contributions of different kinds of FDI to the upgrading of competitiveness of host countries

1 Natural resource seeking	(*a*) Provides complementary assets (technology, management and organizational competence)
	(*b*) Provides access to foreign markets
	(*c*) May or may not lead to local 'spin-off' effects on industrial customers, e.g. secondary processing activities
	(*d*) Raises standards of product quality
	(*e*) May or may not foster clusters of resource-based related activities
2 Market seeking	(*a*) As 1(a) above
	(*b*) Fosters backward supply linkages and clusters of specialized labour markets and agglomerative economies
	(*c*) As 1(d) and also raises domestic consumers' expectations of indigenous competitors
	(*d*) Stimulates local entrepreneurship and domestic rivalry
3 Efficiency seeking	(*a*) Improves international division of labour and cross-border networking: entices comparative advantage of host country
	(*b*) Provides access to foreign markets and/or sources of supply
	(*c*) As 2(b) above
	(*d*) As 1(d) and 2(e) above
	(*e*) Aids structural adjustment
4 Strategic asset seeking	(*a*) Provides new finance capital and complementary assets
	(*b*) As 1(b) above
	(*c*) As 2(d) above
	(*d*) As 3(a) above

the local value added of a foreign affiliate is positively correlated with its age – and, perhaps most important of all, it will depend on the organizational strategies and economic policies adopted by host governments. We shall examine some of these strategies and policies later in this paper, but, in compiling Table 2.5, we have assumed that they are broadly consistent with the dictates of the international marketplace; and that they are primarily directed towards enhancing the dynamic competitive and comparative advantages of the resources and capabilities within their jurisdiction.

The conclusions from Table 2.5, which summarizes a substantial body of research findings,[39] and also the experience of many national authorities, are self-evident. Each type of FDI has its own particular contribution to make to the five ways of upgrading competitiveness identified in Table 2.3, and the four facets of Porter's diamond, illustrated in Figure 2.1. For example, by the resources and capabilities they transfer, the examples they set, their participation in business districts, and their upstream and downstream transactions with related domestic firms, TNCs engaged in both market- and resource-seeking FDI have the potential to raise the productivity of indigenous resources and capabilities, improve quality standards and stimulate economic growth. In the right circumstances, efficiency-seeking FDI can assist the host country to restructure its economic activities more in line with its dynamic comparative advantage; it can reduce the costs of structural adjustment; and it can foster more demanding purchasing standards both by industrial and personal consumers. Strategic-asset-seeking investment may help integrate the competitive advantages of the acquired firm with those of the acquiring firm, and make for additional rivalry between domestic firms. However, this type of FDI, unlike the other three, may be undertaken with the specific purpose of transferring the assets acquiring from the host to the home country; and this may work to the disadvantage of the competitiveness of the former country.[40]

The contribution of each type of FDI will also vary according to the part, or parts, of the value chain in which it is undertaken. In turn, investment in each part may be differently motivated. For example, some kinds of foreign-owned research and development (R&D) activities are truncated replicas of those of the parent companies; some are akin to efficiency-seeking foreign production; and some are designed to gain an insight into the innovatory activities of the host country, and, where permitted, to participate in foreign research consortia.[41] This latter motive explains the presence of foreign TNCs in regional clusters of R&D activities in the USA, and EC and Japan. However, in general, inbound investment, providing it helps advance the dynamic comparative advantage of the host country, is likely to have its most beneficial effects where it is directed to those stages of the value chain where the potential for upgrading productivity is the greatest.

Spatial and country influences

So much for the different kinds of FDI, each of which, as an earlier section of this chapter showed, is likely to be 'pushed' or 'pulled' abroad by different factors, and thus attracted to different countries. Thus, *market-seeking* FDI will be attracted to countries with large and prosperous markets, or to countries with easy access to such markets (e.g. small countries in regionally integrated areas). *Resource-seeking* FDI will almost entirely be determined by the availability and quality of natural resources, together with the level and significance of international transport costs. *Efficiency-seeking* TNC activity will prefer a location consistent with the host country's comparative advantage of that activity in world markets; thus labour-intensive FDI will be directed to countries with low real wages, while TNCs will choose to specialize in high technology activities in the advanced industrial countries and those which offer the best supporting infrastructure. *Strategic-asset-seeking* investment will be partly firm-specific, but will normally take place in countries similar in economic structure and living standards to that of those investing countries, except, perhaps, in the case of natural resource sectors and where FDI is geared towards buying into unfamiliar markets and distribution channels.

Again, the ownership of foreign facilities is not always necessary to achieve the objectives implicit in these four kinds of FDI. In the hotel industry, for example, the major form of foreign involvement by the leading transnational hotel chains is not FDI, but franchising and management contracts (Dunning and Kundu 1994). As large and medium-sized firms are reducing the scope of their domestic value added activities, this is also likely to occur abroad as well. But, in place of vertical or horizontal integration, firms are now concluding a variety of non-equity cooperative arrangements; and, if this pattern is replicated abroad, we might expect the significance of these arrangements to increase in the years to come. Certainly, in considering the impact of foreign TNC activity on the competitiveness of host countries, it is appropriate that all forms of non-equity alliances as well as FDI are considered.

Let us now turn to factors determining the location of TNC activity in the last decade. How do they differ from those of the 1970s? What determines the kind of competitive advantages offered by countries seeking to attract FDI? What should be the attitude and policies of national governments at the turn of the millennium towards FDI, and in the light of globalization? And, how do these attitudes and policies differ from those displayed in the 1960s and 1970s?

In answer to the first question, Table 2.6 sets out a selection of some generic spatial characteristics, which scholarly research has shown to most affect the geography of TNC activity. Broadly speaking, the characteristics fall into two main groups:

1 Those which chiefly affect the *production* costs and revenues of the investing firms and

Table 2.6   Some country–specific attributes affecting FDI

---

(1)   Those which chiefly affect direct production costs and benefits
- Spatial distribution of natural resources, created assets and markets
- Input prices, quality and productivity (e.g. labour, energy, materials, components, semi-finished goods)
- Investment incentives and disincentives (including performance requirements, etc.)
- Comparative economies of centralization v. decentralization of different segments of value chain, namely, production and marketing

(2)   Those which chiefly affect transaction and coordinating costs and benefits
- Cross-border transport and communication costs
- Artificial barriers (e.g. import controls) to trade in goods and services
- Societal and infrastructural provisions (commercial, legal, educational, transport and communication)
- Differences in cross-country political ideologies, language, culture, business, customs and the ethos of competitiveness
- Economic system and policies of host governments; the organizational and institutional framework for resource allocation
- The opportunities to exploit the agglomerative economies of industrial districts

---

Source: Adapted from table 4.1 in Dunning 1993a.

2   Those which chiefly affect the *transaction* and *coordinating* costs and benefits[42] of the investing firms.

Research[43] has established that each of these characteristics – and their constituent components – will have a different effect on each of the kinds of FDI just described. Thus, for example, artificial barriers to trade might encourage defensive market-seeking FDI, but deter efficiency-seeking FDI. Both resource- and efficiency-seeking investors are less interested in the size and character of the local market, which is the main concern of market-seeking investors. Investment incentives and disincentives have been found to be most significant in influencing efficiency-seeking FDI; while sequential investors are less likely to be concerned about cross-country ideological, language and cultural differences than first-time market-seeking investors. Strategic-asset-seeking investors are unlikely to be influenced by input prices or cross-border consumer transport costs to the same extent as are efficiency-seeking investors; while the opportunity to exploit scale economies is likely to be positively correlated with efficiency-seeking FDI, and negatively correlated with market-seeking FDI. Secondly, the significance of the locational variables set out in Table 2.6 will also vary according to the industry[44] of, and the asset portfolios and strategies pursued by, the investing firms.[45] And, finally, they will also depend on the attributes of particular host countries, such as their size, stage of economic development, industrial structure, degree of economic interdependence with the rest of the world, and their physical and psychological distance from the main investing countries.

Now, most of these spatial characteristics, and the industry-, firm- and the country-specific contextual variables which influence them, are well known both to scholars and to the business enterprises alike. Yet, in the past, the expectations of governments – and particularly governments of lower income countries – have been frequently frustrated because they have not sufficiently taken into account the unique characteristics of their own resources and organizational capabilities. The benefits of inward FDI for Nigeria or Taiwan are unlikely to be the same as those for India; those now experienced by Chile and Vietnam are quite different from what they were ten to fifteen years ago; those currently gained in Malaysia and Botswana from efficiency-seeking FDI are scarcely comparable with each other; while those which result from market- and resource-seeking FDI are likely to be highly dependent on the development and macro-organizational policies of host governments, relative to those implemented by other governments competing for the same FDI.

The significance of the spatially related variables set out in Table 2.6 has changed considerably over the last two decades. As their share of total production costs has declined, the drawing power of natural resources and unskilled labour has declined, while that of created assets and the opportunities of networking with local firms has risen.[46] As the unique competitive advantages of TNCs have become both more mobile and systemic, so such firms have increasingly chosen to locate their value added activities in countries which can offer the most cost-effective complementary assets, and the quality of intrastructure and support services which an integrated international production or marketing strategy requires. In this connection, intending investors usually place their need for state-of-the-art facilities for the cross-border acquisition and transmission of information, technology and finance at the top of their locational priorities. An effective and trustworthy legal framework – particularly in its ability to enforce property rights and resolve contractual disputes – comes a close second. At higher levels of economic development, the quality of a country's educational and technological infrastructure becomes more critical.

More generally, as the organizational and transaction costs of economic activity have become relatively more important – and there is some evidence (Wallis and North 1986; Stiglitz 1989) that these are also positively related to the complexity of a nation's industrial structure – countries which can offer a business environment that is conducive to minimizing these costs, are, *ceteris paribus*, likely to gain an increasing share of inbound investment. Recently, two surveys have been conducted – one on the determinants of Japanese direct investment in UK manufacturing and the other on the location of international offices (Dunning 1991). In both surveys, transaction- and coordinating-cost related variables, e.g. those to do with interpersonal relations, information asymmetries, language and culture, searching for and working with subcontractors, learning about the quality of communications and adapting to local business practices and customer needs, and bureaucratic controls were ranked considerably higher as investment determinants than were traditional production-cost related variables.

Host government policies

In various contributions,[47] the present author has written on the ways in which the actions of national governments might affect – for good or bad – the location and structure of TNC activities. In this chapter, we shall focus on the main changes in host government organizational strategies, over the past two decades, which have most affected the level and distribution of FDI.

Foremost among these changes has been a softening in the attitudes of national governments towards FDI. This has resulted in a widespread liberalization of policies which previously constrained TNC-related activity. Since 1990, more than 30 countries have abandoned central planning in favour of market-based policies; and another 80 have liberalized their foreign investment regulations (UN *World Investment Report* 1993). In addition, as we have already mentioned, the criteria by which most countries evaluate inbound TNC activity have shifted from its direct contribution to local value added to its longer-term consequences for the competitiveness of indigenous resources and capabilities.[48] This reassessment has occurred at a time when governments – both of developed and developing countries – have been rethinking their own role and functions in the light of political changes and the globalization of the world economy. The most obvious manifestation of this rethinking has been a widespread deregulation and liberalization of markets and the privatization of many state-owned sectors, together with the removal, or reduction, of a wide range of government-imposed market imperfections, e.g. subsidies, tariff and non-tariff barriers, price controls and all manner of rules and regulations.

However, the fact that governments have lessened their direct intervention in markets does not mean that they have abdicated – or, indeed, they should abdicate – their responsibility as *enablers* and *steerers* of wealth-creating activities, or as *facilitators* of the private enterprise system. Indeed, as firm-specific assets become more internationally mobile, while others increasingly take on the form of public goods,[49] the role of government as a coordinator of markets and hierarchies is becoming a more, rather than a less, critical one. Moreover, because of the demands of modern technology and competitive pressures, the organization of economic activity has become more pluralistic. This places additional responsibilities on governments to ensure the continued existence of resources and capabilities over which they exercise jurisdiction and capture the synergistic benefits of alliance capitalism.

To a large extent, this remoulded role of national government – it being not so much a question of whether or not governments should intervene in markets, but rather *what kind* of intervention and *for what purpose* – reflects the changes now taking place in the relative efficiency of different modes of organizing economic activity. The market – as a systemic organizational entity – has been reinstated and upgraded, except in the case of public goods and strategically sensitive products. The current philosophy is that decisions on what is to be produced in a particular country, and how it is produced, are best left to the collective will of thousands of firms and hundreds of thousands, or millions, of consumers. At the same time, this philosophy also presumes that, underpinning and sustaining the market as a resource-allocative mechanism, is the strong visible hand of government. For without the complementary assets of an efficient and up-to-date legal, financial and commercial infrastructure, an educated labour force, an adequate transportation and telecommunications network, a strong anti-monopoly policy, a sound macroeconomic policy, and a wealth-creating culture, the market cannot do the job expected of it. We believe that besides its various social and strategic responsibilities, it is the government's task to cultivate and support – though not necessarily undertake – all of these market-enabling activities.

Possibly, what we have so far written is not contentious. Indeed, the policy implications may seem all too familiar. However, the real challenge facing governments is how best to implement these policies. The particular point we wish to emphasize is that the globalizing economy of the 1990s is forcing national governments – be they of large or small, developed or developing countries – to re-examine their domestic economic strategies in the light of the fact that they are increasingly competing for competitive enhancing assets, which are much more footloose than they used to be.[50] Macro-organizational policies which, at one time, only affected the domestic allocation and use of resources, are now as likely to affect trade, FDI and cross-border alliances as much as any tariff, exchange rate change or interest rate hike. If nothing else, the world economy of the 1990s is obliging governments to realign their domestic economic strategies more closely to the needs of the international marketplace.

It is our strong contention that governments which are successful in reducing–or helping hierarchies and collaborative ventures to reduce – the transaction and coordinating costs of economic activity, and which best enable firms to surmount the obstacles to structural change are, *ceteris paribus*, likely to be the most successful, not only in attracting the right kind of FDI, but to do so at the least real costs. It is surely no accident that the countries which have recorded the best economic performances in the last two decades are also those which have (*a*) designed and implemented a macro-organizational strategy consistent with upgrading the competitiveness and the dynamic comparative advantage of their location-bound resources and (*b*) sought to attract the right kind of inward FDI.[51]

One final difference between the domestic economic policies now being required of governments in a world of 'quicksilver' capital, and those practised in the 1960s and 1970s, is that, except for cultural or strategic reasons, there is little case for discriminatory action by governments, either in favour of, or against, inbound TNC activity. Though not always admitted, and except for particular types of incentives and performance requirements, most governments have downgraded the significance of FDI policies *per se*. Instead, they are preferring to re-examine the appropriateness of their general macroeconomic and macro-organizational strategies *in the light of the globalization of the economic activity and the growing mobility of the critical wealth-creating assets; and on the understanding that FDI and trade-related FDI are the chief modalities by which countries are linked together.* It is, then, the interaction between these policies and the strategies pursued by TNCs that will determine the extent to which inbound FDI is able to upgrade a particular country's competitive advantage.

Alternatives to foreign direct investment

In an earlier section of this chapter, we observed that some large multi-activity firms were disinternalizing their non-core activities; and in doing so were replacing hierarchical control by a cooperative arrangement. It is also the case that, for many years, some host countries have preferred to purchase the foreign resources and capabilities they need – or the right to their use – on the open market, or by way of a licensing or franchise agreement or management contract, rather than via foreign direct investment. The desire to maintain control over the use of imported technology and organizational competence has always been a powerful one, although it is by no means the case that ownership of equity capital is necessary to achieve this purpose – a fact which many developing countries found out the hard way following a spate of expropriations in the 1970s.

We have seen that the literature distinguishes between a particular set of assets and proprietary rights provided to a host country by FDI, and the control over the use of these assets. Both O-specific advantages are likely to be different if they are internalized within TNCs than if they are exchanged between independent firms. Host countries clearly have to assess whether the net benefits of asset transfer and usage by way of FDI are greater or less than that by a non-equity route. The answer will clearly depend on the form and extent of the market failure leading to the FDI, and how far such failure can be reduced by 'voice' rather than 'exit' type organizational strategies (Hirschman 1970).

The recent experience of Japanese participation in European and US industry has shown that a cooperative venture is sometimes a viable alternative to FDI from an investing firm's viewpoint, although much will depend upon whether, as a result of relational transactions, the proprietary assets of the parties to the exchange can be protected. Earlier, we suggested that technological advances, particularly in inter-firm communications, together with an increasing need for industrial buyers and sellers to tap into each other's assets and work together to ensure that the economies of synergy are fully exploited, are combining to reduce the transaction and coordination costs of alliances or networks. We also averred that various characteristics of flexible production, e.g. the just-in-time inventory system and the greater emphasis on learning from other firms through the exchange and diffusion of superior production technology and organizational routines, etc., together with the increasing inability of 'stand alone' hierarchies to meet the demands of the global marketplace, are increasingly favouring non-equity cross-border relationships.

Over the past decades, the number of high technology strategic alliances has considerably outpaced the number of new foreign affiliates and cross-border M&As – at least in the developed world.[52] And, as we have seen, growth through collaboration and the pooling of assets – particularly among small and medium-sized enterprises (SMEs) – is well suited to transitional economies in which there is a lack of suitable information-processing capability, and/or effective governance mechanisms. Certainly, deficiencies in the socio-institutional infrastructure, inadequate and unreliable legal and commercial rules, a rudimentary banking and accounting system, penal taxes, and a paucity of indigenous trained managers have been the most important causes of the lack of hierarchical inbound investment, i.e. FDI, in the erstwhile planned economies over the last five years or more.[53]

The extent to which host countries should consider producing their own technology and other assets, rather than importing them via FDI or alliances, will strongly depend on the unique characteristics of the countries in question. But, the key to making the right decision rests on (*a*) the setting up of a market-facilitating institutional framework which best ensures the promotion of dynamic comparative advantage, and (*b*) the readiness and ability of the host country's government to pursue the appropriate macroeconomic and macro-organizational policies to foster this advantage.

Japan and South Korea are just two examples of countries which, in seeking to promote their long-term comparative advantages, initially limited the role of inbound FDI and created the economic and technological infrastructure to support these advantages from their own resources and from imported knowledge and technology. In doing so, both countries evolved a socio-institutional system which was a mixture between hierarchical and alliance capitalism, into which, as their economic development proceeded, they incorporated FDI. But, the extent to which a newly developing or transition economy can (or should) follow the Japanese or Korean examples rests largely on its ability to replicate the organizational and institutional structure of those countries, not to mention the culture of its firms and people towards asset creation networking and business districts, the upgrading of product quality and the macro-organizational policies of the government.

The current economic situation of most Central and East European countries is very different from that of Japan, or even Korea, twenty to thirty years ago. None the less, lessons can be drawn from the institutional framework and economic strategies adopted by those countries, which, directly or indirectly, affected the contribution of inbound FDI to their development. Similarly, the experiences of countries as diverse as India, Chile, Nigeria, Portugal and Indonesia, are also worthy of study – sometimes as a guide to what might be done and sometimes as a guide to what ought *not* be done! As we have frequently stressed in this chapter, each country is unique in its economic, social and cultural characteristics, and therefore its assessment of the value of FDI is also likely to be distinctive. Moreover, time may change both the characteristics of a country and its objectives, while techno-economic developments may affect the appropriate way of organizing the creation and use of resources.

It would seem today that the routes by which countries can gain access to foreign-owned resources and markets are considerably wider than they once were. Foreign direct investment is now just one of a plurality of channels which a country may use to upgrade its competitive and comparative advantages. Analysts are agreed that, as a general rule, it should be used to *supplement* the creation and deployment of indigenous assets, rather than replace them: and that any macro-organizational policies of governments should be directed to ensuring that foreign and indigenous resources and capabilities are combined in such a way that their static and dynamic competitiveness are optimized. One thing, however, is certain. Whether technical knowledge, managerial expertise, entrepreneurship, marketing skills, financial acumen or organizational capacity are provided by indigenous firms, FDI, cross-border alliances, or networks of foreign and domestic firms, in today's global marketplace, where economic progress is primarily decided by the ability of private enterprises to innovate new assets and combine these effectively with other assets (some of which will be government supplied), a strong and vibrant techno-economic production system and an efficient socio-institutional infrastructure are essential. And it is only by a conscious and determined effort by government, enterprises and people working together that the critical conditions for the success of both foreign and domestic investment can be achieved.

Conclusions and some caveats

This chapter has sought to identify the main contributions which inbound FDI can make to the static and dynamic competitiveness of host countries, and the conditions which must prevail if that contribution is to be optimized. It has also reviewed the changes which have taken place since 1980, in both the determinants affecting TNC activity, and the attitudes of governments towards it.

Among the most important of these changes has been the globalization of the world economy, the emergence of a new paradigm of production, and the growth of alliance capitalism. These changes and the resulting international division of labour – an integral part of which is the growing mobility of intra-firm intermediate products between countries – is demanding a reappraisal of the economic philosophies and policies of national governments. In particular, the widening locational options of TNCs and the convergence of the industrial structures and trade patterns of advanced countries are forcing national administrations to pay more attention to ensuring that the quality of their location-bound resources and capabilities do not fall behind those of their competitors.

In pursuance of these goals, governments have other critical roles to play, including the elimination of structural and institutional impediments to efficient resource usage; the active promotion of market-facilitating measures; and the encouragement of an ethos of entrepreneurship and promotion of dynamic competitiveness among their constituents. It is the administrations which have gone the furthest in implementing these changes, and in taking a long-term perspective to their economic strategies, which have been the most successful, not only in attracting inbound FDI, but – much more important – in using it in a way which best advances their national interests in a globalizing economy.

We would, however, like to conclude by offering a couple of caveats. The first takes us back to some of the possible costs of FDI as a competitive enhancing vehicle. There is a saying, much beloved by Western economists, that there is no such thing as a free lunch. That means all good things have to be paid for – there is a price. This is certainly true of FDI; the only question is whether the price attached to it is a fair and reasonable one. One difficulty faced by many governments in formulating and implementing policies which affect the costs and benefits of inbound FDI is that they either do not have the knowledge, or are uncertain, about what these costs and benefits actually are. This is partly because most decisions, the outcome of which affect the behaviour of foreign-owned affiliates, are taken by their parent companies on the basis of information and expectations known only to them. This is not to say that these globally oriented decisions necessarily work against the interests of host countries. But it does make life more difficult for a government seeking to optimize the level and pattern of inward FDI and its effects on domestic competitiveness.

We might summarize the main points made in this chapter by reference to Table 2.7, which sets out the main costs and benefits of FDI as have been experienced by host countries over the past two or more decades. The balance between the costs and benefits of each kind of contribution will vary according to the types of investment identified in Figure 2.1 to a variety of *firm-* and *industry*-specific features, some of which we have identified here, and to the age and nationality of the FDI. It will also depend on the characteristics of host countries – and especially, as we have seen, the policies of host governments.

A second caveat relates to the nature of a country's competitiveness. We have already emphasized that competitiveness is a relative concept, and is used by analysts to compare the economic performance between firms, industries or countries, or that of the same firm, industry or country over time. However, whether a country whose firms are uncompetitive in the production of a particular range of goods or services should encourage inbound FDI to upgrade that competitiveness is a debatable point. Very rarely – if ever – can one country expect to be competitive in the production of all goods and services. Obvious examples include growing bananas in Iceland and producing sophisticated electronic equipment in Chad. One of the tasks of the international marketplace – backed by the appropriate government policies – is to allocate resources and capabilities in such a way that each country engages in the kind of economic activities to which it is *comparatively* best suited. FDI can play a useful – and sometimes a decisive – part in this process. What, however, it should not be used for is to 'prop up' activities which can never be internationally competitive. Resources and capabilities must be directed to where they can be most efficiently deployed. After all, one of the functions of trade is to allow a country to import products which it is relatively unsuited to produce for itself and pay for these with products which other countries are relatively unsuited to produce. The success or otherwise of FDI in upgrading the *competitive* advantage of a country's resources and its *comparative* advantage in the international marketplace should also be judged by this criterion.

Appendix: Measuring the impact of FDI – some methodological issues

There have been a considerable number of empirical studies assessing the costs and benefits of inbound foreign direct investment; and it is not our intention to review these in this chapter.[54] We would, however, like to reiterate some methodological points made in chapter 10 of *Multinational Enterprises and the Global Economy* (Dunning 1993). This is because it is our experience that, in their evaluation of FDI, host governments are frequently inclined to overestimate that part of its contribution which is specifically attributed to its foreignness *per se*.

Table 2.7 Some possible contributions of inbound FDI to the upgrading of the competitive advantages of host countries

Positive	Negative	Host country characteristics which favour positive effects
1 By providing additional resources and capabilities, namely, capital, technology, management skills, access to markets.	May provide too few, or the wrong kind of, resources and assets. Can cut off foreign markets, cf with those serviced by domestic firms. Can fail to adjust to localized capabilities and needs.	Availability of local resources and capabilities at low real cost, particularly those complementary to those provided by foreign firms. Minimal structural distortions or institutional impediments to upgrading of indigenous assets. Development strategies which help promote dynamic comparative advantage.
2 By injecting new entrepreneurship, management styles, work cultures and more dynamic competitive practices.	An inability of foreign entrepreneurship, management styles and working practices to accommodate, or where appropriate change, local business cultures. The introduction of foreign industrial relations procedures may lead to industrial unrest. By the pursuance of anti-competitive practices, it may lead to an unacceptable degree of market concentration.	The policies pursued by host governments to promote local entrepreneurship and a keen and customer driven work ethic; the character and efficiency of capital markets; the effectiveness of appropriate market-facilitating policies. Larger countries may find it easier to introduce some of these conditions than smaller countries.

Table 2.7 Some possible contributions of inbound FDI to the upgrading of the competitive advantages of host countries *(continued)*

	Positive	*Negative*	*Host country characteristics which favour positive effects*
3	By a more efficient resource allocation, competitive stimulus and spill-over effects on suppliers and/or customers, it can help upgrade domestic resources and capabilities, and the productivity of indigenous firms; it can also foster clusters of related activities to the benefit of the participating firms.	Can limit the upgrading of indigenous resources and capabilities by restricting local production to low-value activities, and importing the major proportion of higher value intermediate products. It may also reduce the opportunities for domestic agglomerative economies by confining its linkages to foreign suppliers and industrial customers.	The form and efficiency of macro-organizational policies and administrative regimes. In particular, the benefits likely to be derived from FDI rest on host governments providing an adequate legal, commercial and assigning priority to policies which help upgrade human and technological capabilities; and encouraging regional clusters of related activities, e.g. science and industrial parks.
4	By adding to the host nation's gross domestic product (GDP), via 1–3 above, and by providing additional tax revenue for government.	By restricting the growth of GDP via 1–3 above, and by transfer pricing (TP) other devices to lower taxes paid by host governments.	See 1–3 above, and by suitable policies by the tax authorities of host governments to minimize TP abuse. Countries which have most to offer TNCs are likely to be more successful in implementing these policies.

Table 2.7 Some possible contributions of inbound FDI to the upgrading of the competitive advantages of host countries (*continued*)

	Positive	Negative	Host country characteristics which favour positive effects
5	By improving the balance of payments (b of p), through import substitution, export generating or FDI efficiency-seeking investment.	By worsening the b of p, through limiting exports and promoting imports and out-competing indigenous firms which export more and import less.	Need to take a long view of importing and exporting behaviour of foreign affiliates. The key issue is not the b of p *per se*, but the contribution of FDI to economic efficiency, growth and stability. However, countries with a chronic b of p deficit may find it difficult to completely liberalize their b of p policies.
6	By better linking the host economy with the global marketplace, and helping to advance economic growth by fostering a more efficient international division of labour (d of l).	By promoting a d of l based on what the investing firm perceives to be in its global interests, which may be inconsistent with dynamic comparative advantage, as perceived by host country.	As 3 above – and in particular the extent to which host country governments can pursue policies which encourage investing firms to upgrade their value adding activities, and invest in activities which enhance the dynamic comparative advantage of indigenous resources. The gains from 6 are particularly important for smaller countries.

Table 2.7 Some possible contributions of inbound FDI to the upgrading of the competitive advantages of host countries (*continued*)

Positive	Negative	Host country characteristics which favour positive effects
7 By more directly exposing the host economy to the political and economic system of other countries; the values and demand structures of foreign households; to the attitudes to work practices, incentives and industrial relations and foreign workers; and to the many different customs and behavioural norms of foreign societies.	By causing political, social and cultural unrest or divisiveness; by the introduction of unacceptable values (e.g. respect to advertising, business customs, labour practices and environmental standards); and by the direct interference of foreign companies in the political regime or electoral process of the host country.	Extent to which society is strong and stable enough to smoothly adjust to technological and political change. Also, the strength and quality of government-determined regulations and norms; the nature of the host country's goals and its perceived trade-off between (e.g.) economic growth, political sovereignty and cultural autonomy. The difficulties in optimizing the benefits of the openness induced by FDI will be greatest in countries which are most culturally distinct from their trading or investing partners.

The problem of attribution is common to all impact studies. Suppose, for example, it is possible to identify the transactions and performance of MNEs or that of their affiliates. For example, suppose it can be shown that the German-owned affiliates in Brazil record a good export performance; or that Japanese affiliates in the UK are highly productive; or that Swedish subsidiaries in Malaysia pay their workers above the national average wages; or that French-owned hotels in Jamaica import most of their food; or that UK mining companies in New Guinea limit the markets to which their affiliates can sell; or that US subsidiaries in Canada carry out only a limited amount of R&D; or that, as a result of a takeover of a Thai textile company by a Hong Kong foreign investor, a large number of redundancies occur; or that, in order to obtain a permit for building a petrochemical plant, an Italian construction company is found guilty of bribing a Nigerian government official, or that a Dutch and Indian food-processing firm conclude a strategic alliance to drive out a powerful US competitor.

Suppose all these things. To what extent may it then be said that these events are due specifically to the *foreignness* or the *multinationality* of these companies, and to what extent to other attributes they may possess, but which may have little, if anything, to do with their nationality of ownership or degree of multinationality? For it is a fact that, as well as engaging in foreign production, MNEs are often big and diversified; but so are many uni-national firms. They may also influence, if not control, sources of supply or marketing outlets: but, so too, might some of their local competitors. By their marketing and advertising practices they may, for good or bad, affect the purchasing habits and values of consumers; but, so too might indigenous firms or foreign firms exporting to the countries in question! In assessing the unique contributions of MNEs, the scholar needs to be constantly careful only to attribute those which are a consequence of their foreignness and/or their degree of multinationality.

There is another, but related, problem. Let us take just one example. How does one measure the impact of the operations of a foreign affiliate of a MNE on the balance of payments of a host country? We shall demonstrate that it is not sufficient to calculate the external transactions on capital and current account of MNEs or their foreign affiliates; for these must be set against some estimate of the transactions that would have occurred in the absence of such foreign affiliates–the so called *alternative* or *counter-factual* position. For example, suppose that a Dutch MNE company finds that, after two years of operating a foreign affiliate in Pakistan, its exports to that country are only one-half those before the affiliate was set up? How far can this decline in exports be attributed to the foreign investment? The answer depends very much on what would have happened had not the investment taken place. There is also the question of what happens to the resources, e.g. capital and labour displaced by exports. Will these be employed elsewhere in the economy where exports might be earned, or will they remain unused? Much in this instance rests on the supply capacity of the home country, and the kinds of macroeconomic, fiscal and employment policies pursued by the home government. But, depending on the answer to these questions, the net balance of payments effects of outward investment may vary from being strongly negative to strongly positive.

Naturally, any alternative or counter-factual position is bound to be hypothetical, as one cannot be sure what would actually have happened in the absence of the foreign investment. Because of this, some researchers have argued that it is more helpful to try and identify the specific characteristics of the *ownership* of foreign affiliates, by making comparisons between the conduct and performance of foreign and indigenous firms or between foreign firms according to the nationality of their ownership or degree of multinationality. Any differences revealed may then be reasonably attributable to the nationality or multinationality of the firm. This is an interesting estimating procedure. At the same time, it does make the implicit assumption that, in the absence of FDI, the output gap would be met by other firms, that is to say, that the resources released by the foreign firm would be utilized.

Such methodological points are critical if the distinctive impact of MNEs is to be properly appreciated and evaluated. Of course it is quite possible that the main contribution of inbound investment to a particular country may have little to do with country of origin. One suspects that this particularly applies in the case of intra-OECD investment in international industries, where the main competitors of foreign MNEs are domestic MNEs. On the other hand, in some cutting-edge technology and information-intensive sectors, e.g. biotechnology, banking and financial services, etc., the nationality of ownership may be a crucial variable affecting technological or organizational competences; and even in other sectors, since foreign-owned firms are often more efficient than domestic firms, their marginal impact on the competitiveness of indigenous resources may be quite substantial.

Notes

1. For a detailed examination of this system, cf. the scale or mass production system, see e.g. Best (1990), Gerlach (1992), Harrison (1994) and Oman (1994). For a discussion of the interaction between changes in techno-economic production systems and the socio-institutional framework of market economies, see Perez (1983) and Freeman (1998).

2. What Benjamin Gomes-Casseres (1994) has recently referred to as 'group alliances' and Jorg Sydow (1992) has called 'enterprise networks'.

3. There are several such theories or paradigms which are reviewed in Cantwell (1991) and Dunning (1993a).

4. Which, of course, may be an advantage in its own right.

5. Not every scholar accepts the idea of a continuum. Powell (1990), for example, argues that it fails to capture the complex realities of inter-firm connectedness in such organizational structures as industrial and regional networks.

6. Because it is unique to their *ownership*. Advantages of firms other than those which may be attributable to the ownership (e.g. size, etc) we term firm specific advantages. See chapter 4 of Dunning (1993a).

7. These included the heterogeneity and immobility of resources and capabilities and *ex ante* and *ex post* limits to competition (or to the contestability of markets).

8. I cannot accept that the single activity firm is a market-replacing mechanism. The initial *raison d'être* of a firm is the creation of valued goods and services; markets have never fulfilled this function. However, once a firm engages in multiple activities it replaces transactions, which otherwise might have been undertaken by other single activity firms; and at this point they engage in signalling and allocating resources, which would otherwise have been the function of markets.

9. Such products include both intermediate and final goods and services.

10. E.g. product cycle, intangible asset, risk diversification, oligopolistic strategy and sequential theories all seek to explain different types or aspects of TNC activity.

11   Where different stages of the same value chain are linked.

12   For example, to be fully effective, one technology needs to be used jointly with another technology, such as in the telecommunications and biotechnology sectors.

13   For a recent application of the Hirschman concept of 'voice' and 'exit' to customer–supplier relationships in the auto industry, see Helper (1993).

14   Especially when they are part of a spatial network of related firms, e.g. a business district.

15   The risk diversification thesis identified with Alan Rugman (1979) suggests that the existing geographical structure of a firm's investment may affect its attitude to a subsequent investment. Thus, Japanese firms with existing investments in the UK may prefer an additional investment in France or Italy to diversify their risks in Europe.

16   E.g. whether FDI is restricted to certain sectors.

17   E.g. local content and/or export requirements; insistence that a certain proportion of scientific managers, or administrative personnel, be nationals of the host country; the adherence to local environmental standards, etc.

18   Localization economies were first identified by Marshall (1920). More recently, their implications have been taken up by several scholars, notably Piore and Sabel (1984), Porter (1990), Best (1990) and Harrison (1994).

19   This system has a long, practical and intellectual heritage. Its genesis goes back to the introduction of interchangeable manufacturing in the mid-nineteenth century, through the rise of large corporations in the 1870s, to the mass production system which added the principle of flow to that of interchangeability, and the application of scientific management control systems as proposed by Frederick Taylor (1967).

20   As, indeed, has happened in the USA, which has long had a reputation for adversarial labour/management relations. One excellent example of how a working culture may be changed to fit the needs of alliance capitalism is the joint venture of Toyota and General Motors, viz New United Motor Manufacturing, Inc., or NUMMI, which began operations in 1984. For further details, see Wilms and Zell (1994).

21   Although we accept governments may also need to intervene to counteract the anti-competitive behaviour of firms.

22   There still remain exceptions, and sometimes the rhetoric of governmental officials is different from the reality. For a critical evaluation of South Korea's policies towards FDI, see a paper 'Foreigners Cool to Seoul', *International Herald Tribune* (1994).

23   We use the expression 'TNC systems' deliberately, because although there is a good deal of evidence that uni-national – and particularly small to medium size uni-national firms – continue to play an important role in the generation of created assets, sooner or later these firms are forced into a network of complementary activities in which the larger TNCs act as the lead or flagship firms. This idea is further explored in Van Tulder and Junne (1988), Gugler and Dunning (1993), D'Cruz and Rugman (1993) and Harrison (1994).

24   This is especially so in the case of dynamic industries where product life cycles are shortening, and the urgency to innovate new products and introduce more cost-effective production techniques is particularly intense.

25   For some illustrations of the failures of TNCs to acknowledge the significance of inter-country cultural differences, and for some ways in which TNCs may, them-

selves, build upon these differences to their advantage, see an excellent book by the ex-chairman of Smith Kline Beecham (Wendt 1993).

26 The gains of spatial agglomeration or clustering of related industries are one of the four critical variables influencing the competitiveness of firms and countries, as identified by Porter (1990).

27 This definition was popularized in the 1930s, when the nature of the firm as an organizational unit was hotly debated among British economists.

28 These include strategic alliances and long-term contractual relations with suppliers. The widening scope of firms to control at least partially the use of resources and capabilities of other firms in which they have no ownership, and vice-versa, is encouraging scholars to return to the idea of *groups* of related firms as a critical unit of microeconomic analysis.

29 Some writers have contrasted a global system of TNC-organized *intra*-firm activities with a global network of inter-firm activities. For the purposes of this chapter, bearing in mind that the main unit of analysis is the TNC, we embrace each and every 'related transaction of TNCs – be they *intra*- or *inter*-firm – within the context of a TNC system.

30 Estimates of the universe of TNCs, and their affiliates, are constantly being revised upwards. The latest estimates by UNCTAD are that, in the early 1990s, there were at least 37 000 TNCs and 200 000 foreign affiliates (UNCTAD 1994).

31 While this chapter concentrates on the relations to inbound direct investment, an increasing number of governments are also reassessing the benefits of outbound direct investment. Indeed, as we have frequently stressed – notably in Dunning (1993b) – the globalizing economy is forcing governments to take a more integrated view of outward and inward MNE activity, in exactly the way they do of international trade.

32 For example, as usually measured by its gross national product (GNP) per head or rate of increase in its GNP. The term 'productivity' relates to the efficiency at which a nation is utilizing its scarce resources at a given moment of time. The term 'competitiveness' refers to how well that country is doing *as compared with* other countries; or in some cases, compared to its own performance at a past period of time. The main value of competitive-related studies is to help point the way in which a nation, a region within a nation, or a nation's firms, can improve its (their) production.

33 For further details, see Dunning (1992). In this version of the diagram, we have replaced Porter's 'chance' variable by a 'mentality of competitiveness' variable, as we believe this to be a more critically important country-specific factor, which not only is exogenous to each of the four attributes of the diamond, but is closely linked to the government and FDI variables.

34 See e.g. Dunning (1993a).

35 For recent examples, see Wendt (1993).

36 Toyota, Nissan, Honda, Mitsubishi, Mazda and Isuzu.

37 In a very interesting paper, Peng (1993) has argued that, because they are often denied routes of growth through generic expansion or through mergers and acquisitions, firms from planned economies, e.g. Central and Eastern Europe and China, are almost compelled to implement a growth strategy through networking and bilateral alliances. By such a strategy, firms can tap into 'external resources', i.e. assets which are used but not directly owned by them. Although Peng accepts that a network-based growth strategy frequently incurs many of

the bureaucratic costs of hierarchies, he argues that such inter-firm collaboration may well lead to lower bureaucratic costs since it does not require substantial transfers of ownership rights. Peng further argues that a network-based strategy also facilitates organizational learning through the exchange and diffusion of superior production technology and organizational routines.

38   For further examples of sub-national regional clusters of economic activity in which foreign firms are often involved see, for example, Teece (1992), Scott (1993) and Enwright (1994).

39   For a summary of these, see Dunning (1993a).

40   But not necessarily, as much would depend on how the owners of the acquired firm spend the proceeds of the transaction; and how the location bound resources released by the acquired firm are subsequently deployed.

41   For a recent examination of the structure of FDI in US R&D facilities, see Dunning and Narula (1994).

42   Defined as costs and benefits which arise as a direct result of internalizing the market for intermediate products, i.e. hierarchical or bureaucratic costs of administration.

43   As summarized in chapter 6 of Dunning (1993a).

44   According, for example, to differences in input requirements, costs of transporting intermediate and final products, the extent to which products need to be adapted to local customer requirements, the advantages offered by networking with local firms, the behaviour of competitors, and the need to be sensitive to government mandates and policies.

45   Asset portfolios are the accumulated tangible and intangible assets (i.e. resources and capabilities) which a firm owns, or to which it has privileged access. It is these portfolios, their sustainability and the firm's strategic response to them which will determine the kind and range of products it produces, the extent to which it is vertically integrated, the number and character of its associations with other firms, and the geographical distribution of its activities. In turn, the strategy of a firm will be affected by its age, size, organizational competences and long-term objectives.

46   Exceptions include some resource-seeking and manufacturing assembling investments in the poorer developing countries.

47   See especially Dunning (1991, 1992, 1993b and 1994).

48   What might be thought of as a shift from a 'micro-income' to a 'macro-asset' perspective.

49   Examples include many capital- and technology-intensive products and those which, in their exchange, yield external costs and benefits, i.e. to non-market participants.

50   The idea of 'competing' governments has a very respectable intellectual heritage. It has, so far, been used by public choice economists to explain how individuals, by leaving the country, or 'voting with their feet', can act as a constraint to governments in the tax policies, and in the services they offer their tax-payers. See, for example, Brennan and Buchanan (1985). But the idea could be easily extended to explain how a whole range of actions by governments which affect the profitability of firms may also influence their locational preferences.

51   There are examples of countries which have attracted FDI, but have not grown and *vice versa*. But, sensible macro-economic and macro-organizational policies have led to FDI being attracted to most competitive sectors of the economy or those which are potentially the most competitive.

52 For an analysis of strategic alliances concluded in the 1980s, see Hagedoorn (1993).
53 For a recent and vivid account of the difficulties facing foreign firms contemplating investment in Russia, see Goldman (1994).
54 For the reader who is interested in the results of mainstream research on the consequences of FDI on the economic welfare of host countries, see chapters 11, 13, 14, 15, 16, 17 and 18 of Dunning (1993a).

3
Foreign Direct Investment and the Private Sector

Vitalija Gaucaite

Introduction

Increasing attention has recently been paid in the European transition economies to variations in foreign direct investment (FDI) inflows among recipient countries and the extent to which FDI might be affected by the slowdown in privatization. This reflects both the relative importance and the recent slowdown of privatization-related foreign direct investment flows in most advanced transition economies, along with the capacity of their newly emerging businesses to attract foreign capital in the post-privatization period.

At the centre of the debate is the focus on the costs and benefits of foreign investment, namely whether privatization-related foreign investment affects employment and economic growth positively in the short- to medium-terms and whether foreign investments driven mainly by favourable factor cost differentials (in the East European and Baltic countries) and rich factor endowments (in Russia and some other CIS member countries) are sustainable. An understanding of foreign investors' behaviour in the period of mass privatization and the motives behind their decisions to invest in newly emerging businesses is of particular importance for the transition countries, where privatization has until recently accounted for more than half of all FDI inflows. FDI inflows have also been more volatile than might have been expected on the basis of potential growth scenarios because of the high share of privatization-based investment.[1]

In this chapter an attempt is made to place these issues within the context of different privatization schemes employed by the European transition economies as well as within the wider context of macroeconomic reforms undertaken, including liberalization and stabilization. The factors affecting FDI inward flows, the possibilities of host government policies having an effect on foreign investment and the implications of FDI for the transition economies are addressed below in some detail. Many of these issues have been investigated in the recent economic literature on the transformation process in Eastern and Baltic Europe.[2]

Privatization progress

It is widely accepted that privatization can stimulate an infusion of capital, technology, ideas and skills, complementing changes in incentives and boosting the productivity of enterprises, all of which were clearly lacking in the centrally planned economies. However, whether these benefits arise depends to a large extent on the privatization techniques and on the ensuing distribution of ownership.[3] Moreover, transferring property rights to new owners – whether insiders or outsiders –is only one step, which needs to be complemented by the institutions of a market economy. Hence, rapid mass privatization, as pursued in 1991–92 in the former Czechoslovakia and Lithuania and a year later in Russia, did not reach expected results, at least in the short run, partially because of the lagging institutional changes and the lack of complementary support from other reforms, particularly in fiscal and monetary policy. The slower (or in some cases somewhat delayed) privatization programmes, such as in Poland and to a lesser degree in Estonia and Hungary, gained some momentum in 1993–94 and progressed steadily in 1995 following sustainable institutional changes.

Methods and techniques of privatization in the European transition economies[4] have varied widely: from extensive sales to strategic owners, as was done in Estonia and Hungary from the very start of privatization, to programmes based primarily on insider buy-outs, as in Croatia, Romania, Russia and Slovenia, and particularly in Hungary and Lithuania at a later stage, to innovative mass privatization programmes involving the creation of new financial intermediaries in the Czech Republic, Slovakia and Poland.[5] The methods used to privatize medium- and large-scale enterprises and estimates of the extent of privatization by the end of 1995 in selected European transition economies are summarized in Table 3.1.

Generally speaking, mass and speedy privatization at an early stage (often considered as the first phase of privatization) took place mostly in the small-scale sector, while medium- and large-scale enterprises were initially turned into joint-stock companies rather than privatized. Thus, by the end of 1993 the high level of private activities throughout the region still concerned mainly agriculture and the small-scale service sector, such as catering and retail trade: in the Czech Republic, Poland, Hungary, Estonia and Lithuania between 80 and 90 per cent of former state-owned firms had been privatized. In the mean time, large-scale privatization and industry restructuring progressed at a slower pace, if at all, in Albania, Bulgaria, Romania and the European CIS region, with the exception of the Russian Federation. In fact, it gained momentum only in late 1994 and early 1995, when, in addition to direct sales to large outside managers and management–employee buy-outs, privatization through equity offerings gathered pace as capital markets were slowly opening. Increasingly, large

Table 3.1 Main privatization techniques for medium and large-scale enterprises and acquired FDI in selected European transition economies, 1995

(Shares and ratios in per cent, values in million dollars)

| Country | Share of the value of all formerly state-owned firms | | | | | Cumulative FDI[a] | | FDI inflow |
	Sale to outside-owners	Management employee buy-out	Voucher privatization	Other[b]	Still in state hands	Value	Per capita	Ratio to GDP
Czech Republic	5	0	50	5	40	5943	574	5.4
Estonia	60	12	3	10	15	648	437	5.6
Hungary	40	2	0	16	42	11 394	1113	10.1
Lithuania	<1	5	60	0	35	145	39	1.2
Poland[c]	3	14	6	23	54	2751	71	1.0
Russian Federation[c]	0	55	11	0	34	5612	39	0.5

[a]As from 1988, balance of payments cash basis, end of period.

[b]Including restitution.

[c]Share of the number of all state-owned firms.

Source: C. Grey 'In Search of Owners: Privatization and Corporate Governance in Transition Economies', *World Bank Research Observer*, 11: 2 (August 1996), p. 184, and UNECE *Economic Survey of Europe in 1996–1997*, (Geneva and New York, 1997), tables 3.6.15 and 3.6.16.

and powerful intermediaries such as investment banks and privatization funds in the Czech Republic, Hungary, Poland, Slovakia and later on in Russia accelerated the process. This stage is often earmarked as the second phase of privatization and also includes the consolidation of shares originally distributed to employees in insider buy-out cases. In Russia, at this stage, a 'shares-for-loans' campaign was launched and financial-industrial groups – registered as well as unregistered – took possession of important stakes in oil and mining enterprises.[6]

The third phase of privatization started with rapidly increasing market capitalization and efficiently operating public stock exchanges in most of the advanced East European and Baltic economies and Russia. Shares previously held in state hands were often first to appear on these markets, as in Estonia and Poland. This stage was also marked by the direct sales of enterprises in the telecommunications and energy sectors.

The pace of privatization in individual Central European countries was uneven because of differences in levels of decentralization in decision-making power inside enterprises, and privatization techniques adopted. For example, Estonia and Hungary have managed to privatize the bulk of their medium- and large-scale enterprises through direct sales, mostly to foreign investors (Table 3.1). However, whilst Estonia did so in just three years (1992–95), in the first five years (1990–94) Hungary sold only one-third of its enterprises. The high share of privatized assets in Hungary (see Table 3.1) also reflects large sales in the infrastructure and energy sectors in late 1995. Poland and Romania pursued direct sales in the early privatization phase, but with limited success due to little foreign interest and employee–management (insider) resistance.

Management–employee buy-outs widely implemented in Croatia, Poland, Russia and Slovenia from the early stages of privatization and later on in Hungary and Lithuania (1993–94) guaranteed speedy privatization, particularly in the case of government-issued vouchers. For example, Russia's management–employee buy-out, (voucher-based privatization) programme was completed by mid-1994 and resulted in insider ownership of two-thirds of the shares of privatized enterprises.[7] However, as some surveys have shown, enterprises privatized to insiders were much more reluctant to restructure and invest as compared with those sold to outsiders.[8] On the other hand, sales to insiders tended to inhibit competition in the privatization process and, in some cases, hampered capital market development.

Mass privatization via the voucher programmes has been more or less successfully implemented in the Czech Republic, Lithuania, Russia, Slovakia, Estonia and Poland. The Czech Republic and Lithuania launched their privatization in this way in 1991–92 and managed to transfer some 50–60 per cent (in value) of their state-owned enterprises into private ownership via vouchers. Estonia and Poland introduced voucher privatization much later, in 1994–95, opting for sales of a smaller number of state-owned enterprises or a state-owned equity share in already privatized enterprises. In sum, voucher privatization has been a stimulating factor in the development of market institutions. Its drawbacks have included an inability to generate revenues for further investment as well as a widely dispersed ownership. This remains a major concern, as patterns of ownership usually determine the efficiency of private enterprises and their responsiveness to the market environment. This, in fact, delayed FDI inflows in some European transition economies at least until the second or even third privatization phases.[9]

Private sector performance

The expansion of the private sector over the last few years has been one of the most pronounced features of the East European countries' transition to market economies. Newly emerging businesses have become predominant in many non-industrial sectors, while the large- and medium-scale privatization process has gained momentum since 1994–95.

The speed of the reforms has varied greatly between countries, but their content has remained similar: *liberalization*, including the institution of private ownership, price and foreign trade liberalization; *stabilization*, with its fiscal and monetary aspects, and in particular currency convertibility; and *privatization*, starting with small-scale and moving on to large state-owned enterprises.

Countries such as the Czech Republic, Estonia, Hungary and Poland have managed, within a short period of time, to establish the basic conditions for private sector development, including the adoption of laws and regulations related to private ownership and the creation of product and labour markets. Others, like Bulgaria, Romania and most of the CIS member states, have lagged somewhat behind, not only with the practical implementation of the reforms, but also with the establishment of an institutional framework for them.

Nevertheless, as a result of the property transformation of state sector enterprises and the establishment of new private businesses, the share of the private sector has broadened over the past few years. Changes in the structure of total output and employment over the period 1991–95 may be seen as a reflection of this process (see Tables 3.2 and 3.3).

National statistics offer mixed data on the private sector's involvement in the economy, usually reporting output, income and employment of 100 per cent privately owned businesses and partially privatized enterprises (see Appendix). These data suggest that the private sector's share is as high as 50–75 per cent of the East European and Baltic states' GDP. However, the data are inconsistent: statisticians lack uniformity in reporting and processing methodology and face the unreliability of

Table 3.2 Share of major sectors in total output in selected European economies in transition, 1991 and 1995 (per cent of GDP)

Country		Agriculture	Industry	Construction	Services	Total	Share of private sector
Bulgaria	1991	14.5	32.9	4.4	48.2	100	27
	1995	13.9	28.5	5.2	52.4	100	48
Czech Republic	1991	6.0	47.4	6.8	39.8	100	17
	1995	5.2	34.1	7.4	53.3	100	66
Estonia	1991	21.8	35.4	7.9	34.9	100	18
	1995	8.1	22.9	5.3	63.7	100	60
Hungary	1991	8.5	29.0	5.4	57.1	100	30
	1995	7.2	26.9	4.9	61.0	100	65
Latvia	1991	23.2	38.1	5.7	33.0	100	–
	1995	9.8	25.3	7.7	57.2	100	60
Lithuania	1991	20.2	45.2	5.0	29.6	100	16
	1995	9.3	29.0	6.7	55.0	100	65
Poland	1991	6.4	35.8	8.7	49.1	100	42
	1995	7.3	36.0	5.8	50.9	100	58
Romania	1991	19.7	39.5	4.5	36.3	100	24
	1995	20.5	35.8	6.8	36.9	100	45

Table 3.2 Share of major sectors in total output in selected European economies in transition, 1991 and 1995 (per cent of GDP) *(continued)*

Country		Agriculture	Industry	Construction	Services	Total	Share of private sector
Russian Federation							
	1991	14.0	39.3	9.4	37.3	100	–
	1995	7.6	33.5	8.6	50.3	100	70
Slovakia							
	1991	5.7	52.7	7.4	34.2	100	–
	1995	6.3	32.1	5.2	56.4	100	65
Slovenia							
	1991	5.4	40.5	4.1	50.0	100	16
	1995	5.0	32.1	5.1	57.8	100	45

Source: UNECE *Economic Survey of Europe in 1995–1996* (Geneva and New York, 1997), tables 3.2.1, 3.2.2., 3.2.4; also for estimated share of private sector in some countries: EBRD, *Transition Report 1995*, pp. 28–30, and *1996*, p. 11.

89

Table 3.3 Employment by major sectors in selected European transition economies, 1992 and 1994 (employment in thousands, share in per cent)

Country	Agriculture Total employment	Agriculture Share of private sector	Industry Total employment	Industry Share of private sector	Construction Total employment	Construction Share of private sector	Other sectors Total employment	Other sectors Share of private sector	Total economy Total employment	Total economy Share of private sector
Bulgaria										
1992	694	45.7	1 067	3.7	195	15.6	1 318	14.6	3 274	17.7
1994	752	77.1	943	12.3	185	43.4	1 362	28.8	3 242	36.0
Czech Republic										
1992	375	8.0	1 725	27.1	396	57.8	2 270	33.3	4 766	31.1
1994	323	39.3	1 623	55.1	434	87.3	2 427	47.3	4 807	53.0
Hungary										
1992	460	–	1 214	–	217	–	2 135	–	4 026	–
1994	328	–	1 036	–	201	–	2 128	–	3 693	–
Latvia										
1992	269	70.3	340	15.3	89	34.8	647	23.6	1 345	31.6
1994	232	90.5	253	43.5	62	72.6	658	33.4	1 205	52.5
Lithuania										
1992	364	91.9	535	36.5	169	39.6	787	21.6	1 855	41.3
1994	392	96.5	378	56.5	111	84.4	795	43.4	1 675	61.5
Poland										
1992	4 028	–	3 778	–	1 014	–	6 191	–	15 011	56.0
1994	4 054	95.9	3 717	46.1	853	78.2	6 300	44.1	14 924	60.6
Romania										
1992	3 422	81.5	3 430	7.2	524	19.4	2 990	23.5	10 365	37.0
1994	3 707	86.9	2 965	14.8	580	50.1	2 930	31.5	10 182	47.9

Table 3.3 Employment by major sectors in selected European transition economies, 1992 and 1994 (employment in thousands, share in per cent) (continued)

Country	Agriculture		Industry		Construction		Other sectors		Total economy	
	Total employment	Share of private sector	Total employment	Share of private sector	Total employment	Share of private sector	Total employment	Share of private sector	Total employment	Share of private sector
Russian Federation										
1992	10 336	62.9	21 324	7.9	7 887	20.7	32 524	10.5	72 071	18.3
1994	10 528	82.1	18 576	24.1	6 788	44.2	32 592	19.9	68 484	33.0
Slovakia										
1992	246	–	576	–	128	–	697	–	2 013	30.5
1994	183	–	517	–	93	–	722	–	1 977	40.5
Slovenia										
1992	70	–	289	–	31	–	397	–	797	–
1994	68	–	252	–	30	–	402	–	752	–

Source: National statistics and UNECE common database.

primary data providers – private enterprises, which tend to hide actual output, income and payroll figures.

According to EBRD estimates, the share of the private sector in the total output of the most advanced European transition economies (including Russia and Romania) in mid-1996 accounted for some 60–75 per cent, up from 10–30 per cent in 1991, while in Bulgaria and Slovenia its share did not exceed 45 per cent and was even lower in the European CIS: 15–40 per cent.[10] The highest share of the private sector was registered in the output of agriculture, construction and some services.

However, the rapidly growing importance of the private sector in terms of its share of total output may be misleading if the changes in output structure throughout the region are not taken into account. The drastic contraction in industrial output (particularly manufacturing), which is generally attributed to the break-up of Comecon and adverse changes in the terms of trade in the early 1990s, was followed by a significant drop in industry's share of total value added. The drop varied from 20 to 10 percentage points over the period 1991–95 in most countries, with the exceptions of Hungary and Poland, where reforms started early, and Bulgaria and Romania, where the transition had yet to start in earnest.

Service sector output, which now accounts for more than 50 per cent of GDP throughout the region (with the exception of Romania) compared with some 30 per cent in 1990, has increased in real terms since 1990. This increase was brought about by the 'new service' sector, namely banking, financial intermediation and real estate, while traditional services tended to contract.

In order to assess the changes in the behaviour of privatized enterprises we attempt to look at their performance and types of ownership. However, there are no systematic data on the performance of privatized enterprises; some surveys carried out by researchers indicate that restructuring is occurring, albeit slowly, in the internally-privatized firms.

The first evidence of post-privatization restructuring is generally translated into employment policies and the financial situation of private enterprises. For instance, according to one survey conducted among Hungarian, Polish and Russian internally privatized enterprises (where the highest level of resistance to employee lay-offs can be expected) in a period of 1–3 years after privatization, employment was known to have been reduced significantly.[11] In Poland, where the survey covered 110 enterprises, in 21 per cent of cases employment was more than halved, in 40 per cent of enterprises it fell in a range of 30–50 per cent and only in 9 per cent of enterprises was employment increased. In Hungary, employment was known to have increased only in one out of 17 enterprises, whereas in seven cases the reduction in employment varied between 10 and 31 per cent. In Russia, a fall in employment exceeding 10 per cent had occurred in 38 per cent of cases, while a slight increase was registered in 6.5 per cent of enterprises.[12]

These changes, which suggest restructuring at the micro-level, have had undesirable macroeconomic effects at least in the short- to medium-terms. In centrally planned economies, public enterprises tended to hoard more labour than they actually needed to meet production targets. The larger the enterprise was in terms of employment, the more bargaining power its management had in securing subsidies and special treatment from the planners.[13] Because of the large size of enterprises and the high level of labour surpluses, the employment effects of privatization on the macro-economy have been problematic. The above-mentioned survey suggests that privatization usually involves immediate job losses: the introduction of more capital-intensive techniques in a period of slow growth or decline – as in the Baltic states in 1990–94 – lead to less demand for labour. An improvement in the employment situation of privatized enterprises can only be expected in the longer term, stemming from an increase in the profitability of privatized enterprises and resulting increases in investment and demand for labor. However, privatization in the European transition economies was usually accompanied by redundancies and the introduction of hard budget constraints on enterprises, which added to job losses (open and/or hidden). These developments created a pool of unemployed workers which could not always be absorbed by other privatized or new firms.[14]

The financial situation of enterprises in the post-privatization period varies widely and shows some improvement in cases of outsider ownership (foreign in particular). In cases of management–employee buy-outs, changes, at least in the first two to three years after privatization, were more often on the negative side (Poland was an exception).[15] For instance, the aforementioned survey indicates that in Hungary, where initial post-privatization conditions were more favourable than in many other European transition economies, only 30 per cent of sample enterprises were faced with financial problems as a result of difficulties in adjusting to market conditions. Conversely, in Russia, a fall in sales volume was registered in almost 60 per cent of sample firms, and the increasing value of outstanding credits continued to be an important source of finance.[16] For the majority of these enterprises, the most important sources of finance were funds raised through the sales of assets and new bank loans. The position of Russia's privatized enterprises remains precarious, as the ongoing 'shares-for-debts' campaign indicates. Working capital shortages and the mutual indebtedness of enterprises have become particularly depressing factors in the European CIS.

In the European transition economies, cuts in subsidies, the collapse of the Council for Mutual Economic Assistance market and trade liberalization have left some enterprises in a hopelessly uncompetitive situation, not only because of their obsolete technology and the poor quality of their products and productivity but also because of the scarcity of new investments and the lack of marketing skills.

Employee redundancies apart, the most important sources of productivity gains in newly privatized enterprises have been innovations in products and production. The modernization of capital equipment, adequate supplies of materials, and a more efficient organization of production have raised productivity and improved quality, but need to be backed by commensurate financial resources, which are often lacking.[17] Evidence of increasing capital investment, financed domestically and, increasingly, through foreign sources and unrelated to privatization, has emerged in many European transition economies since 1995–96.

The scope of inward foreign investment in transition economies

Inward foreign direct investment to Eastern Europe has been growing rapidly in recent years, thanks to the removal of many barriers to goods and capital movement within these countries and in the world market as a whole. The aggregate stock of FDI in the European transition countries is estimated to have risen from $3 per capita in 1990 to $123 per capita in 1996, while net flows of FDI in the region rose to above $10 billion in 1996, as compared with just over $1 billion in 1990.[18] In respect of aggregate world FDI inflows, the share of the European transition economies rose from 0.77 per cent on average in 1988–92 to 3.8 per cent in 1995.[19]

Data in Table 3.4 indicate that the most noticeable changes were recorded in the period 1990–96, when aggregate FDI stocks rose from $10 to $281 per capita, and net foreign direct investment flows peaked in 1995, totaling $9 billion or 2.9 per cent of GDP. The Baltic states were also able to attract foreign direct investment, notwithstanding their late start in post-Soviet reforms: in just five years (1992–96) cumulative FDI stocks in their region grew from $14 to $233 per capita with net FDI inflows peaking at a level of $518 million in 1995, when they accounted for 3.7 per cent of GDP. Estonia was the most attractive to foreign investors: with a FDI stock of $507 per capita by the end of 1996, it was ranked third among the European transition economies. By contrast Russia and other European CIS countries were lagging far behind: this region's aggregate FDI stocks by the end of 1996 had reached only $41 per capita and net FDI inflows accounted for only 0.4 per cent of the region's GDP.

The overall level of foreign investment in the European transition countries rose sharply in 1995, when most countries doubled their inflows in dollar terms, when compared with 1994.[20] However, FDI inflows in 1996 fell by some $2.2 billion, if compared with the previous year for the region as a whole.

Foreign investments have increasingly been concentrated in the non-manufacturing sectors of countries most advanced in reforming their economies (see Figure 3.1). However, FDI flows into the manufacturing

Table 3.4   FDI inflows into the European transition economies, 1991–96

Year	Total	European transition economies		
		Of which		
		Eastern Europe	*Baltic states*	*European CIS*
Value (millions of dollars)				
1991	2 326	2 326	–	–
1992	3 921	3 120	101	700
1993	5 339	3 999	241	1 098
1994	4 822	3 469	536	817
1995	11 972	9 152	457	2 363
1996	10 050	7 171	443	2 436
Share in total (per cent)				
1992	100	79.6	2.6	17.9
1993	100	74.9	4.5	20.6
1994	100	71.9	11.1	16.9
1995	100	76.4	3.8	19.7
1996	100	71.4	4.4	24.2
Growth rate (per cent)				
1992	68.6	34.1	–	–
1993	36.2	28.2	138.6	56.9
1994	–9.7	–13.3	122.4	–25.6
1995	148.3	163.8	–14.7	189.2
1996	–16.1	–21.6	–3.1	3.1
Memorandum item:				
Cumulative FDI per capita				
(dollars)				
1992	25	61	14	8
1995	93	215	175	30
1996	123	281	233	41

Source: UNECE, *Economic Survey of Europe in 1996–1997* (Geneva and New York, 1997), table 3.6.16, appendix table B.16.
Note: Aggregates for *Eastern Europe* include FDI inflows into Albania, Bosnia and Herzegovina, Bulgaria, Croatia, the Czech Republic, Hungary, Poland, Romania, Slovakia, Slovenia, The FYR of Macedonia and Yugoslavia; aggregates for the *Baltic states* include Estonia, Latvia and Lithuania; the aggregates for the *European CIS* include Belarus, Moldova, Russia and Ukraine.

sector still prevail in the other transition economies: for instance, the composition of foreign investment in Russia has been overwhelmingly and increasingly industrial: in 1993, FDI in Russia's industrial sector accounted for 88 per cent of total FDI, and in 1994, for 94 per cent. Moreover, investment in Russia's industrial sector has become increasingly focused on the fuel and energy industries. In 1993 this sector accounted for 16 per cent of all FDI, and in 1994 for nearly one half.[21]

The OECD economies account for most FDI to the European transition economies. In Eastern Europe and the Baltic states the main FDI contributors are from the European Union (EU), which accounts for some three-quarters

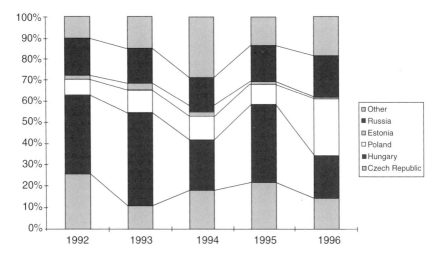

Source: UNECE, *Economic Survey of Europe in 1996–1997* (Geneva and New York, 1997), appendix table B16.

Figure 3.1   FDI inflow concentration in European transition economies

of FDI stock in Hungary and Bulgaria, two-thirds in the Czech Republic, Poland, Slovakia and Slovenia, and half in the Baltic states. Within the EU, Germany and Austria are the major investors. In Russia, the USA and Switzerland account for more than half of FDI stock.[22]

These FDI developments have been accompanied by a significant change in the trade pattern of the European transition countries: the Western economies have increased their importance as trade partners and through their exports of machinery, equipment and intermediate goods to the area. The share of the developed market economies in the total imports of the East European countries rose from 44 per cent in 1989 to 66 per cent in 1996, with imports of investment goods from the developed world accounting for more than one-third of total imports. For the Baltic countries, this change is even more marked: the share of imports from developed countries rose to nearly 60 per cent in 1996 from almost negligible figures in 1989.[23] On the export side, the most notable change in trade with developed countries has been the rapidly rising share of textiles, apparel and footwear, and assembled cars.[24]

Privatization-related FDI

Privatization-based equity investments can produce heavy swings in FDI inflows in smaller economies.[25] The empirical data on FDI inflows and the privatization process in the European transition economies confirm the aforementioned trend. For example, at the beginning of the large-scale privatization process in 1991–92, FDI inflows into Central Europe and the Baltic states rose at a rate of nearly 40 per cent with FDI flows from privatization accounting for almost three-quarters of total FDI inflows. A year later, by the end of the first stage of privatization in many Central European countries, the aggregate privatization-related inflows fell to just above one-half of total FDI, with the latter slowing down to 30 per cent. In 1994, total FDI inflows into the region remained broadly stagnant: however in Bulgaria and Romania, where privatization was well under way, and the Baltic states – in particular Estonia and Latvia, whose privatization progress was catching up with the more advanced Central European economies – the privatization-related foreign investment share in those countries remained almost unchanged, at some 50 per cent. Conversely, in the Czech Republic, Hungary, Lithuania and most of the European CIS, privatization-related FDI inflows dropped significantly. This coincided with the start of the second phase of privatization in many Central European and Baltic countries; privatization in the European CIS was still in its infancy (see Table 3.5).

Table 3.5 FDI and privatization proceeds in selected European transition countries (values in millions of dollars, shares in per cent)

	1991	1992	1993	1994	1995	1996
Czech Republic						
FDI inflows	511	1004	568	862	2562	1296
Privatization proceeds	–	–	–	1077	1205	944
Hungary						
FDI inflows	1459	1471	1471	1146	4453	1983
Privatization proceeds	–	–	1842		3813	880
Poland						
FDI inflows	117	284	580	542	1134	2741
Privatization proceeds	–	–	734	642	1156	495
Russian Federation						
FDI inflows	–	700	900	637	2017	1907
Privatization proceeds	–	–	344	339	1018	493
Memorandum item:						
European transition economies[a]						
FDI from privatization	1868	2657	2932	1121	–	–
Share of region's FDI inflows	76.3	71.0	52.5	19.0		

Note: Privatization proceeds reflect gross privatization proceeds in domestic and foreign currency.
[a]Coverage as in Table 3.1 except for successor states of former Federal Republic of Yugoslavia.
Source: UNECE, *Economic Survey of Europe in 1996–1997*, (Geneva and New York, 1997), table 3.6.17, appendix table B.16; *Russian Economic Trends*, 1997/1, p. 133, and UNCTAD, *World Investment Report 1996*, (Geneva and New York), 1996, table 1.3.

The second stage of privatization was complete by 1995 in the most advanced Central European economies, and a noticeable growth of privatization-related FDI inflows occurred. In Hungary, the Czech Republic and Poland these inflows accounted for all the increment in total FDI inflows in 1995, as compared with 1994.[26] The same, to some extent, could be said about the rapid increase of FDI inflows in Moldova and Ukraine, where privatization was finally getting under way. In the Baltic states, where the second phase of large-scale privatization had been exhausted by late 1994/early 1995 and conditions for a third phase were not yet in place, FDI inflows fell and, with them, privatization-related investment.[27] Privatization slowed down in 1996, as a large number of state-owned enterprises had already been privatized during the first two phases in most advanced European transition economies; this, in turn, was reflected in lower levels of FDI to those countries.

The fear, however, that the ending of privatization of state-owned enterprises, which attracted the bulk of investment to the European transition economies in the period of 1991–95, would drastically cut FDI inflows may have been overstated. Observers point to the Latin American experience where FDI continued to flow in the post-privatization period, with additional investment required for the modernization of acquired assets.[28] This is particularly relevant to the telecommunications and energy sectors.

Conclusions

The massive privatization launched in the European transition economies, along with the reforms pursuing liberalization and stabilization in the post-Soviet period, provided a sound signal to foreign investors about the region's aim to integrate into the world economy. Given that FDI promotes integration into the international marketplace while being essential for the efficient allocation of resources, the transition economies have actively tried to encourage inward FDI. FDI has also been perceived as an inevitable vehicle for domestic economic revival, in particular through the restructuring of large and uncompetitive enterprises.

The foreign investors' response followed: foreign participation in the transition process was largely related to privatization, at least at the outset. In the first phase (1991–92), privatization-based FDI accounted for some three-quarters of total foreign investment with its share falling to one-half in 1993 and one-fifth in 1994. In 1995, privatization-related FDI doubled and even tripled in most advanced transition economies. However, this growth was not sustained in 1996 as privatization in the region started to show mixed signals.

FDI's dependency on privatization raised concerns about the transition economies' prospects of attracting FDI in the post-privatization era.

Moreover, the factor cost advantages based on low wages, which attracted many foreign investors at an early stage, are likely to disappear as income levels converge towards West European levels in the wake of EU accession.

However, the Latin American experience does suggest that privatization-related FDI often leads to reinvestments and creates the environment and demand for additional FDI. The presence of FDI often reassures other potential investors that the host country is committed to liberal policies. In addition, privatization-based FDI may lead to follow-up investments in related sectors, including infrastructural and environmental projects.

Finally, recent questionnaire surveys in many of the European transition countries indicate that FDI has become market motivated rather than cost oriented. Factors such as the widening of selling potential, technical development and high-skilled labour have attracted a growing number of investors.

Appendix: Private sector measurement

Any estimate of the size of the private sector in the countries in transition is very tentative and highly questionable because of certain methodological and statistical issues.

Firstly, up to the present time, no clear distinction between the public and private sectors on a classification level has been achieved by researchers or statisticians. While newly emerging small enterprises are counted as private sector establishments, the state enterprises which have been through the privatization process are not as easy to classify. The majority of these enterprises are still under some state control and sooner or later enter a second stage of privatization according to the privatization schemes employed by individual countries. Some enterprises have already gone through the second stage of privatization in the Czech Republic, Poland, Hungary and the Baltic states but the state, for one or another reason, holds part of their stock, and quite a high proportion in some cases. For instance, at the end of 1994 this state portion in privatized enterprises accounted for 23 per cent in Lithuania, while in Estonia the state usually holds a minority stake of up to 30 per cent in enterprises which have been sold by tender. The question naturally arises to which sector – public or private – should activities of such enterprises be ascribed.

The most common approach when evaluating the private sector impact in the transition economies is to include all enterprises where a majority of shares (at least 51 per cent) is in private possession. Another option is to include all kinds of mixed ownership enterprises as long as any private capital involvement occurs, while the other extreme takes into account only companies with 100 per cent of private ownership. The choice of a particular methodology might lead to an overvaluation as well as an undervaluation of private sector importance for the state economy at this stage. For example, according to the enterprise register monitored by the Estonian Statistical Department there are nine groups of enterprises depending on their ownership: private property, state property, municipal property, cooperative property, property of public organizations, property of rented enterprises, property of foundations, joint property with foreign participation, and property of foreign countries. Activities of at least three or four groups in this register might be questionable when defining them as private or public sector activities: for example, in the group of joint property with foreign participation there are enterprises with different levels of state capital involvement, and likewise in the cooperative property group.

Notes

1 UNCTAD, *World Investment Report 1996* (Geneva and New York, 1996), chapter II.c.
2 Among more recent studies, see G. Hunya and J. Stankovsky, *Foreign Direct Investment in Central and East European Countries and the Former Soviet Union* (Vienna: Vienna Institute for Comparative Studies, 1996); H. Lankes and A. Venables, 'Foreign Direct Investment in Economic Transition: The Changing Pattern of Investment', *Economics in Transition*, 4 (1996); K. Schmidt, 'Foreign Direct Investment in Eastern Europe: State-of-the Art and Prospect', in *Transforming Economies and European Integration*, ed. R. Dobrinsky and M. Landesmann (Aldershot: E. Elgar, 1996); R. Stern, 'Putting Foreign Direct Investment in Eastern Europe into Perspective: Turning A Macroeconomic Failure Into Microeconomic Success Story', in the same volume; M. Lansbury, N. Pain and K. Smidkova, 'Foreign Direct Investment in Central Europe since 1990: An Econometric Study', *National Institute Economic Review*, 156 (May 1996); Z. Wang and N. Swain, 'The Determinants of Foreign Direct Investment in Transforming Economies: Empirical Evidence from Hungary and China', *Weltwirtschaftliches Archiv*, 131:2 (1995).
3 Among more recent studies on these issues, see I. Filatotchev *et al.* 'Buyouts in Hungary, Poland and Russia: governance and finance issues', *Economics in Transition*, 4(1), 1996; C. Grey, 'In Search of Owners: Privatization and Corporate Governance in Transition Economies', *World Bank Research Observer*, 11:2 (August 1996); B. Katz and J. Owen, 'Optimal Voucher Privatization Fund Bids When Bidding Affects Firm Performance', *Journal of Comparative Economics*, 24 (1997); D. Willer, 'Corporate Governance and Shareholder Rights in Russia', *Emerging Markets*, CEP Discussion Paper 343 (April 1997); and studies in *Corporate Governance in Central Europe and Russia*, ed. R. Frydman, C. Grey and A. Rapaczynski, (London: Central European University Press, 1996).
4 'European transition economies' here and elsewhere in this chapter refers to the East European countries, Baltic states and European CS countries.
5 C. Grey, 'In Search of Owners: Privatization and Corporate Governance in Transition Economies', *World Bank Research Observer*, 11: 2 (August 1996).
6 See Y. Adjubei's chapter on Russia in this book.
7 Between the end of December 1992 and the beginning of June 1994 more than 13 000 medium and large state-owned enterprises in Russia became private companies. Total employment in these companies amounted to 15.7 million or 76 per cent of total industrial employment. *'Obsor Ekonomiki Rossii'*, *Osnovniye Tendentsii Razvitiya*, 2 (Moscow 1994), pp. 125-6.

8 See for instance, J. Earl and S. Estrin, 'Worker Ownership in Transition', in *Corporate Governance in Central Europe and Russia*, ed. R. Frydman, C. Grey and A. Rapaczynski (London: Central European University Press, 1996).

9 There is, in fact, very little information on actual post-privatization ownership. Since governments tend to keep only very general records of who purchased assets at the time of official transactions, little is known about the present structure of the privatized sector. However, it seems that the vast majority of all voucher-privatized assets ended up in the hands of three major ownership groups: employees, management and investment funds. Foreign ownership occurred in a very small number of enterprises.

10 EBRD, *Transition Report 1996* (London, 1996), p. 11.

11 I. Filatotchev *et al.*, 'Buy-outs in Hungary, Poland and Russia: Governance and Finance Issues', *Economics in Transition*, 4:1 (1996).

12 Ibid., pp. 71, 74, 77.

13 J. Kornai, *Economics of Shortage* (Amsterdam: North Holland, 1980).

14 R. Jackman, 'Economic Policy and Employment in the Transition Economies of Central and Eastern Europe. What Have We Learned?', *International Labour Review*, 133:3 (1994).

15 In Poland, re-emerging growth of manufacturing output in 1993 was more evident in the private sector (> 10 per cent growth on average). However, in general, output growth was fairly widely dispersed, though more marked in the private sector, while employment growth was concentrated in new private firms. Privatized enterprises were mostly profitable, but with a significant proportion making substantial losses (margin < –10 per cent); state-owned and corporatized enterprises were nearly profitable, but with a large portion making substantial losses and fully one-fifth in serious financial distress (profitability < –25 per cent). For more details see M. Belka *et al.*, *Enterprise Adjustment in Poland: Evidence from a Survey of 200 Private, Privatized, and State-Owned Firms*, Centre for Economic Performance, London School of Economics, Discussion paper 233, April 1995.

16 Filatotchev *et al.* (1996).

17 For instance, among Polish enterprises the greatest obstacle to investment was felt to be high interest rates; next, the poor financial situation of firms; and third, the unwillingness of banks to lend (Belka *et al.* 1995).

18 UN/ECE, *Economic Survey of Europe in 1996–1997* (Geneva and New York, 1997).

19 UNCTAD, *World Investment Report, 1996* (Geneva and New York, 1996), p. 4.

20 The dollar's depreciation by some 8–14 per cent against other major convertible currencies in 1995 (year-on-year) should be borne in mind when considering these figures.

21 *Russian Economic Trends*, 1996.

22 UNCTAD, *World Investment Report 1996* (Geneva and New York, 1996), p. 65.

23 UNECE, *Economic Survey of Europe in 1996–1997* (Geneva and New York, 1997), chapter 3.5 and appendix table B.13.

24 UN/ECE Common database and UN Comtrade Database.

25 J. Agarwal, 'European Integration and German FDI: Implications for Domestic Investment and Central European Economies', *National Institute Economic Review*, 2(1997).

26 UNCTAD *World Investment Report 1996* (Geneva and New York, 1996), p. 67.

27 These are purely speculative observations, as data on FDI flows from privatization for 1995–96 were not available for most of the European CIS or for the Baltic states at the time of writing.

28 J. Agarwal, 'European Integration and German FDI: Implications for Domestic Investment and Central European Economies', *National Institute Economic Review*, 2 (1997).

4
Direct Investment in South-East Asia and Eastern Europe: A Comparative Analysis

Klaus Meyer

Introduction

The countries of Central and Eastern Europe are undergoing an unprecedented transition from centrally planned to capitalist market economies. Aside from macroeconomic stabilization, which has been a top priority in the early years of transition, this necessitates an almost complete microeconomic restructuring, including large-scale changes in ownership and the establishment of market institutions. It was expected that Foreign Direct Investment (FDI) could play a very important catalytic role in the transition, and transfer capital and urgently needed technological and management skills to the region (Dunning 1993a; McMillan 1993). Some countries made FDI an integral part of their transition strategy and the international financial institutions considered it 'crucial' for the success of the transition (IMF, World Bank, OECD and EBRD 1991, p. 75).

Widespread expectations of major FDI inflows in response to the needs of these economies have, however, not been fulfilled. The expectations were partly built on the very successful role that FDI appeared to have played in East Asia over the last decades, in a region at roughly the same level of income and in geographical proximity to advanced developed countries. This chapter will review the role of FDI in the economic development of East Asia by focusing on the economic environment and the process of structural change. The objective is to assess how FDI can be expected to contribute to development in Eastern Europe. In the second section we survey the trends in FDI in emerging markets over the last three decades. The third section develops a model that synthesizes the arguments on the role of factor costs as determinants of FDI in Asia. This model is then briefly assessed in the context of the empirical literature. The fourth section discusses the implications for Eastern Europe.

Trends in FDI in emerging markets

Worldwide FDI surged upwards in the late 1980s but this trend could not be maintained in the 1990s as the recession took effect. The developing countries have received more than 20 per cent of worldwide FDI in past decades: inward investment to emerging markets increased in absolute terms from $12 billion in 1985 to $30 billion in 1990 and $70 billion in 1993. Their relative importance fell in the late 1980s as the FDI surge affected mainly the industrial countries. As a group, they continued to increase FDI inflows in the early 1990s against the trends set in the OECD countries. As a proportion of worldwide FDI, their share fell from 24.5 per cent in 1985 to 13.7 per cent in 1989 and climbed to 40.4 per cent in 1993. FDI inflows have, however, been very uneven, as illustrated in Figure 4.1. Developing countries have been aggregated in groups to depict long-term trends since the late 1960s. The data are taken from IMF balance of payments statistics which may not cover all FDI, but are the most comparable sources of data (Meyer 1995a).

In the 1970s and early 1980s, the oil-exporting countries of OPEC (Organization of Petroleum Exporting Countries) attracted large amounts of FDI, but the pattern was erratic: some years recorded large net withdrawals of investment – even at this high level of aggregation. In recent years, OPEC countries have been of minor importance for multinational investors as investment has shifted from natural resource exploration to manufacturing and sales operations.

The leading destinations for FDI in emerging markets are in South-East Asia and Latin America. The five ASEAN countries, led by Singapore and Malaysia, received more than $16 billion of investment in 1993. China had a very restrictive regime governing foreign investment until 1991, and since then has become the most important location for investors. Its market of 1 billion potential customers and low labour costs often proved irresistible to foreign firms. In relation to the size of its economy, however, inflows to date have not been exceptional.

The Latin American countries were major recipients in the early 1980s, and again from 1988 onwards. Within this group, Brazil was replaced by Argentina and Mexico as preferred destinations. In these countries, the privatization process opened up large opportunities for foreign investors (UN *World Investment Report* 1994, p. 85). Figure 4.1 also includes a group of Mediterranean countries, which topped the FDI inflow league from 1986 to 1992. This group is dominated by Spain, which is no longer considered as an emerging economy.

Eastern Europe is a latecomer in attracting direct investment. Given that values are reported in nominal terms, Figure 4.1 would suggest that this region is at the same stage as ASEAN, Latin America and the Mediterranean group some ten years ago, which suggests a bright future.

104

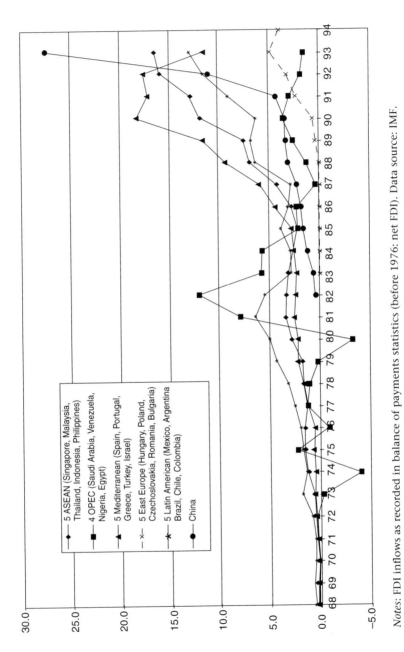

Notes: FDI inflows as recorded in balance of payments statistics (before 1976: net FDI). Data source: IMF.

Figure 4.1 FDI in emerging markets: selected groups, 1968–93 ($ billion)

Figure 4.2 illustrates FDI inflows into South-East Asia. It is remarkable that the small country of Singapore has been the most attractive location in the region in all but one year over the last 15 years. The annual inflow is approaching $7 billion and there is no evidence of a saturation level being reached. Singapore is also heading the list of top recipients when adjustments are made for the size of the economy. The average FDI inflow from 1990 to 1993 amounted to $2145 for each inhabitant, or 10.9 per cent of GDP per capita (Table 4.1). Its large neighbour, Malaysia, came second in the early 1980s as well as in recent years receiving over $5 billion of FDI annually – more than the whole region of Eastern Europe at the time.

Other East Asian countries have attracted far less direct investment: South Korea received more than $1 billion in only one year, and Taiwan has received larger inflows only since 1989. These two countries followed a policy of technology acquisition by other means to strengthen the technological capabilities of indigenous firms. Hence, the restrictive policy on FDI did not have a negative effect on their economic development (Urban 1992; Lall 1994; UN *World Investment Report* 1994). The Philippines, on the

Table 4.1   Major recipients of FDI among emerging markets
(Balance of payments recorded FDI, 1990–93: rankings of 34 emerging markets)

Rank	Cumulative FDI in $ billion		Average FDI per capita, $		Average FDI as % of GDP, 1993	
1	China	46.5	Singapore	2145	Singapore	10.9
2	Singapore	24.0	Hong Kong	245	Malaysia	6.5
3	Malaysia	16.7	Malaysia	220	Hungary	3.7
4	Mexico	16.1	Portugal	210	China	2.7
5	Argentina	14.8	Hungary	138	Portugal	2.4
6	Thailand	8.3	Argentina	109	Nigeria	2.4
7	Portugal	8.2	Greece	102	Czech Republic	1.7
8	Taiwan	6.8	Israel	74	Greece	1.7
9	Indonesia	6.4	Czech Republic	53	Thailand	1.7
10	Hong Kong	5.7	Chile	48	Hong Kong	1.6
11	Hungary	5.6	Estonia	38	Estonia	1.2
18	Poland	2.8	Slovenia	34	Slovakia	0.9
21	Czech Republic	2.2	Slovakia	19	Poland	0.8
29	Slovakia	0.41	Poland	18	Slovenia	0.6
30	Romania	0.32	Albania	5	Bulgaria	0.4
31	Slovenia	0.26	Bulgaria	4	Romania	0.3
32	Estonia	0.24	Romania	4	Albania	n/a
33	Bulgaria	0.16				
34	Albania	0.07				

Sources: FDI from IMF (International Financial Statistics), GDP and population from the World Bank (World Development Report 1995). Data for Hong Kong and Taiwan are from national statistics. Slovenia is understated because the 1990 FDI datapoint is missing.

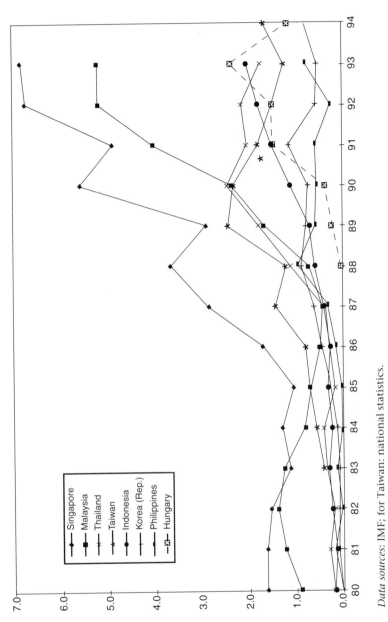

Data sources: IMF; for Taiwan: national statistics.

Figure 4.2   FDI in emerging markets: East Asia, 1980–94 ($ billion)

other hand, has performed poorly in terms of economic development as well as in attracting FDI. Thailand, Indonesia, Hong Kong and Taiwan[1] now hold the middle ground with $1 billion to $2.5 billion annually since 1990. These four countries reached the top 10 emerging markets by cumulative FDI over the 1990–93 period, but not necessarily so if FDI was adjusted to take account of the size of the economy (Table 4.1).

In Eastern Europe, FDI is a very recent phenomenon, as the region was almost closed to foreign investors until 1989. Reliable data on FDI in Eastern Europe, however, have been scarce, and the FDI trends shown in Figure 4.3 may have a larger than usual margin of error. Hungary has been the clear leader from the beginning of the transition due to early advantages in establishing business contacts with Western businesses as well as the chosen mode of privatization, which concentrated on sales of enterprises to foreign investors (Lane 1994; Meyer 1995a). Hungary is now host to as much FDI as Thailand and Indonesia (Figure 4.2). Among emerging markets, it is ranked fifth in terms of FDI per capita and third by FDI as a percentage of GDP (Table 4.1).

Czechoslovakia chose a different approach to privatization, a voucher scheme, which offered fewer opportunities for foreign investors in the early stages of the transition (e.g. Estrin 1994). Nevertheless, its larger successor state, the Czech Republic, came third in the region in terms of absolute FDI inflows in 1991 and 1992 (Figure 4.3) and is among the top 10 emerging markets both in terms of per capita FDI and FDI/GDP ratio (Table 4.1). Poland was a relative latecomer, considering that it is the largest market in the region with 38 million potential customers, compared to 10 million in Hungary and the Czech Republic. Inflows reached $1.7 billion in 1993, according to IMF data.[2] Relative to the size of the economy, FDI in Poland is still fairly small.

Some small countries in the region have been relatively successful in attracting FDI, especially Estonia and Slovenia. The performance of the South-East European countries, namely Albania, Bulgaria and Romania, has been rather disappointing (Meyer 199a), even if the small size of their economies is taken into account. Interestingly, the trend in Romania was reversed by a major investment undertaken by Daewoo in the automotive industry in 1994.

In sum, both Eastern Europe and South-East Asia have seen very unequal inflows of FDI, with Hungary and Poland taking the lion's share of FDI in Eastern Europe, as did Singapore and Malaysia in Asia. The total volume of FDI in Eastern Europe is still less than that of the two leaders in Asia. Considering that the region was practically closed to foreign investment until 1989, and current inflows have grown over five years to a level comparable to that of South-East Asia ten years ago (in real terms), it may augur well for Eastern Europe's future. Also, the East European reforms came at a time when worldwide FDI flows were reduced as the surge around 1990 was not maintained in the new decade.

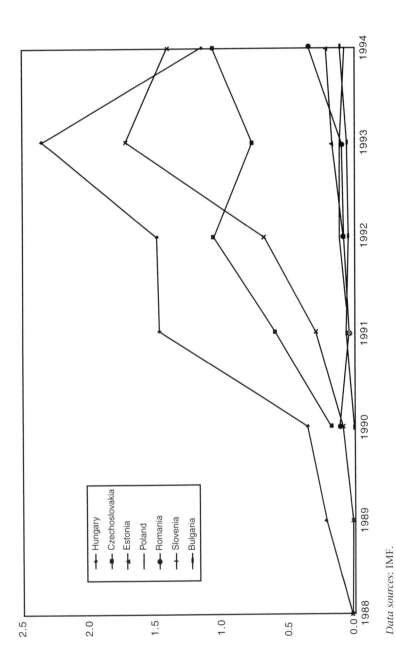

Data sources: IMF.

Figure 4.3   FDI in emerging markets: Eastern Europe, 1988–94 ($ billion)

Next, we discuss whether the Asia patterns could be used to predict the future role of FDI in Eastern Europe. The Asia pattern of development has often been characterized as the 'flying geese' pattern of development, in which spill-overs from advanced countries to second-range countries contribute to their development. FDI is an important mechanism affecting such spill-overs (Ozawa 1992).

FDI and development in South-East Asia

The model

It is generally recognized that FDI contributes to development in the host economy through the transfer of technology and managerial know-how. A foreign subsidiary has spill-overs through 'leakages and linkages' into the local economy. Hence, the investor's knowledge is eventually diffused throughout the host economy and strengthens its locational advantages, particularly its human capital. FDI can thus contribute to the accumulation of knowledge and upgrading of factors of production in the host economy.

On the other hand, FDI can itself be a consequence of developmental adjustment processes. The change in locational advantages and especially in comparative cost advantages over time creates the environmental conditions which are the basis of a dynamic macroeconomic interpretation of FDI (Lee 1990). In the process of development, some industries become uncompetitive in more advanced countries and move to less advanced countries, where the factor endowment is more appropriate for their production technology. This structural change creates conditions that favour factor-cost oriented FDI, as some countries lose their competitive advantage in sectors that other countries try to attract (Markusen 1991). The mechanisms underlying this interactive process of development and FDI are described below.

Mechanisms driving factor-cost oriented FDI

Economic development can be interpreted as a process of accumulation of physical and human capital. In this process, economies move towards more sophisticated production technologies through the acquisition of necessary resources. In particular, higher levels of human capital enable economies to reach higher productivity and income; as a result, the factor endowment of the economy becomes more capital and human-capital intensive. As the economy moves towards higher levels of production sophistication, the industrial structure of the economy changes towards more skill-intensive sectors.

In this 'structural change', certain types of production, stages in the value chain or whole production processes become unprofitable as they face import competition. The supply of untrained labour decreases as workers have the opportunity to increase their skill level. This shortage of low-

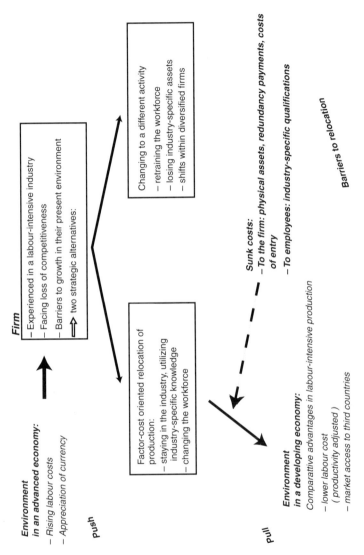

Figure 4.4 Economic Forces driving the Asian model of FDI

skilled labour, combined with maximum spreads of wages between skilled and unskilled, undermines the international competitiveness of production processes based on unskilled labour. The core of untrained workers will then move to sectors that are not exposed to international competition, in particular the service sector.

Rising labour costs, often in connection with currency appreciation, create strong push factors for labour-intensive firms. If they are unable to redesign their production processes by substituting low-skill labour for capital- and knowledge-intensive technologies, they face barriers to growth in their present environment and lose international competitiveness. Nevertheless, they possess valuable assets that can be utilized through restructuring. Businesses in this situation face two strategic alternatives to maximize their assets and capabilities:

- They could move into another sector, acquiring new technological knowledge and retraining their labour force, but losing their industry-specific assets, especially knowledge-based intangibles such as employee experience or exclusive technological knowledge; or,
- They could move their production facilities – or labour-intensive parts of the production process – abroad, utilizing their industry-specific assets but changing their labour force as they close down domestic operations in the long run, and use the locational advantages of the host economy (Kojima and Ozawa 1985).

The choice between these alternative strategies is a function of

1 The attraction of potential low cost locations,
2 The nature of the firm's core competencies, and
3 The sunk costs of implementing the relocation strategy.

The attraction of a potential foreign location for production creates pull factors to induce factor cost oriented investment. The attraction is dependent on local labour costs, adjusted for labour productivity and taking into account all non-wage expenses such as training and social payments. In addition, investors consider a wide range of secondary factors in assessing the attraction of an investment location. For instance, the costs of local inputs vary, including the access to raw materials as well as the existence of local supplier networks for intermediate inputs. The costs of bringing products to the market will depend on the geographical proximity of important markets, the trade regime and infrastructure. The regulatory environment, including tax regimes and bureaucratic procedures, can also raise costs substantially.

The nature of a firm's core competencies is always a major determinant of strategic decisions. Diversified enterprises, mainly with financial assets or capabilities embodied in employees that are not mobile, may prefer to shift into other industrial sectors. On the other hand, if assets are highly industry-specific and intangible, then the preference will be on relocation, as this strategy can profitably combine lower local factor costs abroad with existing capabilities. Such assets include technological and managerial know-how, including knowledge of markets and reputation with customers (Wells 1993). Due to their intangible or tacit nature these assets are not often transferred via markets, as markets for knowledge-based assets are highly imperfect. The more intangible the assets, the more the firm will prefer an internal mode of transfer over a contractual relationship to internalize the transaction costs of markets (Williamson 1981; Buckley and Casson 1976; Hennart 1991).

The implementation of either strategy involves, however, one-off expenses, which are often an unrecoverable sunk cost. A relocation incurs fixed costs to the firm as well as to its employees that have to be weighted against the net present value of the reduced production costs. Firms incur costs from exploring potential new locations and setting up new production facilities, as machinery may be immobile and has to be written off. In addition, labour laws may require high redundancy payments to former employees. The human capital of laid-off workers is lost and new employees need firm-specific training.

Workers in the relocating firm face a loss of human capital as their industry-specific training becomes worthless (sunk costs) at home after the structural change has been completed. As they are usually immobile, they have to invest in education and training or face 'structural' unemployment. This explains the strong resistance of labour unions to structural change. The job specificity of qualifications and the inter-sectoral labour mobility thus affect the costs to individuals and indirectly to the firms which have to restructure their workforce. These costs are highly dependent on the institutional environment in the home country.

The factor-cost oriented FDI described in this model is a special case of Dunning's general paradigm: structural change threatens the ownership advantages of certain firms at their established location. They can continue to utilize their ownership advantages in a less advanced country, which has complementary locational advantages, especially labour supply, but they can do so only by direct investment because they need to internalize the markets for their intangible assets.

The model can explain the temporality of certain features of FDI, especially the high labour intensity of investment of young outward-investing countries. It provides a rationale for the 'investment-development-cycle' (Dunning 1986) that hypothesizes a relationship between the national stage of development of the home economy and the characteristics and composition of its FDI outflow: early FDI tends to be resource-oriented, first towards raw materials, later using a cheap labour supply. FDI from mature industrial countries is more likely to be market-oriented and thus determined by the international competitive situation in the marketplace.[3]

Implications of factor-cost oriented FDI

It is generally presumed that, in the absence of market distortions such as protectionism, multinational enterprises make locational decisions in a socially efficient way by optimizing both production-cost and market-related locational advantages. Investors will not, however, consider the spill-overs of their investment on the host economy (Markusen 1991). The externalities of FDI arising from the mechanisms described in the model often lead to a very positive assessment of the impact of this type of FDI. It has distinct implications for technology transfer, export performance and the involvement of small and medium-sized companies.

This type of FDI will usually come from countries whose technological standards are not very far above those of the host economy, and thus be relatively labour intensive. Its main transfer may not be capital but managerial and technological knowledge, at a level of technological sophistication that is only slightly above the standard of the host economy (Kojima 1978). Such relatively 'appropriate' technology matches the host country environment, especially the availability of labour and the level of general and specific education. At this level of technology, investors are likely to compete with local entrepreneurs with similar technological standards. Domestic enterprises in the host countries may be able to imitate the technology and acquire management skills within a fairly short time. Then, they can establish contacts and reputation with international customers themselves, following the example set by the foreign investors (Wells 1993, p. 182). This demonstration effect may have a significant impact on the indigenous businesses and the growth of domestic firms rather than developing an economy that is dominated by multinationals.

Thus, structural-change FDI is by its motivation 'comparative advantage augmenting' (Ozawa 1994b), that is its complementarity to the domestic human and capital resources makes its externalities particularly useful. It is considered 'desirable from the viewpoint of the developing countries' factor endowment' (Ozawa 1979b) and contributes to a steady and balanced economic growth. Hence, multinational enterprises are not only 'a facilitating institution which helps to organize world production to optimally exploit comparative advantages' (Markusen 1991), but its externalities contribute to 'FDI facilitated development' (Ozawa 1992b).

Factor-cost oriented FDI is generally more trade-creating than investment, which is primarily motivated by the objectives of entering or sustaining a position in the local market. Factor-cost oriented FDI improves the trade balance of the host economy by promoting exports and replacing imports with local production (see Kojima 1978, Lee 1990). MNEs, however, have comparative advantages in both export and import businesses, and 'import substitution FDI' may well expand local sales in such a way that increasing intermediate imports outweigh reduced imports of final goods. FDI is increasingly attracted by market-related locational advantages due to modern production and marketing techniques (Meyer 1994).

FDI induced by structural change involves established multinationals as well as small and medium-sized enterprises (SMEs), many of whom move abroad for the first time. The relative importance of SMEs in structural change FDI depends on the business structure of the home economy. Since structural change creates very strong push factors, it induces a major change in corporate strategy which a first step in the internationalization process of an enterprise necessitates. Thus, structural change induces relatively many first-time investors and SMEs. As their investment behaviour differs from that of established MNEs, this will influence the characteristics of FDI. The strategies of new investors develop gradually, step by step, and emerge shaped by the experiences gained in the internationalization process (Johanson and Vahlne 1977; Jansson 1993). These investors have a strong preference for locations in close proximity to their home base, where gathering experience is less costly. Thus, they prefer to invest where cultural, linguistic and informational barriers are lower and historical relationships stronger.

Host countries may particularly welcome SME investment because of the larger spill-overs to the economy. As many SME investors lack financial resources, bargaining power and country-specific information, they are more likely to enter into a joint venture with a local firm[4] and are more responsive to host country government incentives (Hiemenz *et al.* 1987, p. 77).

To sum up, a certain type of FDI has a desirable impact on economic development, for which the model suggests the following characteristics:

- Industries that are in the process of restructuring due to a loss of competitive advantages in their home location move their production activities to less-advanced countries.
- This FDI comes from industries that are labour intensive by standards of the home country, but technology intensive by host economy standards.
- This investment would generate more exports than other FDIs and concentrate on industries where the host economy has comparative advantages in international trade.
- A relatively high share of this type of FDI comes from SMEs, which tend to prefer locations in close proximity to the home economy.

Evidence

Structural change

After the Second World War, Japan experienced rapid economic growth that was accompanied by a substantial reallocation of resources from the primary to the secondary and tertiary sectors, and within the manufacturing sector from low-productivity light manufacturing to high-productivity industries. A similar development was experienced a decade later by the Newly Industrialized Economies (NIEs) of Korea, Taiwan, Hong Kong and Singapore. They took the second row in the 'flying geese' pattern of East Asian development.

FDI from Japan began in the 1950s and 1960s, and from other Asian countries a decade later, with small FDI flows compared to later stages of their development. Such early FDI was in large-scale projects in mining, petroleum extracting, refining and other natural resources (Whitmore *et al.* 1989, p. 5), the main motivation being to secure resources for the home economy. Since Japan is heavily dependent on imported raw materials, resource-securing FDI was of special importance for Japanese investment strategies, with primary sectors accounting for up to 36 per cent of FDI in developing countries, especially Indonesia, in the 1960s and 70s. The share of this sector fell to below 5 per cent in the late 1980s (Takeuchi 1990, p. 8). The second type of first-wave FDI from developing countries consisted of 'small scale operations that turned out standardized, low technology, labour intensive products highly sensitive to relative production costs' aimed at the local market (Whitmore *et al.* 1989, p. 5).

The second wave of FDI, that is Japanese investment in the 1960s–70s and Asian NIEs in the 1980s, had a strong labour-cost orientation for relatively simple manufacturing processes, sometimes in the form of subcontracting, producing both for the local and increasingly for the export market. A labour shortage, especially for young workers (Ozawa 1979a, p. 80), led to a rapid rise of wages in Japan, while wages in neighbouring countries remained lower. In this situation Japan rarely allowed inward migration as did the USA or West Germany at the same time.

More serious problems still arose in Japan due to the shortage of land, rising prices and environmental pollution. Thus firms sought suitable foreign locations at reasonable prices where congestion and pollution were not yet a problem or where there was less public sensitivity to these problems (Ozawa 1979b; and Sekiguchi and Krause, 1980). The stronger current account led to an appreciation of the yen and the accumulation of financial reserves, thus increasing relative labour costs and providing the necessary financial resources for overseas investment. Segments of the industrial structure with low productivity were given away to neighbouring developing countries, securing a concentration of Japanese industry at home in high productivity sectors (Ozawa 1979a). Under the active 'guidance' of the Ministry of International Trade and Industry the economy shifted from 'pollution-prone' and 'resource-consuming' heavy and chemical industries towards clean and 'knowledge intensive' industries. Hence, overseas investment served as a catalyst to the restructuring of the economy. It was facilitated by host-country policies that moved towards the promotion of labour-intensive FDI.

The development of the Asian NIEs in the 1980s closely shadowed the Japanese experience of the 1960s and 1970s. Today the 'Asian Tigers' are major investors within the region, led by Hong Kong, Singapore and Taiwan, and catching up with Japan's dominant role in the last decade (see Table 4.2). The NIEs experienced rapid industrialization and development and achieved large current account surpluses. Real labour costs increased dramatically, with shortages of unskilled and semiskilled labour and appreciating currencies. Under the competitive pressure of world markets on export-oriented businesses, the rationalization and relocation of export-oriented labour-intensive industries – most vulnerable to cost fluctuations – led the outward flow of FDI. At the same time, firms from Asian NIEs lost their preferred trading status and exhausted their quotas: hence, new ways to gain access to American and European markets were needed.[5]

As labour costs in South-East Asia rose in the 1980s and host countries tried to attract foreign investment in more sophisticated technologies, labour cost oriented investment had to turn southward. The preferred location for factor-cost oriented investment shifted from the (now) NIEs to the relatively advanced ASEAN countries (Malaysia, Thailand, Indonesia), and more recently to Southern China and Vietnam (see Freeman 1994). Development in East Asia appears to be a continuous process of structural change of all countries in the region: a number of studies in Ramstetter (1991) confirm the facilitating role of MNEs in this process in manufacturing industries in Asia.

Technology transfer and labour intensity

The theory suggests that marginally efficient firms moving abroad are using technology that meets the endowments of the host economy relatively well. Since the technological gap between the NIEs and the host countries is smaller than between other industrial and developing countries, they have a comparative advantage in transferring the industrial knowledge of labour-intensive small-scale manufacturing operations. Therefore, Hill (1990) observed that the problems of 'appropriate' technology were less evident in East Asia than elsewhere.[6]

Empirical evidence for differences in labour intensity, however, yields mixed results. Ozawa (1979b) observed that, in the 1970s, Japanese firms transplanted mainly general, mature technology fundamental to the establishment of an industry, a technology hardly considered to be an advantage by oligopoly standards. Kojima (1978) reported Japanese-owned plants to be more labour intensive than their American counterparts. Unlike Kojima, Lee (1983) in Korea and Hiemenz (1987) in the ASEAN countries did not find labour intensity to be significant.

Wells (1993) reported that Japanese investment in Indonesia used to be more capital intensive in the 1970s compared to NIE investors, but that in the 1990s it was producing with the lowest capital intensity, below that of

Table 4.2 Cross country pattern of FDI flows in East Asia (share of FDI from neighbouring countries of origin)

Source economies		Japan	Korea	Taiwan	Hong Kong	Singapore	Europe	USA	Total
Host economies									
Korea	(82–88)	22.4	–	0.1	3.0	0.7	–	–	100
Hong Kong	(80–87)	22.4	–	0.5	–	1.3	–	–	100
Taiwan	(60–69)	12.3	0.52	–	12.9	0.3	10.4	42.4	100
"	(70–79)	18.7	0.10	–	7.9	7.4	12.2	31.8	100
"	(80–89)	29.5	0.03	–	10.3	3.0	12.0	26.5	100
"	(90–94)	26.3	0.18	–	10.6	6.1	11.4	21.1	100
Singapore	(71–76)	16.6	–	–	–	–	29.9	32.4	100
"	(77–82)	17.9	–	–	–	–	35.5	34.6	100
"	(80–88)	33.7	–	0.1	4.8	–	–	–	100
Malaysia	(71–77)	23.5	–	0.3	11.8	21.8	15.7	13.7	100
"	(78–83)	20.4	4.3	–	5.7	7.7	–	20.4	100
"	(80–88)	23.2	0.9	3.4	5.6	11.3	–	–	100
Indonesia	(71–76)	17.1	1.0	1.2	5.2	1.0	12.8	50.5	100
"	(77–83)	10.6	0.5	0.1	2.7	1.0	9.6	49.0	100
"	(80–88)	12.9	2.3	1.3	10.0	4.4	–	–	100
"	(90–91)	14.0	21.8	7.1	8.0	13.2	–	2.9	100
Thailand	(66–70)	29.5	–	0.2	3.8	0.0	5.0	34.6	100
"	(71–76)	29.2	–	0.1	10.2	8.1	13.7	31.5	100
"	(77–83)	27.9	–	0.2	11.3	5.8	18.8	24.2	100
"	(84–89)	51.0	1.3	13.5	6.9	5.5	–	–	100
"	(96–91)	31.1	2.1	11.7	16.5	3.3	–	10.3	100
Philippines	(71–76)	28.1	2.4	3.8	1.1	0.3	10.6	31.2	100
"	(77–83)	11.7	0.4	–	6.1	0.7	12.5	55.7	100
"	(80–88)	14.4	0.2	5.8	3.9	0.7	–	–	100
PR China	(79–85)	7.8	–	–	62.7	2.1	7.4	13.0	100

Sources: Pangestu 1987; Riedel 1991; Schroath, Hu and Chen 1993; Wells 1993; Whitmore, Lall and Hyun 1989; Investment Commission of the Ministry of the Economy, Republic of China (includes 'overseas Chinese' and 'foreign' FDI).

NIE investors and far less than investors from other developed countries. He offers the explanation that earlier investments in Indonesia were often geared towards a protected market, which had since become more open. In addition, Japanese investment in raw material exploration in Indonesia contributed to high capital intensity data.

Schroath, Hu and Chen (1993) analysed FDI into China for the period 1979–85 and found major differences in project characteristics across countries of origin. Labour intensity was found highest for investors from Hong Kong and lowest for Europeans, although the latter had the highest share in manufacturing (77 per cent) and only 9 per cent of projects in service industries. Technology was considered 'low technology' for 75 per cent of investors from 'other' countries, presumably mainly Asian neighbours, 64 per cent from Hong Kong and 63 per cent of Japanese projects, but only 56 per cent of both US and European investments. These findings confirm that technology and labour intensity appear to be influenced by proximity, as low-technology and labour-intensive investment tend to come from neighbours.

Export performance

The last decade has seen a significant increase of intra-regional and intra-firm trade in regions which appear linked to surges in FDI (Primo-Braga and Bannister 1994). Moreover, FDI is generally found to be more export oriented in East and South-East Asia than in other regions of the world (Riedel 1991; Fry 1993); for instance, Japanese FDI within South-East Asia used to be more export oriented than in other regions (Takeuchi 1990).

A stream of research focused on differences between investors within the region and American or European investors. Kojima (1985) compared Japanese and American investment in the region empirically and observed that export-orientation was more important for Japanese overseas affiliates. Lee (1980; 1983) obtained similar results for Korea, thus supporting Kojima's hypothesis. Others found evidence to the contrary: Chou (1988) found no support for the hypothesis of different export orientation in Taiwan; neither did Gross (1986) in a study on FDI in ASEAN countries.[7] Only in the case of Korea was there strong evidence in favour of this hypothesis. The regional proximity and historical relations, as well as restrictive Korean government policy towards inward FDI may have caused this specific development. The difference in market orientation, if it actually existed, disappeared, and the export orientation of all Japanese manufacturing affiliates declined substantially between 1974 and 1979 only to recover slightly thereafter, while US affiliates increased their exports (Hiemenz 1987). The sum of various studies again yields mixed evidence, suggesting that, at some stages and in some countries, Japanese investment had a higher export orientation, but this was not a general feature (Hill 1990).

For NIE investors, Wells (1993) observed an export orientation in the first, relatively small, wave of FDI, and a focus on the local market in the second wave, competing on the basis of price rather than brand names and using cost-minimizing technology, often second-hand plants. In the third wave, at the turn of the 1990s, Wells observed 'mobile exporters' coming to Indonesia and Thailand and producing at a low-cost location for worldwide markets. Investors from both NIEs and Japan exported 71 per cent, compared to 53 per cent for other developed country investors (based on approval data). In contrast, for European investors in the region, the low labour costs of local production seemed to be a minor factor in investment decisions (Jansson 1993, p. 89).

The pro-trade nature of Japanese (and NIE) investment was based less on cultural differences, as implied by Kojima (1978; 1985), than on specific economic factors: (i) the short distance between the developing and advanced countries reduced transportation and other transaction costs; (ii) the existence of Japanese trading companies facilitated small projects that could be integrated in their international trade network; (iii) a large, unsaturated domestic market absorbed imports; (iv) due to its immigration policy, Japan experienced a more significant labour shortage than other countries.

It should be noted that exports by Japanese and other regional multinationals were not initially focused on the home markets, but primarily on third country markets. There are two reasons for this: FDI focused on industries that were subject to quantitative import restrictions in the USA and Europe which could be circumvented by producing in a less advanced country (Sekiguchi and Krause 1980, p. 425; Wells 1993). Second, tariffs in Asia, especially Japan and Korea, were higher and had a larger degree of escalation than OECD (Organization for Economic Cooperation and Development) tariffs (Safadi and Yeats 1994). This implies that investment and location decisions were made in dynamic and highly competitive world markets, where costs of production were more important than within domestic markets with established supplier relationships. On the other hand, intra-firm exports to Japan became a way of easing access to the Japanese market, as they accounted for most Japanese imports from neighbouring countries in recent years (Encarnation 1993).

Small and medium-sized enterprises and proximity

The advantages of proximity are particularly relevant to small and medium-sized enterprises, as is evident in the cases of Taiwanese FDI and early Japanese direct investment in Korea and Taiwan. Nearly half of Japanese investments in Asia originated in SMEs; in Taiwan they accounted for 58 per cent and in Korea for 70 per cent (Ozawa 1979a, p. 26). Hence, investment per project is smaller than US investment, especially in Korea (Lee 1980) and Taiwan: 70 per cent of the total number of Japanese manufacturing ventures

ated in Asian countries, accounting for only 40 per cent of the total value of investment, due to small business investment in this region (Ozawa 1979a, p. 28). Table 4.2 illustrates the relative importance of Japan and neighbouring Asian countries for FDI inflows in East Asia. Over the past four decades, the relative dominance of the US has declined as intra-regional investment has become the main source of FDI.

Interviews with firms from Asian NIEs (Whitmore *et al.* 1989) showed that geographical proximity and familiarity were overriding factors behind the decisions to invest within Asia. Economic proximity is defined as the characteristics of economies that contribute to closer business relationships, including geography, language, information and historical, cultural and ethnic links:

- Economic relationships between neighbouring countries face far lower natural barriers to trade than those at intercontinental levels. Most obvious are the transportation costs of low-cost production abroad for the home market.
- A common language facilitates cooperation with local people, especially for firms without a pool of managers trained in foreign languages. Thus, small Japanese firms used to find it easier to communicate with Koreans or Taiwanese, where the older generation could speak Japanese (for historical reasons), while Taiwanese and Hong Kong firms had a natural advantage in any other Chinese economy.
- The availability of information on potential locations is a major precondition for investment. Young investing countries and small firms have more problems in obtaining and evaluating this information. The bulk of small country investors target their activities where transactional and informational cost disadvantages are least.[8] Japanese trading firms often provide business information, and large MNEs, including the Korean chaebols, have an internal information network. This may be the main reason why Japanese and Korean firms are investing more outside their region than, for example, Taiwanese investors.
- Historical ties were the basis for the relative concentration of firms from Europe and America in their former colonies: British firms in Hong Kong, Singapore and Malaysia, Dutch firms in Indonesia and US firms in the Philippines. For Japan, the history of the Second World War was a major obstacle to its economic activities in East Asia. Economic relations were established between Japan and its neighbours only after several years, and anti-Japanese sentiments still persist.
- Cultural, historical and ethnic ties are particularly important for economic relationships between the Chinese communities of Hong Kong, Taiwan and their neighbours. Thus firms from these countries tend to prefer locations where ethnic Chinese play a major role in the business community. Informal Chinese multinational networks extend across

East Asia. Lower cultural barriers can also enable investors to move outside the major business centres, as did 85 per cent of Hong Kong investors in China (Schroath, Hu and Chen 1993).[9]

Implications for Eastern Europe

The regions of Eastern Europe and East Asia have two important characteristics in common: they are middle income economies within geographical proximity of developed nations; and they have well-educated workforces, relative to their income levels.

These conditions would, according to the model presented above, be favourable for labour-cost oriented FDI. Starting from the economic theory of location, Acocella (1995), Arva (1994) and Borsos (1995) concluded that lower labour costs in Eastern Europe should attract major foreign investment.

Although the similarities are evident, East Asia and Eastern Europe have very different economic development processes. In addition, the regions have very different cultures which strongly influence individuals' behaviour and their reaction to an economic environment. None the less, the emphasis on social values rather than individualism has been considered a common virtue.

This discussion will focus on differences in the economic environments. Following the model, the environment in Western Europe is analysed with respect to push factors on labour-intensive production processes and the costs of relocation; the East European environment is analysed in respect of its attractiveness to potential investors.

The West European environment

Compared to North-East Asia, the West European economies are growing only at a modest pace, with unusually high unemployment throughout the last decade and without much prospect of substantial improvement. The industrial structure has changed gradually, but without the flexibility and dynamism of the economies of Japan, Taiwan or Korea.

Therefore, the nature of businesses affected by structural change differs substantially. In East Asia, the last three decades saw rapid growth led by export industries facing the competitive environment of world markets. Utilizing low labour costs was essential for their success, as was a 'managerial frame' that was more growth- than profit-oriented, and integrated international business at the core of business strategy. In the Chinese economies, especially in Taiwan, small businesses have been driving forces, but now face a loss of competitiveness in their important third-country markets.

By contrast, European businesses are more mature and better established multinational enterprises and are competing in relatively stable markets.

Their reaction to new opportunities would thus involve a more fundamental corporate change, which would take more time to implement. German business, however, is made up of many dynamic SMEs, which have the option of investing in Eastern Europe as a first step in their internationalization. As SMEs tend to be more flexible, German and Austrian businesses reacted more promptly to East European reforms than British and American multinationals.

In addition, the specific economic regime imposed by the European Union (EU) has reduced incentives for adjustment. The EU is undergoing a structural adjustment process in which overcapacities in agriculture, textiles, steel and chemicals are gradually being reduced in a highly regulated fashion. The EU regulations include protection against imports as well as subsidized exports. As the countries of Eastern Europe have overcapacities in exactly the same industries, they would become part of this exercise of capacity reduction on becoming members of the Union. This serves to justify the fact that these sectors have not been liberalized in line with other industries as part of the recent 'European Agreements' with Eastern Europe (see Nuti 1994; Baldwin 1994). Hence, in sectors where these countries may have current comparative advantages, the protection of the West prevents them from taking full advantage and discourages export-oriented FDI into these industries. Opening up international trade in these areas is linked to the issues of: reform of the EU's common agricultural policy; dumping, as East European energy and other inputs are still subsidized in some cases; and whether the region would be able to gain long-term competitiveness in sectors where it has overcapacity (Nuti 1994).

The specific push factors of Asian economies arose from a loss of competitiveness in labour-intensive production processes due to rising local wage rates and the appreciation of currencies as well as shortages of land. Many firms were highly outward oriented and dependent on their main market, the USA. Therefore, they were especially hit by the appreciation of their local currencies *vis-à-vis* the US dollar. European companies, by contrast, are competing on global markets mainly in up-market segments based on superior quality. Therefore, they do not have the necessary ownership advantages in the management of low labour cost production. If they transplant the technology currently being used in Western Europe, they may be at odds with local factor costs.[10]

In up-market segments, they face a lower price elasticity of demand and are thus less sensitive to currency fluctuations. Their main international markets are in other European markets where they are mainly concerned about currency fluctuations within the European Monetary System. This saw, in the early 1990s, an appreciation of the Deutschmark and currencies closely linked to it *vis-à-vis* sterling and Southern European currencies. Together with relatively high increases in real wages and the costs of German unification, this weakened the competitiveness of the German economy *vis-à-vis* for instance, Great Britain. Thus, German companies would experience more competitive pressures to relocate than British firms.

The shortage of land is a major constraint in Japan, Taiwan and Hong Kong which are amongst the most densely populated countries in the world, and consist mainly of mountainous islands, which are difficult to utilize economically. By contrast, overcrowding is a minor issue in Europe, where the population density is highest in Belgium, a country about the same size as Taiwan but with half the number of inhabitants spread out in an essentially flat terrain. Relocation to avoid strict environmental regulations in Western Europe may be encouraged by the current legal frameworks, but faces ethical concerns which would make enterprises politically vulnerable.

Hence, the push factors in the West European home economies create less pressure for relocation, apart from the loss of German competitiveness *vis-à-vis* other European countries. Factor cost orientation should be less prevalent, in particular from those countries whose currencies were recently devalued.

Moreover, the cost of relocation can be presumed to be higher. Job mobility tends to be higher in a Western society between firms, but much lower across professional boundaries, compared to Japanese or Chinese business. A typical German worker learns specialized tasks in an apprenticeship; a change of employer may be considered, but the worker generally stays within the same profession. Japanese in-house education is general and less task specific, and the typical employee will change jobs within the company rather frequently while staying with the same company (Okimoto and Rohlen 1988). This structural difference, together with industry–based rather than company-based unions, makes structural changes more difficult to implement in the European environment. The legal framework in Germany discourages lay-offs as high redundancy payments are required if large numbers of employees are laid off simultaneously. The job specificity of qualifications and the social protection of employment thus create higher adjustment costs.

In conclusion, the less dynamic business community and the similarity of the East and West European industrial structures create inertia in structural change in Western Europe which induce protectionism and inhibit FDI of the type described in the model. The scope for structural change FDI is thus limited to technologies that are in need of restructuring, but are not established in Eastern Europe so as not to pose the threat of an immediate large inflow of goods.

The East European environment

Based on GDP, the gap in development between Western and Eastern Europe appears to be much larger than between different stages in the 'flying geese' pattern of East Asia.

Labour costs in Eastern Europe are only a fraction of West European labour costs. Wages in the Czech Republic are about 20 to 30 per cent of wages over the border in Bavaria. The qualifications of the local workforce tend to be reasonably high in technical skills, even though they may lack familiarity with the latest Western technology. Their high standards and industrial tradition enable them to adopt it relatively quickly. Finally, transportation costs are lower than for trade with Asia and some raw materials are still relatively inexpensive. Thus, the potential for factor-cost oriented relocation appears obvious, especially for medium-skilled tasks.

Nevertheless, a number of recent questionnaire surveys among investors in the region indicate that the factor-cost motivation is of secondary importance. Labour-cost advantages are utilized only if there is an attractive local market (Gatling 1993; OECD 1995; Meyer 1995a; Estrin, Hughes and Todd 1996). Several factors reduce productivity and thus the cost advantage for factor-cost utilizing FDI:

- Although the general level of labour qualifications in technical skills is high, employees need substantial training in management and marketing to compete in Western markets.
- The labour cost advantage may not be sustainable in the long run, as geographical proximity encourages migration of the most qualified individuals. Recent data report an increase in the $ wage rate in excess of productivity increases (Table 4.3). Uncertainty surrounding future labour costs inhibits projects based on the factor-cost advantage and with long pay-back periods.

Table 4.3   Labour costs in Europe

	US$ wage monthly 1994	*US$ wage change 1990–94*	*Productivity change 1990–94*	*Unit labour cost change 1990–95*
Bulgaria	86	+52%	+15%	+33%
Czech Republic	240	+25%	–23%	+61%
Estonia	138	–	–	–
Hungary	317	+41%	+12%	+27%
Poland	241	+82%	+40%	+30%
Romania	–	–42%	–18%	–29%
Russia	96	–	–	–
Slovakia	196	+10%	–5%	+17%
Germany	–	–	–	+7%
United Kingdom	–	–	–	+5%

Source: EBRD 1995, pp. 174–5.

- The poor infrastructure, old physical capital stock, overstaffing and low morale have resulted in very low productivity in the region. Foreign investors may have an advantage in increasing productivity, but this comes at an extra cost.
- The region lacks local entrepreneurs who would make joint venture partners, and suppliers of intermediate inputs, which can match the standards required by Western investors.

East Asia did build on relatively stable political systems and a predictable economic and legal environment, as well as a strong and active role of government guiding the economy. In contrast, Eastern Europe went through a systemic transformation, in which macroeconomic stabilization generally was given priority over microeconomic restructuring (Portes 1994). A new institutional framework needs to be created with new laws and institutions such as stock exchanges and regulatory bodies: such a fundamental task cannot be achieved overnight (Murrel, Clague and Rausser 1992). Due to the lack of market institutions, investors currently face additional uncertainties and operating costs. The countries in Central Europe have made considerable progress, but problems remain in areas such as bureaucratic approval procedures and contract enforcement (EBRD 1994).

The political system has stabilized in most countries, but the return of reformed Communist Parties to government has created uncertainties and policies that are less favourable to multinational businesses. In addition, the economic environment is still unstable, making cost predictions in the long run very difficult. This would inhibit factor-cost seeking FDI more than market-seeking investment because the latter depends mainly on local demand, which for consumer goods may be approximated to Western patterns of consumption. Apart from these general differences, two specific areas of policy have direct implications for the structure of FDI:

1. A large share of early FDI has been attracted by opportunities in the privatization process (Estrin 1994; Rojec and Jermakowicz 1995). The characteristics of this FDI would thus be directly shaped by the priorities of the privatization programmes and the nature of assets available for sale.
2. No government policy in the region has explicitly encouraged an export orientation based on tariff exemptions or export-processing zones. At the current stage of development there are few opportunities for successful 'special economic zones' (except in Russia) because the countries of the region have already made very strong commitments to systemic transformation and complete liberalization (Ahrens and Meyer-Baudeck 1995).[11] By contrast, multinationals seem to have been successful in negotiating a degree of protection for the domestic markets in which they invested (EBRD 1994).

Cultural differences and language barriers exist but should not be major obstacles. Both German and English are commonly used languages throughout the region. Personal contracts and special cultural relations often date back to the pre-socialist era and can now release substantial economic activity. The expatriate community made up of refugees of the socialist regimes does not have the business power of the 'Chinese network' across East Asia, but still makes a contribution to new business relationships. In spite of these differences, the pattern of proximity could be clearly observed in the early flows of FDI to Eastern Europe: the leading countries of origin are Germany and Austria and some special relationships between neighbours have emerged, such as Finnish investment in Estonia and St Petersburg, Swedish firms in Poland and the Baltics, and Turkish investment in Central Asia and Romania (Meyer 1995a). Table 4.4 reports the patterns of countries of origin in Eastern Europe by concentrating on the role of neighbouring investors.

In terms of proximity patterns, Eastern Europe displays similarities to Asia: many SMEs have had little experience of operating overseas plants, use more readily available information in Europe and have personal contacts with the region. For the formation of joint ventures, existing contacts with potential partners have been of major importance for the choice of partner (Meyer 1995b). The proximity advantages apply in particular to Austria, which had extensive trade relations with the area during the years of socialism and personal contacts dating back to the Austro-Hungarian period (Bellak 1995).

Conclusions

This chapter developed a model of FDI that applies reasonably well in the context of East and South-East Asia. The model is used as a framework for analysing the potential of West–East European direct investment. This analysis has shown that there are still many obstacles to overcome before major factor-cost oriented investment flows can be expected. The reasons are to be found in the economic and institutional environment in both Eastern and Western Europe.

The discussion may have raised more questions than it answered, indicating a need for further research. Nevertheless, some general conclusions can be inferred:

- The general implication of the developmental approach holds for Eastern Europe as well: by making the best use of their competitive advantages or 'aligning pattern of comparative advantage and its stage of development with advanced countries' (Ozawa 1992b), countries can attract and make best use of foreign investment.
- The extent to which Eastern Europe can integrate in the world of multinational production depends on the process of structural adjustment in the West. The more Western Europe can move on to new economic

Table 4.4 Cross-country pattern of FDI flows in Eastern Europe (shares of countries in stock of FDI)

Source economies	Germany	Austria	France	Italy	Netherlands	UK	Switzerland	USA	Total
Host economies									
Albania (12/93)	8.0	10.3	8.0	35.2	–	–	–	–	100
Bulgaria (8/94)	40.6	4.2	–	–	10.2	4.5	9.2	6.5	100
Czech Republic (6/94)	30.0	6.8	12.1	3.2	1.9	–	4.8	25.2	100
Hungary (12/92)	18.5	25.1	5.1	3.2	8.9	4.9	4.3	12.4	100
Poland (9/94)	9.4	3.8	6.6	9.0	6.5	3.9	4.8	34.2	100
Romania (4/94)	10.5	–	13.0	15.0	–	11.7	–	11.7	100
Slovakia (6/94)	21.3	25.4	9.5	3.1	3.7	–	1.0	11.5	100
Slovenia (12/93)	44.9	20.7	7.1	16.0	–	–	3.6	–	100

Data sources: Bundesministerium für Wirtschaft (for Albania), Presseschau Ostwirtschaft (for Bulgaria), Czech National Bank, Hungarian Statistical Office, PAIZ (Poland), Romanian Development Agency, PlanEcon (for Slovakia), and Slovene National Bank.

activities, the more Eastern European countries may find markets in which they can compete on a lower cost basis.

- The factor-cost differences are a major asset of these economies that have not yet been fully utilized. Performance may improve as recent projects expand to supply worldwide markets once they have saturated the domestic market.
- The main parallel to the Asian 'flying geese' pattern may emerge within the region: in a few years investments by Hungarian or Czech companies can be expected to make a major contribution to the development of their Eastern neighbours. They may pass on their acquired know-how combined with their understanding of the local environment.

Notes

1 The data for Taiwan have been obtained from national statistics, which may differ from IMF definitions and statistics.

2 National Bank of Poland statistics (also used by the EBRD) report less than half this figure because of a narrower definition of FDI.

3 See Ozawa (1992).

4 Lee and Beamish (1995) showed that Korean firms in less-developed countries were more likely to enter joint ventures because of their need for the partners' knowledge of the local environment.

5 For FDI from NIEs, see Lall 1991; Whitmore *et al.* 1989; Wells 1993; Primo-Braga and Bannister 1994; and Blomqvist 1995.

6 See also Lall and Streeten (1977) and Jenkins (1991).

7 Lii (1994) examined the impact of more recent Japanese FDI in the region on both exports and imports, and found a negative net effect on the balance of trade, suggesting the dominance of market-access motivation.

8 Caves (1982, p. 64) and Dunning (1993a, p. 156) report several studies that support this point.

9 An important cultural link within the region is the philosophy of Confucianism. Its role should not be underestimated in analysing South-East Asia, because Japan as well as the Asian NIEs of Taiwan, Singapore and Hong Kong have a similar social philosophy. Also, in some countries such as Malaysia, the Chinese tend to be more successful businessmen than local Malays or Indians. Therefore Confucianism is more than just a link connecting East and South-East Asia, but an ethic on which they could build economic growth.

10 The experience of Volkswagen is illustrative: its investment in Spain (Seat) was based on a high-technology, capital-intensive strategy, that was not sustainable. When the problems with Seat became evident, VW changed its strategy for Skoda in the Czech Republic to make better use of low labour costs (*Financial Times*, 8.11.94).

11 In Russia, free economic zones have been established, but have to date been generally unsuccessful because of the inconsistent and unstable legal framework (Kuznetsov 1995).

Part II
Empirical Country Studies

5
Foreign Investment and Privatization in the Czech Republic

Alena Zemplinerova

Introduction

Before 1989 the number of FIEs operating in the Czech economy was negligible. Since 1990 FDI has grown markedly, thanks to several large privatization deals, principally joint ventures like Volkswagen-Skoda, Nestlé-Cokoladovny or TelSource-Telecom. At the same time, a large number of small FIEs appeared, often not recorded in official statistics, but with an important' and dynamic role in the economy.

According to balance of payments statistics, investment by foreign firms in the Czech Republic reached $7.2 billion by year-end 1996. Between 1991 and 1995, FDI investment had been determined on the whole by privatization policy. As elsewhere, investors' decisions to expand or relocate production abroad have been influenced by both macro- and microeconomic policies. The key macroeconomic reforms in the Czech Republic were put in place in January 1991, when prices were decontrolled, the currency was declared to be 'internally convertible', and foreign trade was liberalized. Since then, conservative fiscal and monetary policies have produced a relatively stable and reliable investment climate.

Microeconomic reforms – such as the creation of a new legal framework, privatization, and enterprise restructuring – have also progressed steadily since reforms began, but naturally at a slower pace than the macroeconomic measures. Privatization, for example, has been a mixed blessing. On the one hand it has created investment opportunities, but on the other it has also thrown up barriers that have slowed or in some cases deterred altogether the involvement of foreign investors. Other than splitting up unwieldy conglomerates and monopolies, the problem of restructuring has been left with few exceptions to the post-privatization owners. Relatively high expectations for the restructuring of former centrally planned economies were related to foreign investment. It is the main purpose of this study to contribute to the knowledge of the extent, structure, dynamics and performance of FIEs in the Czech economy in general and privatization in particular.

The analysis is based on both traditional and non-traditional sources. The 'standard' source of data on FDI capital flows is the balance of payments series. This refers to cash payments made through banks from outside the country, recorded by percentage ownership of the firms' assets. After an examination of the general features of foreign capital inflows, FDI is analysed according to sector, geography and size, beginning with foreign capital flows and followed by a look at developments between 1990 and June 1996.

Balance of payments statistics do not, however, give an account of more detailed foreign penetration by economic sector, nor do they allow for the evaluation of the efficiency of foreign investments.

Therefore, in the third section we look at additional sources related to foreign direct investment. These include data on individual enterprises obtained from the Czech Statistical Office (CSO) which allow identification by owner. Firms are divided into two groups, FIEs and domestic enterprises. We focus on distribution patterns among foreign investors, as well as on the size and structure of firms. We then compare the performance of domestic and foreign enterprises, first for the economy as a whole and its sectors, then for the manufacturing sector and its component industries. Such an approach is particularly useful in revealing several important aspects of foreign involvement in the Czech economy, especially with respect to its restructuring.

In the next section we discuss government policies affecting FDI, and in the final section we examine the privatization process as it has affected foreign investment, and put forward empirical evidence of the experience and behaviour of foreign investors during privatization and of the linkages with domestic industry.

General features of foreign capital inflows

The worldwide asset value of FDI can be estimated at about $2500 billion, of which the volume in 1995 amounted to $235 billion, according to the United Nations Conference on Trade and Development. The Czech Republic's share in the flow of FDI worldwide was just over 1 per cent in 1995. FDI stock ownership, however, was lower, at only 0.2 per cent, indicating how far the Czech Republic has still to go before it is successfully integrated into the world economy (see Table 5.1).

It needs to be stressed, however, that Czech balance of payments statistics may not describe all performing FDIs. For example, some share transactions may escape public monitoring, and thus remain unidentified within group portfolio investments. Other deals, especially in the case of small businesses, may not be reported as foreign buy-outs, as FDIs valued at less than 100 000 korunas often escape statistical monitoring altogether. Also the reinvested profits of foreign companies are not always included in FDI figures.

Table 5.1 FDI, portfolio investment, foreign credits and deposits in the Czech Republic, 1990–95 (in $ mn)

Foreign Capital Inflows	1990	1991	1992	1993	1994	1995
FDI	49	595	1003	568	862	2559
FDI/GDP in current prices (in %)	0.09	2.45	3.53	1.80	2.39	5.45
FDI/total gross investment	0.7	10.7	14.1	6.5	7.4	16.3
Portfolio investment	n.a.	n.a.	-26	1059	819	1651
Long-term capital	n.a.	n.a.	320	528	860	3173
Short-term capital	n.a.	n.a.	–1275	535	–75	233
Total foreign cap./GDP (in %)	n.a.	n.a.	n.a.	9.6	9.2	18.4

Source: Bulletin of the Czech National Bank (1993–4–5).

Before 1993, FDI was the prevalent form in foreign capital influx to the Czech Republic. Later, portfolio investment[1] as well as the extension of credit by foreign banks also became important. There was significantly less foreign investment during 1993 and 1994, as compared with either 1992 or 1995. Accordingly, the figures for FDI as a percentage of gross investment or GDP fell in those years as well. A number of factors contributed to the investment decline:

- Political uncertainties related to the separation of the Czech and Slovak Republics in January 1993.
- Voucher privatization which excluded foreign investors from more than a third of privatized assets.
- Warning signals picked up by the international investing community. One widely cited example was the repurchasing of shares in CSA airlines, originally sold to Air France, because of a failure to meet restructuring commitments. Another was the decision by the City of Prague not to approve the construction of a major new Canadian hotel in the old city centre.
- The success of domestic investors over foreigners in several important tender offers, coupled with the failure of several key foreign privatization bids, such as that by Mercedes for the state truck manufacturers.

The low volume of FDI in 1993 and 1994 was partially compensated for by an increase in investments by foreign mutual funds and other institutional investors, which are, in reality, hard to separate from FDI. These reached $819 million in 1994.[2] Despite some speculative investing, the majority of foreign institutional holdings are long- or medium-term.[3]

There have also been large amounts of foreign capital flowing into the country in the form of foreign loans. Since the first half of 1994, credit extended to Czech enterprises by foreign banks accelerated, reaching a level of $3.6 billion by the end of 1995. Large loans represented only 15–20 per cent of the total. The majority were small and medium-sized loans, or were related to the establishment of new joint ventures. Some 30 per cent of loans went towards investments in technology, 40 per cent for the purchase of real estate, 26 per cent for trade activity, both domestic and international, and the remaining 4 per cent for other miscellaneous investment. Most of the credit was extended by German banks.

Foreign capital inflows increased radically in 1995, especially in the form of FDI, for the following reasons:

- the acceleration of economic growth;
- progress in the privatization of large enterprises, particularly in telecommunications, and the final instalment in the transfer of Škoda to Volkswagen;
- continuing macroeconomic and political stability, reflected in a general perception of low risk by the investment community;
- membership of the OECD in September 1997;
- full convertibility of the koruna in current account transactions, as established by article VIII of the IMF Agreement, and partial deregulation of capital account transactions;
- relatively low share prices on Czech securities for portfolio and institutional investors, coupled with anticipated high returns;
- high interest rates on the domestic money markets coupled with a fixed exchange rate, which attracted foreign loans and portfolio investment.

Regarding the balance of payments, high foreign capital inflows were partially counterbalanced by a trade deficit, which reached 8 per cent of GDP in 1995. Thanks to the surplus in services, the current account deficit was in the end only half the trade deficit, just under $2 billion. Thus, 1995 closed with a balance of payments surplus as in previous years and a doubling of foreign exchange reserves at the Czech National Bank. Hence, the Czech Government had no need to attract additional foreign direct investment to correct a balance of payments deficit, as was the case in Hungary. On the contrary, thanks to the real appreciation of the currency resulting from a policy of fixed exchange rates and relatively high inflation, the National Bank needed to sterilize the money supply of any net foreign exchange inflows. More FDI would have added inflationary pressure and complicated the efforts of the National Bank to curb the growth in money supply.

FDI by sector, size and country of origin

While no details are available of industrial sectors in balance-of-payments source statistics, a clear pattern of foreign direct investment emerges, as seen in Table 5.2, that varies significantly with the sector and time period

Table 5.2 FDI inflows to the Czech Republic by sector, 1990–June 1996 (in $millions)

	1993	1994	1995	1996 Jan–June	1990–June 1996
Transport, telecommunication	n.a.*	n.a.*	1 349.8	n.a.*	1 364.5
Automotive	10.0	266.1	307.8	n.a.*	1 025.2
Consumer goods and tobacco	244.0	59.2	179.3	40.0	851.9
Construction	65.0	107.9	n.a.*	27.6	490.6
Banks and insurance	55.0	132.4	n.a.*	n.a.*	443.0
Foodstuff	35.0	71.2	121.5	n.a.*	478.1
Engineering	57.0	n.a.*	158.2	n.a.*	n.a.*
Chemicals	19.3	43.6	89.7	214.9	n.a.*
Trade	40.0	n.a.*	147.3	71.7	n.a.*
Electronics	22.4	86.2	n.a.*	20.0	n.a.*
Fuel and energy	n.a.*	n.a.*	n.a.*	56.5	n.a.*
All others	20.3	95.9	204.9	27.4	1 402.2
Total	568.0	862.4	2 558.5	458.0	6 039.4
of which percentage manufacturing**	70.0	38.8	37.5	63.0	57.7

Source: Czech National Bank, 1995
* Individual statistics not available; included under 'others'.
** Data include only the Czech Republic; Slovak enterprises are excluded for the period 1990–92.

involved.[4] During the period 1990–June 1996, the highest level of FDI was directed at the telecommunications industry (22.6 per cent of the total), followed by the automotive industry (17 per cent) and the tobacco industry. In all, over 50 per cent of the FDI investment total was in manufacturing, including those manufacturing investments listed under 'other industries'.[5] Nevertheless the percentage of investment in manufacturing appears to be declining over time as other sectors – such as telecommunications, oil refineries and banking – open up to foreign investors.

Data about the size distribution of FDI based on the balance of payments statistics are not very detailed. Alongside major foreign investments, there are numerous cases of small and medium-sized foreign investments, as illustrated in Table 5.3. Very small foreign investments (up to $18 500 or 0.5 million koruna) are not recorded in the National Bank survey of business activity and are therefore excluded from these statistics. We can assume on the basis of personal observation and informal reports that this figure is made up of a great number of separate small investments. Therefore the average size of these investments must be rather small, often with only the minimum capital requirement of 100 000 koruna.

The volume of FDI grew dramatically thanks to five large privatization deals. Almost half of the total foreign direct investment comes from these large projects – Skoda-Volkswagen, Tabak-Philip Morris, Cokoladovny-Nestlé, Technoplyň-Linde and SPT Telecom-Telsource, four of which are in manufacturing.

The first large deal was signed in April 1991 between Skoda, Mlada, Boleslav and Volkswagen. The Volkswagen investment was divided into three stages. The first stage took place in 1991, the second in 1994 and the last in 1995, after which Volkswagen altogether acquired 70 per cent of the equity in Skoda Auto for $0.9 billion. Philip Morris acquired 77 per cent of Tabak Kutňa Hora for about $0.5 billion, and Nestlé-BSN 69 per cent for $0.2 billion. The last and largest foreign investment to date was in late 1995 by the Dutch/Swiss consortium Telsource for 27 per cent of SPT Telecom at a price of $1.3 billion.[6]

Table 5.3   Size of FDI in the Czech Republic

Foreign investment ($)	Number of enterprises (% of total)
18 500–37 000	25.2
37 000–370 000	22.3
370 000–3 700 000	29.4
3 700 000–37 000 000	21.1
more than 37 million	2.0

*1 USD = 26.55 CZK
Source: Czech National Bank, 1995; Ministry of Privatization.

Table 5.4   FDI in the Czech Republic by country of origin, 1990–96 (%)

Country	1990–June 1996
Germany	29.6
USA	14.5
Switzerland	13.7
Netherlands	13.5
France	8.8
Austria	5.8
Other	14.0
TOTAL	100.0

Source: Czech National Bank, 1996.

Altogether, the German-speaking countries (Germany, Switzerland and Austria) represent 50 per cent of the total FDI in the Czech Republic. The EU countries as a whole make up 68 per cent and the OECD countries 97 per cent (see Table 5.4). In 1994 the Czech Republic was the sixth most important recipient of all German FDI. With transfers of DM1132 million by 1994 the Czech Republic became the second largest recipient of German capital of all the Central and Eastern European countries after Hungary. Germany's position as the largest foreign investor remained unchallenged through 1996. The FDI ranking of the Czech Republic's Western neighbours may be even stronger than it appears, because of numerous small foreign investments which are often excluded from statistics. Small foreign business owners often come to the Czech Republic from Austria or Bavaria, with which traditional trade and investment links were recently revived.

In 1994 and 1995 'other industries' in Table 5.4 included investments from the Bahamas (Stratton Investments), Italy, the European Bank for Reconstruction and Development, Britain, South Korea, Norway and Sweden. After a two-year setback the position of the USA picked up in 1996. A solid presence by French and Austrian investors is in marked contrast with the rather slack performance of Japan. Japanese multinationals have only recently started to show an interest in Central Europe, particularly in the case of greenfield investments involving new infrastructure and facilities.

Foreign and domestic enterprises by sector and size

In this section, we examine in greater detail the patterns of foreign investment by sector and size, and the investment performance of both foreign and domestic enterprises.

We begin with data from the Companies' Register, which includes the total population of firms from all size categories, with location (address), form of ownership, activity and size (number of employees). It was not feasible from these data to establish how many firms (especially small businesses) were operational.[7]

In order to obtain more information, we used a reduced set of data based on financial statements of output, investment and profit. According to the methodology used by the Czech Statistical Office (no. 8, April 1993), eight types of ownership are distinguished.[8] For our purpose, we divided the enterprises into two groups according to ownership: FIEs, that is enterprises with any foreign participation, and domestic enterprises (all others, both private and state owned).

First, the analysis was carried out for the whole economy and included all registered enterprises (all sizes and sectors as well as individual entrepreneurs): 1.31 million firms were registered in 1995, of which 32 946 were partially or fully owned by foreigners. The second stage involved non-financial enterprises, of which 365 were under foreign control. This group included enterprises fully owned by foreigners and those in which foreigners had a majority or controlling interest. Our findings confirmed that this group was almost identical to the group of FIEs. We also found that, in most cases, foreign investors preferred to acquire a majority position, and calculated that FIEs were primarily under foreign control.[9] This is supported by the evidence in the next section, which addresses foreign investment and privatization.

Our enquiry concluded with an analysis of manufacturing enterprises. At year end 1995 there were 2288 manufacturing businesses (with 100 or more employees), of which 216 were wholly or partly foreign-owned. For the period 1992–94, we have complete balance sheet and export data for all businesses with 25 or more employees. As of 1995, however, the Czech Statistical Office altered its methodology and started to record balance sheets for enterprises with 100 or more employees, limiting comparability. Since 1995 export data have not been recorded. Hence, we have conducted our own analysis of the manufacturing sector for 1994 and of the economy as a whole for 1995. Company Register data also became available in mid-1996.

Our first observation is of startling growth – an increase of 85 per cent in the number of FIEs in just over 2 years, as compared with an 11 per cent increase for all firms. For firms that are totally foreign owned, the rate of increase is a dramatic 264 per cent, revealing growing investor confidence in the Czech economy. By mid-1996, 23 721 of the 1 390 459 registered firms were wholly foreign owned, and another 13 772 partially foreign owned, amounting to 2.7 per cent of all registered firms, up from 1.1 per cent in 1993.

The percentage of foreign enterprises varies considerably according to sector, showing a markedly different pattern of investment from domestic businesses. Foreign investment is concentrated in real estate, mining,

wholesale trade and services. By June 1996, the percentage of foreign businesses in real estate had reached 11.4 per cent and that in wholesale trade
8.7 per cent (see Table 5.5).

In absolute terms, there are now more than 22 700 FIEs in wholesale and
retail trade and in excess of 6500 in manufacturing and construction. There
are some 3700 FIEs providing business services and 1400 in real estate.
Between 1993 and mid-1996 the number of FIEs increased dramatically in
all sectors: it grew six-fold in construction, four-fold in retail, three-fold in
real estate, and doubled in manufacturing and transport.

Table 5.5   FIEs in the Czech Republic by industry, 1993 and 1995

	Percent of total number		*Number of foreign enterprises*	
	1993	*1995*	*1993*	*1995*
Mining and quarrying	1.54	6.11	16	37
Manufacturing	0.65	1.55	1 488	2 863
Electricity, gas and water supply	0.74	1.07	10	16
Construction	0.33	1.86	574	2 647
Sale and repairs of motor vehicles	0.82	0.99	169	235
Wholesale trade	7.40	8.56	4 600	11 263
Retail trade	1.18	3.37	2 491	8 578
Hotels and restaurants	0.50	0.93	332	502
Transport, storage, communication	0.78	1.21	374	563
Financial intermediation	2.66	1.93	101	161
Real estate activities	8.04	10.86	438	1 201
Renting of machinery	0.34	2.26	68	116
Computer and related activities	1.25	1.71	204	333
Research and development	3.21	4.50	35	30
Other business activities	1.46	1.96	2 593	3 453
Public administration and defence	0.29	0.01	47	85
Education	0.12	0.56	24	56
Health and social work	3.04	0.21	27	69
Sewage, sanitation, similar activities	1.09	4.80	257	304
Recreation, cultural, sporting activities	0.07	0.12	21	54
Other service activities*	0.46	0.38	140	147
Total	1.12	2.51	14 052	32 946

*Includes public administration, extra-territorial organizations and home-based businesses.
Source: Register of Firms, Czech Statistical Office, 1993–95.

Most foreign businesses are small, following a similar pattern to that of domestic enterprises documented in Table 5.6. Only nine companies employed more than 2000 employees and only three foreign companies had more than 5000 employees.

For businesses with 100 or more employees, foreign penetration is highest in the hotel and restaurant sector, where almost one-quarter of all employees work for foreign companies (see Tables 5.7 and 5.8). In real estate, trade and other services, foreign employment is also well above average. A similar pattern holds for the share of foreign companies in total output. Even in healthcare and education, where only a small part of the

Table 5.6　Czech Republic: size distribution of enterprises between 1993 and 1996

| | | % of total | | |
| | Domestic | | Foreign | |
Number of employees	1993	1996	1993	1996
1–5	76.37	74.25	76.80	66.61
6–24	10.25	18.67	16.03	23.90
25–99	7.68	5.18	4.94	6.80
100–499	4.41	1.59	1.72	2.22
500–999	0.71	0.19	0.34	0.27
1000 and more	0.57	0.12	0.17	0.20
Total	100.0	100.0	100.0	100.0

Source: Register of Firms, Czech Statistical Office, 1996.

Table 5.7　Share of FIEs in total workforce, output and other indices by industrial sector in the Czech Republic, 1995 (%)

	Workforce	Output	Wage fund	Own capital	Book VA	Fixed capital	Investment
Mining and quarrying	0.58	0.82	0.53	0.43	0.91	0.45	0.57
Manufacturing	7.88	13.19	9.49	10.90	11.59	10.07	22.04
Construction	1.41	1.92	1.60	2.07	1.84	1.59	1.69
Wholesale, retail trade	8.72	14.16	12.41	5.24	11.52	10.71	24.60
Hotels, restaurants	24.35	24.73	23.39	10.75	21.72	11.70	18.83
Transportation, Communication	0.36	3.20	0.69	0.15	2.68	0.16	0.56
Real estate activities	9.21	12.73	11.46	1.32	9.90	2.27	10.01
Education, healthcare	3.81	13.97	7.18	4.19	14.89	3.72	10.24
Total of above	5.15	8.66	6.23	4.48	7.38	5.00	8.88
Total economy	8.50	11.20	n.a.	n.a.	8.5	n.a.	n.a.

Sources: Czech Statistical Office, 1995, and author's own computation.

sector is made up of enterprises operated as separate legal units available for investment, foreign businesses accounted for a remarkable 14 per cent of total output. This situation should continue, as FIEs account for a high percentage of total investment, especially in manufacturing, but also in trade, hotels and restaurants, and services generally.

Foreign enterprises are more productive and invest more than domestic firms, and also achieve higher value added per employee and pay higher salaries. The profitability of FIEs varies significantly according to sector and is highest in mining, construction, trade, hotels and restaurants, education and healthcare. These findings are illustrated in Table 5.8.

FIEs in manufacturing

Foreign manufacturers in the Czech Republic employ 70 per cent of all FIE workers and staff and produce 80 per cent of total FIE output. In 1995, FIEs employed 9.6 per cent of total workforce in manufacturing companies of more than 100 employees, compared to only 2.6 per cent in 1992. Their share of output increased from 5.6 per cent to 16.5 per cent. They earned 27 per cent of total manufacturing profits and 27.5 per cent of total manufacturing investment in 1995.

Foreign manufacturing enterprises also restructure faster than enterprises owned solely by domestic investors, getting rid of redundant employees and investing in new technology. FIEs also pay higher average salaries than domestic firms by about 20 per cent, reflecting higher labour productivity and an apparent ability to attract more managers and skilled workers.

On average, capital endowments per employee are also higher in FIEs than in non-foreign enterprises, belying the general opinion that foreign companies invest primarily in low-wage, labour-intensive industries (see Table 5.8). The average rate of depreciation reveals that foreign plant and equipment are usually more modern than that in domestic companies, reflecting a concentration of foreign investment in state-owned enterprises with the most recent equipment.

Labour productivity is markedly higher in firms with foreign capital involvement than in domestic firms, because of both higher capital investment and greater capital efficiency. Foreign enterprises invest four times more per employee than domestic firms and are also major exporters (see Table 5.9).

The role of FIEs differs significantly by industry. The period 1992–94 saw large privatizations that included acquisitions in the automobile industry (Volkswagen, Steyer Daewoo), food processing and tobacco (Nestlé, Philip Morris, Pepsi-Cola, Bass Breweries), rubber and plastics (Intercontinental), printing and publishing (the majority of newspapers and magazines are owned by foreigners, many of whom have invested heavily in private production facilities), non-metal minerals (Glaverbel-Asahi Glass, Italcementi), chemicals (Linde, Dow Chemicals, Procter & Gamble), and electronics (Siemens AG, Asea Brown Boveri).

Table 5.8 Comparison of enterprises by ownership and sector in the Czech Republic, 1995 (in thousands)

	Output/ employee	VA/ employee	Average salary	Profit/ output	Fixed capital/ employee	Investment/ employee
Mining and quarrying						
Domestic enterprises	642	321	10 306	4.47	1550	92
Foreign enterprises	905	503	9349	23.93	1182	91
Manufacturing						
Domestic enterprises	844	245	7870	3.53	982	58
Foreign enterprises	1500	376	9649	3.08	1285	192
Construction						
Domestic enterprises	819	216	9017	3.63	439	29
Foreign enterprises	1123	285	10 302	9.46	497	35
Wholesale, retail trade						
Domestic enterprises	452	209	7442	4.74	950	58
Foreign enterprises	781	285	11 040	6.96	1194	198
Hotels, restaurants						
Domestic enterprises	552	231	8313	-0.82	1475	115
Foreign enterprises	564	199	7885	0.66	607	83
Transportation, communication						
Domestic enterprises	434	181	8350	11.90	1295	140
Foreign enterprises	3920	1364	15 865	3.76	570	216

Table 5.8 Comparison by ownership and sector in the Czech Republic, 1995 (in thousands) *(continued)*

	Output/ employee	VA/ employee	Average salary	Profit/ output	Fixed capital/ employee	Investment/ employee
Real estate and like						
Domestic enterprises	653	286	9823	9.60	1266	50
Foreign enterprises	939	310	12 530	5.85	290	54
Education, healthcare						
Domestic enterprises	531	273	8287	9.25	817	59
Foreign enterprises	2179	1208	16 206	29.28	797	169
Total						
Domestic enterprises	776	253	8254	6.14	1163	95
Foreign enterprises	1358	372	10 114	3.48	1128	171

Source: Czech Statistical Office, 1995, and author's own computation.

Table 5.9   FIE share of total employment, output, value added, investment and export of manufacturing in the Czech Republic, 1992–95 (%)

	1992	*1993*	*1994*	*1995*
Labour force	2.6	6.2	7.2	9.6
Output	5.6	9.8	11.6	16.5
Fixed assets	3.4	n.a.	10.2	14.9
Value added	4.0	8.2	9.2	19.1
Own capital	n.a.	n.a.	12.6	16.7
Wage fund	3.1	7.4	8.9	11.6
Investment	n.a.	22.4	26.9	27.5
Export	9.9	15.1	16.0	n.a.

Source: Czech Statistical Office, 1995.

In 1994 foreign investment expanded into textiles (Marzotto, Shoeller), paper (Assi Doman) and furniture (Lyra). In other industries, the development of foreign involvement was more gradual, occurring through re-invested profits and cash-flow retrenchment. This was the case in processed metals, communications, equipment, machinery and wood products. Measured by the share of output and labour force, foreign participation in manufacturing is concentrated in the automobile sector, printing and publishing, rubber and plastics and non-ferrous minerals. A high foreign presence is also reported in electrical equipment and medical instruments.

Thus, FIEs in the Czech Republic are very active in the export market, often considered one of the positive effects of foreign direct investment. And in most manufacturing industries – cars and trucks, rubber and plastics, processed foods and tobacco, as well as electrical equipment and medical instruments – the export market penetration of FIEs is significant. In addition, foreign firms export substantially more than domestic firms: this is most evident in the cases of rubber and plastics, metals, electrical equipment, medical instruments, transportation equipment and furniture and wood products. Three-quarters of all FIEs' sales in apparel, wood products and furniture, and more than half of sales in leather goods and shoes, chemicals, metals, medical equipment, automobiles and furniture are destined for the export market.

FIEs are more productive than domestic businesses, especially in manufacturing, where economies of scale play a large role and foreign investments have been substantial – as in automobiles, chemicals, paper, printing and publishing, and food products and tobacco. The same set of industries also records both high productivity and high levels of investment per employee.

Capital endowments are generally higher in FIEs, particularly in large-scale industries such as paper, printing, publishing, chemicals, non-ferrous metals, automobiles, food products and tobacco. In the more traditional industries, such as textiles, leather products, shoes and machinery, domestic firms have a higher level of capital investment, as well as in newer industries such as business machines and recycling.

Government policy towards FDI

Over the last few years, the Czech government has taken the position that the best way to encourage economic development is to provide a stable economic and political environment, and liberalize key regulations that have slowed the formation or expansion of business activity.[10] In the long run, it is assumed that this approach will create and maintain a climate conducive to sustained economic growth and mitigate risks.

After the first free elections of 1990, the Czech government experimented with a variety of investment subsidies – as in the Skoda–VW venture – with mixed success. The programmes were expensive, and the company results rarely as promised. They also created a climate of favouritism, which discouraged competitors. After the June 1992 elections, the new government adopted a significant policy shift, aiming instead for a 'level playing field' of stability and equal opportunity for all entrepreneurs, domestic and foreign. We can expect this approach towards foreign business to remain unchanged in the foreseeable future.

This is good news for investors, as the Czech Republic has attained a solid foundation of stability, both politically and economically. The country continues its reintegration with the developed world market through macroeconomic stabilization and the orientation of its trade towards the European Union market. At the time of writing (1997), the Czech Republic was the only post-communist country with an investment grade rating for government bonds from Moody's Investors' Service, a Baa1 grade (as of November 1995), a BBB+ from Standard and Poor's and 'A' rating from the Japanese Bond Research Institute. According to the *Institutional Investor* magazine, the Czech Republic is ranked 13th out of 135 countries in terms of creditworthiness.

With a low level of foreign debt and high foreign reserves, the Czech Republic is enjoying somewhat easier access to international capital markets than other Central European countries. It also has a relatively highly skilled labour force, a strong work ethic and a long tradition of industrialization which preceded the communist era. Because of this the Czechs do not feel the same pressing need for foreign investment as some of their Central European neighbours, and have had fewer problems sourcing managerial skills and technology from the domestic market.

But even though foreign direct investment may not be deemed crucial to the successful transformation and privatization *per se*, it is expected that foreign investors will play a significant role in restructuring enterprises. In the medium term – once equity markets are operating efficiently – the Czech Republic should become readily integrated into international capital markets.

At present, foreign investors can become owners of a company by:

- purchasing shares on the stock exchange;
- participating in tenders for shares;
- purchasing shares directly from the property's owners;
- participating directly in a new stock issue; and
- setting up a greenfield subsidiary.

Under the current law, foreign persons and legal entities can conduct business in the Czech Republic on equal terms with Czech investors with a few minor exceptions, where special provisions apply.

The Czech Republic has set no upper limit to the level of foreign investment or ownership; other than in banking and insurance, no state approval is required for the establishment of a corporate body with foreign participation. The repatriation of profits and capital abroad is guaranteed through various foreign currency and investment protection agreements. Foreigners can also freely repatriate any foreign assets in the form of commercial paper, bonds or other securities in foreign currency which relate to their business activities in the country.

There are very few special incentives[11] for foreign investors; in fact, some protective measures were enacted in recent legislation in an attempt to strengthen the position of domestic firms. One new regulation introduced in 1995 requires that foreign firms underbid domestic firms by 10 per cent in order to win a public contract bid. An amendment to the Trades Licensing Act in November 1995 set a deadline of 31 December 1996 for all representatives of foreign companies (joint stock, limited liability or subsidiary office) to receive work and residence permits, prove unimpeachable character, and demonstrate proficiency in the Czech language.

The equal treatment standard has been set aside in the case of certain large and prestigious FDI projects – but at the regional, rather than the national, level. Recently, Matsushita decided to invest $66 million into a plant at Pilsen for the assembly of Panasonic TV sets. Although the Czech government refused to provide special incentives for the Japanese investor, the local Pilsen government not only sold the land (17 hectares) at below market price ($11.5 per square metre), but also agreed to install the necessary infrastructure, valued at some $4 million, as part of a planned industrial zone in the area. They also agreed to provide assistance with training employees, public transportation links, and housing for Japanese staff. The Czech producers of television sets (Tesla TV), which control 20 per cent of the domestic market, feel threatened by the Matsushita project, because of what they perceive as 'the unfair legislative relief conceded to the Japanese'.

Although Matsushita promises to cooperate with Czech suppliers, some experts have expressed doubts, as Czech parts producers lack the skills and experience of foreign competitors. The expectation is that the new plant will be an assembly line for imported parts, preferentially imported under a tariff shield; a six-year tariff deferment has also been discussed.

The Czech legal environment is still in its infancy: it is over-regulated and often bureaucratic. Laws are often difficult to interpret and burdened with inconsistencies and loopholes. Many informal codes of ethical or corporate behaviour are missing altogether or are going through a slow process of evolution. In addition, the state judiciary infrastructure is overburdened to the point of paralysis, lacking both the human and financial capital necessary to enforce either statutes or contracts.

FDI and privatization

From the outset in 1991, privatization has been considered the key to the transformation of the economy. It began with the restitution and privatization of small-scale assets, now complete except for a few restitution claims being settled through the Ministry of Finance. For large privatization projects, the Czech Republic has combined standard methods[12] with voucher privatization.

The large-scale privatization programme involved property valued in excess of 930 billion koruna ($35 billion) over 5–6 years, of which about one-third was done through voucher privatization (see below). Out of this property list, 93 per cent was privatized by the end of 1995. Today (1997), the Czech economy has the largest share of private ownership in Eastern Europe – between 60 and 80 per cent depending on the source and methodology of data gathering.

Institutionally privatization has been handled primarily through the National Property Fund, the Ministry of Privatization, and other economic branch ministries. Recently the Ministry of Privatization was closed and the National Property Fund became the government's repository for state shares and only institution responsible for the final stages of the privatization process. In some cases, the administration of state shares has been delegated to the Ministry of Economy and Trade.

The programme's goal was to privatize about 80 per cent of the country's assets by mid-1996, with the goal of achieving a ratio of private to state-owned entities similar to that of developed market economies. Postal and telecommunications services have been separated, with the former remaining under government control, and other telecommunications activities and services being partially privatized. Of these, 27 per cent are held by foreign investors. Public utilities have also attracted foreign interest. Recently, it was decided that banks and financial intermediaries would also be privatized. So far, 30–45 per cent of shares in these financial institutions have been sold under the voucher privatization programme; the remainder are held by the National Property Fund.

Natural resources and most traditional public utilities will remain in the public sector. Nevertheless, general disillusionment with central planning, state ownership, and the role of the state bureaucracy has led to a refusal to accept any co-ordinating role for the state in guiding economic activity. This has lent support to an important faction of politicians and economists advocating the extension of privatization to almost all types of economic activity, including public utilities such as electric power, transportation, education and healthcare. If implemented, these would result in more far-reaching privatization programmes than in some established market economies.

Privatization and foreign investors

Although foreign participation represents only 1.2 per cent of all projects submitted, foreign investors have been the source of more than half of all proceeds from large-scale privatization (in all a total of $4.6 billion). Because of investment commitments over the next few years, foreign investment is expected to become an increasingly important factor in company restructuring. Given the penalties for non-fulfilment of contracts, foreign investor privatizations have been closely monitored by the National Property Fund and other officials, and most commitments so far have been fulfilled. Table 5.10 illustrates the size of foreign investment commitments at end-1995.

A total of 315 privatization projects involving in excess of 200 enterprises with proposed foreign participation were submitted. Of these, 144 with a total transaction value of $4.2 billion were approved. The remaining privatization projects were either turned down by the Czech authorities or collapsed as the foreign partners withdrew, often losing interest in the lengthy negotiation process. The average purchase price has been close to book value, but the market to book value ratio ranges widely, between 0.5 and 4.5.

Table 5.10   Size of foreign investments in Czech privatization

Value of privatization transaction	Per cent of the total number of transactions
less than USD 1 mn	6.9
1–5 mn	30.6
5–10 mn	19.4
10–20 mn	21.5
20–50 mn	13.9
50–100 mn	4.2
more than USD 100 mn	3.5
Total	100 per cent

Source: Ministry of Privatization, 1996.

Projects with foreign participation have been subject to particular scrutiny and, as they affect the best enterprises, have tended to be controversial. In evaluating projects with foreign investment, specific attention has been paid to both the deal structure (debts versus equity, plans to increase equity) and social issues such as employment and environmental protection. Newly privatized companies have normally taken over the obligations of the former enterprise, including environmental liabilities.

A Standard Purchase Contract form and two separate standard contracts for the sale of assets (Enterprise Purchase Agreement) and equity (Share Purchase Agreement) are in circulation. These have been helpful in unifying contractual conditions and improving and accelerating the negotiation process. As a rule, foreign investors are given the standard contracts at the initial meeting to highlight the relevant business and legal issues of privatization in the Czech Republic. Negotiations would follow before the project is submitted for review to the Approval Commission. These standard agreements have been continually updated to reflect new governmental resolutions and policies.

The process of privatizing a company through the National Property Fund varies from several months to more than a year. The bid may be initiated by submitting a takeover intention to the relevant Ministry, which may tender out for competing projects. The procedure requires the approval of the Ministry of Privatization. Other government authorities may also be consulted, including the Council of Economic Ministers, the Ministry of Finance and the Ministry of Economic Competition. To accomplish this, a thorough review of business plans, financial statements, environmental audits, and other relevant information must be conducted. Successful bids often involve commitments by the foreign firm to invest, train management and employees, improve the environment and provide new technology and access to export markets. Pricing policy, remuneration strategy and guarantees to preserve domestic competition are other important considerations.[13] Table 5.11 shows that foreign investors prefer majority ownership of the shareholding: over 88 per cent of all investors acquired majority ownership.

Table 5.11   Stakes acquired by foreign investors in Czech privatization

% acquired	% of transactions
1–30	4.9
31–50	6.9
51–70	32.6
71–99	21.5
100	34.1
Total	100.0

Source: Ministry of Privatization, 1996

The National Property Fund and privatization

By the end of 1995, the National Property Fund held equity positions in some 1500 Czech companies. In 410 – nearly a third – it held an interest above 20 per cent, including 38 companies where it was the sole owner. In another 94 companies, it held more than two-thirds of the stock; in 80 companies it had a majority interest, and in another 100 companies a qualified minority of more than 34 per cent. In yet another 1000-plus firms, it held up to 20 per cent of the equity.

The Czech state ultimately intends to privatize much of the aforementioned portfolio, but will probably continue to hold permanent or provisional stakes in about 228 of the 410 companies referred to above. Of these 228 companies, 58 companies have been selected as 'strategic': these are mainly in finance, energy, mining, metallurgy, chemicals and transportation, as well as telecommunications and healthcare.

Privatization and restructuring

In most cases, the government has avoided restructuring enterprises prior to privatization, leaving it to the new owners to reorganize as they judge best. In cases where companies were sold outright to foreign investors, as with Skoda or Cokoladovny, control was transferred immediately to the new owners/managers who rapidly began improving company performance. By contrast, if the ownership remains ill-defined, with neither direct state control nor effective private owners, the restructuring can be delayed and necessary changes slow in coming.

The acquisition of the chocolate producer Cokoladovny by Nestlé/BSN is a good example of restructuring by a foreign owner. Following privatization, the Cokoladovny-Nestlé/BSN company headquarters were completely reorganized with a new emphasis on marketing and sales. First, a marketing department was established to provide market research, new product ideas and improvements in packaging. For instance, the company decreased its number of candy varieties from 500 to 150 to market them more effectively.

Second, there was a new focus on human resources and training. The company restructured the personnel department and provided better training. It also prepared a social programme to improve the working environment and help prepare workers for lay-offs arising from job duplication. The new management also initiated a major campaign to improve communication within the company: by giving workers more insight into company planning and development, it sought to increase their motivation: with this programme in mind Czech middle managers are sent abroad for training.

Third, the company centralized all materials purchasing from domestic suppliers and importers.

Fourth, the company separated the sales operation from both distribution and logistics and set up a local sales network and four regional distribution warehouses to improve the efficiency of product delivery. Previously, customers were resupplied monthly by each production unit with an often incomplete range of goods. Now, the company is able to deliver virtually the entire assortment (90 selected products, representing 80 per cent of sales) every two weeks. The sales department was increased from 10 to 200 employees, reflecting an increase in the number of clients and a new emphasis on improving customer service.

Fifth, the company created two production-management divisions at headquarters for chocolates and non-chocolate sweets, for which there are eight production locations; and biscuits, with seven.

Sixth, the company installed a new computer network with Nestlé management software; new cost control modules now generate complete financial profiles on individual plants.

Once the management changes were in place, the objective was to replace the former top-down management with a more horizontal, collaborative approach preferred by Western managers. Plants receive targets for quantity, quality, efficiency and production deadlines. Financially, the plants are accountable only for operating within a budget; they are not responsible for pricing their end-product, nor do they deal with marketing or market research. Investments are focused on concentrating production, increasing specialization, and adjusting capacities to market size.

Nestlé estimates that productivity has been improved by some 25 per cent through the more efficient use of existing resources, better management and higher capacity utilization. Having learned the specifics of their new business as a result of these changes, Nestlé committed themselves to additional large capital injections.

Privatization and monopoly

Before 1990, the supply of most commodities was controlled by a handful of Czech state enterprises, and monopoly was a general phenomenon in the economy.[14] The centrally planned system set up numerous administrative and legal barriers isolating industries from external competition and regulating the entry and exit of firms. Since 1990, the legal restrictions that institutionalized the monopoly control of various industries have been relaxed, and the market pressure for rational economic behaviour is expected to increase. In general, firms are getting smaller, both through the break-up of large state enterprises prior to, and during, privatization, and through the spontaneous, explosive growth of small independent businesses.

In January 1991 parliament passed the Competition Protection Act. The law is similar to EU legislation and the German Anti-Cartel Law; it has been amended twice since 1991. The Ministry of Economic Competition, which had jurisdiction for this law, will now be turned into an independent agency.

During privatization, the Ministry was empowered to approve each privatization project with a view to reducing industry concentration. The heavy volume of privatization projects led to administrative overload and serious delays. In market economies, anti-monopoly (anti-trust) offices usually deal with tens of cases per year. In the Czech Republic, as in other transitional economies, there were hundreds of enterprises with market shares exceeding 30 per cent. Therefore, the Ministry chose to rely more extensively on direct methods of de-monopolization, by removing entry barriers and creating a favourable climate for fair competition.

In such a small country, the legal system and regulatory ministries are necessarily relatively weak vehicles for maintaining a competitive environment. To date, the application process for merger approval has not been frequently used.

During privatization, the government was usually faced with a choice of selling the monopoly control of an entire market to one foreign investor, or breaking up the enterprise for the benefit of a particular investor. There are no clear guidelines as to the most appropriate way to handle this, although the development of competitive markets is certainly an important consideration. In evaluating the Czech FDI record to date, it seems that, in several cases, it might have been preferable to have set a lower initial purchase price for the company, and to have strengthened a free market by refusing the high levels of protection that so dampen competition. However, this can still be done. By opening up the Czech economy to foreign trade and improving conditions for the growth of new firms, some of the more important market sectors should gradually adjust of their own accord.

Conclusions

Although foreign penetration in the Czech Republic (as measured by the level of foreign direct investment) is still limited in comparison to that in open market economies of a similar size, it is increasing steadily. In manufacturing, the share of FIEs in the total workforce increased to almost 10 per cent in 1995 from 2.6 per cent in 1992. Although foreign companies account for over 20 per cent of manufacturing employment, foreign involvement in the Czech Republic is about half of that in developed market economies. Real GNP growth was about 5 per cent in 1995 and the economy is expected to continue growing in the future. Although inflation has been curbed to single figures, salaries are growing at about 17 per cent a year. The recent increases in the foreign trade and current account deficits call for compensating growth in foreign direct investment to finance these deficits in a more stable way than more mobile capital would provide.

The Economist Intelligence Unit expects this 'catch up' to continue, and estimates the amount of FDI to the Czech Republic during 1996–2000 to reach $15.5 billion. Nevertheless, the real FDI inflows, and by implication the expansion of FIEs in the Czech Republic, can significantly differ from this forecast depending on economic growth rates, the balance of payments situation, exchange rate and trade policies, labour-cost developments, taxation, the existence of bureaucratic obstacles to investment, and the progress of integration to the European Union. New foreign investment will also be influenced by outstanding government privatization decisions.

Prior to 1995, the main source of FDI was privatization. FDI amounted to $1.4 billion in 1996, down from $2.6 billion the previous year. This was primarily because of the absence of large deals such as the Telecom privatization of 1995. Large-scale privatization is essentially over, although there are some existing investment commitments which should come to fruition over the next few years.

Privatization has generally slowed down. Future inflows of foreign investment arising from privatization will depend on developments in the banking sector, the utilities and strategic sector enterprises. There are also large outstanding blocks of shares in state hands which could be privatized. The Ministry of Industry and Trade, for example, administers holdings which will probably be privatized, at least partially, in the future. These include raw materials industries, such as coal mines and steel works, and a variety of manufacturing enterprises. Holdings in the oil giant Unipetrol and other energy-distributing enterprises are also likely to be partially privatized.

The bulk of future FDI is likely to be channeled into modernizing and restructuring companies that have already been privatized, or into greenfield investments. Our analysis has shown a sizeable level of investment activity by FIEs in the Czech economy. The foreign managers of these projects are planning for the long term and developing strategies beyond the turn of the century. Domestic investors have so far not paid much attention to strategy or long-term planning; instead, they have directed their efforts towards acquiring operational control. They also face the additional problem of how to finance such a strategy and carry the responsibility of repaying or servicing a heavy debt burden. Foreign companies usually have both the expertise and the financial means for their strategic and restructuring objectives. Foreign investors have also helped establish the small business sector, which did not exist at the beginning of the transformation process.

Notes

1   The stock exchange opened in spring 1993, and the shares of more than 600 companies were originally traded, primarily companies privatized in the voucher privatization. Voucher shares that do not qualify for the Stock Exchange are traded in the RM-system 'over-the-counter-market', which was based on the technology originally developed to implement bidding in voucher privatization.

2 The origin of portfolio investment at the end of 1995 was as follows: Britain 50 per cent, USA 22 per cent, Germany 6 per cent, Slovakia 5 per cent (voucher privatization holdings excluded), Austria 5 per cent, Cyprus 3 per cent and other countries 9 per cent. The industrial structure of portfolio investment in 1995 was as follows: banking (including government bonds mediated through the Czech National Bank) 54 per cent, energy 17 per cent, transport 17 per cent, construction 3 per cent and other industries 9 per cent.

3 In 1994 Prague Townhall bonds worth $250 million were sold abroad, as well as $126 million of Eurobonds held by the Czech National Bank.

4 The sectoral structure is too aggregated, and detailed information was not available from the Czech National Bank.

5 'Other industries' in Table 5.2 include not only services and transport, but also machinery, electronics and other manufacturing industries.

6 There was a disinvestment in the case of Air France, when the state repurchased Air France's share in CSA.

7 Recent results from the PANEL PECO PROJECT, published by the Czech Statistical Office (edition 'Reports and Analysis', Publication No. 27 01-96), assessed the quality of the Company Register in the Czech Republic. According to this analysis 36 per cent of units in the Register are non-active. The most frequent reason for non-operation was closure (57 per cent).

8 *Foreign ownership (FEs)*: unit established by a foreign physical or legal unit, non-resident of the Czech Republic, owning 100 per cent of assets (total equity);
International ownership: joint ventures established jointly by domestic and foreign units, that is units with domestic and foreign capital (enterprises with any foreign contribution, with the exception of total equity);
Private ownership of private domestic physical or legal units;
Cooperatives:
State ownership: units of public administration, enterprises founded by the ministries or other central administrative bodies, or other institutions set up from state sources, joint stock companies where the state is the only shareholder;
Municipal ownership:
Non-governmental organizations: ownership of parties, associations and church;
Mixed ownership of more than one domestic founder with a mixed ownership. Mixed ownership is a combination of private and state ownership. In 1994 some large firms were still under this indeterminate arrangement.

9 A. Zemplinerova (1995) 'Evolution and Efficiency of Concentration', in J. Svejnar (ed.) *Manufacturing in the Czech Republic and Economic Transition in Eastern Europe*, Academic Press.

10 Among the comparative advantages which have attracted foreign investors to the Czech Republic are more than 150 years of established industrial tradition, the high technical skills of the workforce, a steep learning curve, a stabilized political climate and long-lasting experience with parliamentary democracy, acquired in the 1920s and 1930s, a European cultural heritage, social peace and a favourable geographical position.

11 As of 21 July 1993 joint venture companies in the Czech Republic with at least 30 per cent foreign ownership (equaling no less than $1.7 million) were allowed one year's exemption from customs duties on raw materials or semi-processed goods imported through the foreign partner for manufacturing. The law, intended to encourage new companies, was valid for established enterprises until July 1994 or, in the case of new enterprises, for one year after their foundation.

12 Restitution to original owners or their heirs; sale of property to domestic or foreign investors through public auctions and tenders; direct sale to a designated owner; transformation into a joint stock company with the subsequent sale of shares; and free transfer of property to the municipalities.

13 The assessment is usually carried out by an independent international real estate company or a team of foreign advisers paid by the Czech government. Though relatively free of corruption, this process has been criticized for being bureaucratic, subjective and slow.

14 See Zemplinerova, 1995.

6
Foreign Investment and Privatization in Poland

Wladyslaw Jermakowicz

Although Poland has been a recipient of foreign direct investment (FDI) since 1976, the real acceleration in FDI began after the first free elections of June 1989 and the 'Big Bang – Balcerowicz Programme' of January 1990. These political and economic factors influenced the new FDI legislation and dramatically improved the business climate.

Over the past nine years, the number of new firms with foreign participation has grown considerably. The evolution of FDI went through various phases. We examine in turn the influx, origin and strategy of FDI, and use a well-established investment development path model to determine whether Poland's FDI development fits within a more global pattern.

The investment development path model

John Dunning[1] has developed an investment development path model which corresponds to three types of adjustment mechanisms. Taking into account Narula's contribution, this model comprises four stages: factor-driven, domestic-investment driven, export-investment driven, and innovation-driven (see Table 6.1).[2]

The factor-driven stage

At this stage nations draw their advantages mostly by mobilizing an abundance of basic and inexpensive factors. Little technology is created locally, and domestic firms use imported technology mostly through licensing and joint ventures. Factor-driven development is supported by a relatively low level of inward investment and, more importantly, by subcontracting and outward processing. Usually a large number of small firms arise: joint-ventures and minority foreign investment are dominant. Traditional industries based on local resources are prevalent.

Table 6.1   Investment development path model

Investment strategy stage	Characteristics of firms	Strategy seeking	Entry modes
• Factory-driven	Large number of small firms	Resources Cost efficiency	Licensing Joint-ventures Subcontracting
• Domestic-investment driven	Limited number of average-sized firms	Domestic market	Inward Direct Investment direct acquisition
• Export-investment driven	Limited number of large firms	Foreign market	Inward direct investment Greenfields
• Innovation-driven	Investment in R&D institutes	Human capital R&D assets	Inward direct investment equals Outward direct investment non-equity

Sources: J.H. Dunning, 'The Prospects for Foreign Direct Investment in Eastern Europe', in P. Artisien-Maksimenko, M. Rojec and M. Svetličič (eds) Foreign Investment in Central and Eastern Europe (Macmillan, London, 1993); J.H. Dunning and R. Narula, Transpacific Foreign Direct Investment and the Investment Development Path: The Record Assessed (Maastricht Economic Research Institute on Innovation and Technology, Maastricht, 1993).

The domestic-investment-driven stage

This stage is dominated by investment in manufacturing standardized products for the domestic market. Domestic market conditions, buttressed by import-substitution policies, are dominant with regards to balance of payments constraints. Inward FDI through direct acquisitions develops as a major source of technology transfer.

The export-investment-driven stage

At this stage, advanced factor conditions attract investments to the export-driven mass production of medium-technology products. Inward FDI increasingly concentrates on economies of scale, because low labour costs are no longer sufficient grounds for establishing local production. Growth measured by the number of FDI slows down as the ownership advantages of MNEs *vis-à-vis* domestic firms weaken. The average size of firms is high. Firms enter the market with global investment strategies. Greenfield inward investments predominate.

The innovation-driven stage

During this stage the national innovation system reaches a level of maturity which enables the economy not only to appropriate and improve from foreign locations, but also to create its own innovations. The bulk of inward investment now seeks strategic assets through applied and basic research. Outward investment grows rapidly, and inward and outward investment become increasingly complementary. Thus, the national innovation system becomes the main source of a country's competitive advantage, systematically acquired through generating new knowledge and technological capabilities.

Historical development of FDI in Poland

Calculating inward FDI in Poland is fraught with difficulty. The Polish State Foreign Investment Agency publishes only data for large firms with investments exceeding $1 million, whilst the Polish Statistical Office's data sources are not always reliable or comparable. In this chapter data from the Ministry of Privatization and the State Foreign Investment Agency will be used.

Table 6.1 includes data for all firms as well as large firms with investments exceeding $1 million. The data for all firms come from the Ministry of Privatization for 1987–96; for larger firms, the source is the Polish State Foreign Investment Agency for 1989–96. Whilst at the beginning of the period large investments were practically non-existent, by 1996 they constituted 93 per cent of all investments.

Poland has experienced increasing FDI inflows since 1987: in 1988 it played host to a mere 30 investments with a total capital value of $6880; in

1989, as many as 518 foreign firms invested $96 410 (Table 6.2). The ten-fold increase in capital and joint ventures in 1988 was exceeded the following year when the number of joint ventures increased by a factor of 16.7 and capital by 13.7. Such growth levels clearly could not be sustained in the medium term.

The second wave of FDI growth occurred in 1992, when new laws and economic reforms gave foreign investors the security needed to enter the Polish market. In 1992 the amount of invested capital tripled over the previous year. The average size of firms with foreign participation more than doubled, and the share of large firms exceeding $1 million was over 50 per cent of all investment.

The third wave of inward FDI took off in 1995, when the value of annual investment nearly doubled in comparison to 1994, accumulated capital grew 1.5 times, and the ratio of large investments to all investments exceeded 80 per cent. The stock of small firms with capital below $1 million became marginal. By 1996 the total value of inward FDI exceeded $12.5 billion.

The statistical data on FDI to Poland confirm the usefulness of Dunning's Investment Development Path model. The first wave resembled a typical factor-driven stage: during this period the Polish advantage lay in the abundance of cheap raw materials and an inexpensive labour force. Local firms provided infrastructure, buildings, labour and materials, whilst foreign partners supplied the capital and technology. At this stage a relatively low level of inward investment was observable. The second wave resembled the domestic-investment driven stage, with large firms exceeding 50 per cent of all FDI. Average-sized firms grew and the import of technology became more visible. The third wave witnessed export-investment-driven activities: large firms with a clearly global approach prevailed. As yet, there is no sign of the beginning of the fourth stage in FDI development.

Greenfield v. acquisitions

A foreign company's decision to invest abroad involves selecting the most appropriate investment mode. This decision depends, to a large degree, on the investor's motives and the nature of the industry. There are three basic investment modes: greenfield investment, indirect acquisition – via joint ventures, and direct acquisition – through the purchasing of shares in local companies. The last mode is most frequently used in the privatization process.

Table 6.3 illustrates the changes in the structure of investment modes between 1988 and 1996. Although the value of all modes of investment significantly increased, the proportions of greenfields and privatizations changed most over these years. First, an impressive increase in greenfield investment flows is observable: from only $82 000 in 1987 to $1.8 million at end 1996. This suggests an increase in confidence in the Polish market

Table 6.2 FDI stock and flows to Poland, 1987–96

| | Growth of FDI by number | | Growth of FDI by Capital | | | Average size of the firm | | | |
	Number	Accumulate	Capital	Accumulate	Dynamic (%)	Large	$ in all (%)	Yearly	Accumulate
1987	3	3	696	696			0	232.0	232.0
1988	30	33	6 880	7 576	1 089		0	229.3	229.6
1989	518	551	96 413	103 989	1 373	8 000	8	186.1	188.7
1990	1 493	2 044	204 458	308 447	297	97 000	47	136.9	150.9
1991	3 125	5 169	425 096	733 543	238	219 000	52	136.0	141.9
1992	3 456	8 625	1 500 645	2 234 188	305	1 084 000	72	434.2	259.0
1993	4 179	12 804	2 014 657	4 248 845	190	1 633 000	81	482.1	331.8
1994	4 023	16 827	1 675 437	5 924 282	139	1 280 000	76	416.5	352.1
1995	3 421	20 248	3 045 874	8 970 156	151	2 511 000	82	890.3	443.0
1996	3 654	23 902	3 578 942	12 549 098	140	3 323 000	93	979.5	525.0

Source: Author's own calculations based on data from the Ministry of Privatization.

Table 6.3 Greenfield investment, indirect and direct acquisitions in Poland (1987–96)

Year	Greenfield $	%	Indirect acquisition $	%	Direct acquisition $	%	Total $	%
1987	82	11.8	614	88.2	0	0.0	696	100
1988	1 686	24.5	5 194	75.5	0	0.0	6 880	100
1989	26 514	27.5	54 399	56.4	15 500	16.1	96 413	100
1990	58 066	28.4	91 266	44.6	55 126	27.0	204 458	100
1991	126 254	29.7	126 796	29.8	172 046	40.5	425 096	100
1992	454 695	30.3	398 673	26.6	647 277	43.1	1 500 645	100
1993	689 013	34.2	276 853	13.7	1 048 791	52.1	2 014 657	100
1994	646 719	38.6	187 541	11.2	841 177	50.2	1 675 437	100
1995	1 495 524	49.1	165 436	5.4	1 384 914	45.5	3 045 874	100
1996	1 800 208	50.3	152 365	4.3	1 626 369	45.4	3 578 942	100
Total	5 298 759	42.2	1 459 137	11.6	57 912 014	46.1	12 549 098	100

Source: Author's own calculations based on data from the Ministry of Privatization.

and a growing willingness to start new ventures. A second observable trend is the increase in receipts from direct acquisitions: from $15.5 million in 1989 (16.1 per cent of all inward investment), to $1.6 million (or 45.4 per cent of the FDI total) in 1996. Third, there has been a decline in the number of joint ventures (4.3 per cent in 1996): this suggests that greenfield investments and privatizations have become more attractive modes of entry. Fourth, greenfield investments have grown relatively faster than direct-acquisition investments (privatizations). Although privatization made up over half of all FDI in 1994, we believe that greenfield investments are now set to increase at a faster rate than privatizations. Poland has already privatized its most attractive enterprises, and privatization is meeting increased resistance among the population. Adding to the interest in greenfield investments is the growing investor confidence in political stability and the potential for high returns.

The role of greenfield investment is even more impressive in terms of the number of enterprises. In 1995, a total of 10 422 greenfield investments constituted 88.3 per cent of all FDI, compared with 1115 indirect acquisitions (9.4 per cent of foreign investors), and 266 direct acquisitions (a mere 2.3 per cent of all cases). In terms of capital invested, however, direct acquisitions have contributed 30 per cent more capital than greenfields.

Investors acquiring Polish firms in the framework of privatization between 1989 and 1993 contributed $1 938 741 million or 45.6 per cent of total FDI. But the average foreign share in capitalization per firm differed significantly: greenfield investments amounted to only $130 100 per firm, joint ventures $855 400 (nearly six times more), and direct acquisitions $7 288 500 (56 times more). Greenfield investments involved mostly small investments in retail premises; by contrast, direct acquisitions comprised mostly large firms.

Table 6.4 compares the modes of market penetration in selected East European countries. Foreign investors entering the Polish market have chosen greenfield investments more often than their counterparts in other post-communist countries (32.9 per cent v. 17 per cent). This is partly the result of Poland's more liberal investment climate. Table 6.4 also shows that indirect acquisitions through joint ventures have been more prevalent elsewhere in Eastern Europe (50 per cent against 22.4 per cent in Poland). This would suggest that the Polish economy has entered a more mature stage in terms of attracting FDI, as joint ventures are normally associated with infant economies.

In the Russian Federation joint ventures predominate, and greenfield investments are negligible: this supports the argument that high risk levels have prompted foreign firms to take the shared-risk approach offered by joint ventures. In the Czech Republic, the extensive voucher privatization schemes have encouraged direct acquisitions. Hungary's position bears similarities to that of Poland, with one exception: a higher share of joint ventures. The

Table 6.4 FDI distribution by types of investment in Eastern Europe (December 1993)

Modes of investment in Poland	Number	%	Capital	%	Average size
Greenfield	10 422	88.3	1 356 309	32.9	130.1
Indirect Acquisition	1 115	9.4	953 795	22.4	855.4
Direct Acquisition	266	2.3	1 938 741	45.6	7 288.5
Total	11 803	100.0	4 248 845	100.0	164.3
Modes of investment in the Russian Federation					
Greenfield	2 077	26.0	31 525	1.0	15.2
Indirect Acquisition	5 672	71.0	2 774 816	88.0	489.2
Direct Acquisition	240	3.0	346 852	11.0	1 447.2
Total	7 989	100.0	3 153 200	100.0	394.7
Modes of investment in the Czech Republic					
Greenfield	1 650	33.0	102 650	5.0	62.2
Indirect Acquisition	1 650	33.0	656 960	32.0	398.2
Direct Acquisition	1 700	34.0	1 293 390	63.0	760.8
Total	5 000	100.0	2 053 000	100	410.6
Modes of investment in Hungary					
Greenfield	6 011	28	1 741 653	29.0	289.7
Indirect Acquisition	7 728	36.0	2 162 052	36.0	279.8
Direct Acquisition	7 728	36.0	2 101 995	35.0	272.0
Total	21 468	100.0	6 005 700	100.0	279.8
Modes of investment in CEE					
Greenfield	9 738	28.0	1 875 835	17.0	192.6
Indirect Acquisition	15 051	44.0	5 593 828	50.0	371.7
Direct Acquisition	9 668	28.0	3 742 237	33.0	387.1
Total	34 457	100.0	11 211 900	100.0	325.4

Source: Author's own calculations based on data from the Ministry of Privatization

investment-path model thus suggests that in 1993 Russia was still at Stage I, whilst the Czech Republic, Hungary and Poland were entering Stage II. Since 1996 Poland has entered Stage III, with neighbouring countries being expected to follow suit (with the exception of Russia).

Majority and minority stakes

Table 6.5 shows the relationship between acquisitions and greenfield investments in terms of equity ownership. The general trend suggests an investor preference for majority holdings, although some discrepancies occur between greenfield and acquisition-type investments. The past nine years have witnessed a radical increase in majority interests (from 9.6 per cent in 1988 to 79.6 per cent in 1996).

The first stage (1988–92) was characterized by minority foreign involvement, with the exception of larger firms entering the market as greenfield investments such as Intercell, Sigma and Hyatt Regency. Foreign acquisitions dominated the second period (1993–95), when both acquisitions and greenfield investments helped secure foreign majority control. In the third period (1996 onwards), greenfield investments have shown steady growth; at the same time, a surprising decline in foreign acquisitions has also been observed.

Sectoral patterns of FDI

The FDI stock shifted between sectors in the first two years of the transition (1990–91), when foreign investors faced high levels of uncertainty and essential changes took place in target industries for FDI. During 1992–94, a gradual level of stabilization was introduced; since 1994 sectoral stabilization has occurred.

Table 6.6 shows that the two highest-ranked sectors (in technological terms) (1 and 2) received the smallest portions of FDI (about 10 per cent) in the first period. Sector 3, characterized by low human and physical capital, was dominant, and included such industries as footwear, clothing, metals and furniture. FDI in this period was attracted by location advantages. During this factor-driven stage – dominated by subcontracting – access to resources and low production costs motivated foreign investors.

The second period was export-driven: sector 4 became dominant with low human capital but high physical capital, including such industries as motor vehicles and textiles. The principal reason for the strong performance of sector 4 was the drive to capture the strongest share of the domestic market. Investment into scale-based industries attracted less investment, not because of cost-efficiency considerations, but rather because of lagging demand for standardized, mass-consumption products.[3]

Table 6.5 FDI distribution in Poland by foreign capital shares, 1988, 1993 and 1996

Foreign share in capital (%)	Total		Foreign acquisitions		Greenfield investments	
	50% and less	51% and more	50% and less	51% and more	50% and less	51% and more
1988	90.4	9.6	100	0	39.1	60.9
1993	28.9	71.1	43.3	56.7	26.9	73.1
1996	20.4	79.6	57.6	42.4	17.3	82.7
Total	60.4	39.6	64.4	35.6	26.3	73.7

Source: Author's own calculations based on data from the Ministry of Privatization.

Table 6.6 Sectoral distribution of FDI in Poland, 1990–95

Sector		1990	1991	1992	1993	1994	1995	1990–95 % point change
Stock structure in %	1	1.9	15.3	12.8	12.6	21.5	18.4	+16.5
	2	8.5	19.2	14.9	11.8	14.1	17.4	+8.9
	3	64.4	22.2	17.0	11.8	11.5	12.5	−51.9
	4	6.3	30.2	21.5	37.1	35.3	30.5	+24.2
	5	19.0	13.1	33.7	26.7	17.6	21.2	+2.3
Flow structure in %	1	1.1	19.3	11.6	12.5	48.9	12.9	
	2	3.4	22.4	12.7	9.6	21.3	23.3	
	3	71.2	9.8	14.4	8.3	10.3	14.3	
	4	5.8	37.2	17.1	47.7	29.7	22.0	
	5	18.4	11.4	44.1	21.9	−10.2	27.5	

Source: Author's own calculations based on companies' balance sheets from the Central Statistical Board.

In the third period, a clear increase in human-capital-related sectors (sectors 1 and 5) seems to indicate that export-driven factors are gradually beginning to dominate.

Origin of investors

A comparison of FDI over time shows important changes not only in the size of invested capital but also in the ranking of different countries. In the first period, the most striking trend is the dominance of countries bordering Poland. Germany, including West Berlin, made up 29.8 per cent, followed by Sweden and Norway (Table 6.7).

In the second period (up to December 1993) geographical proximity played a lesser role. Italy and the United States topped the table, followed by Germany. Low costs, abundance of resources and proximity to markets took on greater importance. During the third period (1994–96) the United States was ranked first, followed by Germany. Little deconcentrating of inward foreign investment has taken place so far. In 1988 the top ten investor countries provided 92 per cent of all capital; in 1993, of the 93 countries with capital invested in Poland, ten accounted for 87 per cent of all FDI. Italy occupied first position with 30.2 per cent of all foreign capital. The average size of Italy's firms amounted to $887.9 million, the result of large capital investments by Fiat, the Luccini Group, and Frotrade Financing. Germany, by contrast, has invested in a large number of firms with an average capital of $67 900 per firm. The situation changed in 1996: the ten major investing countries engaged just under 70 per cent of all inward investment.

The impact of historical relationships on the size and structure of investment warrants some attention. In the first period they were important, as investors relied on familiarity with the region. Firms from Germany, Sweden and Austria were less wary of Poland and tended to invest greater amounts.

In the third period, more non-European firms entered the Polish capital market. Australian, South Korean, Canadian and Japanese firms significantly increased their investing profile. Yet another trend was the growth of multinational capital in the form of international investment funds and institutions, particularly in the post-1993 period.

In terms of FDI structure, two-thirds of EU investments consisted of acquisitions and one-third of greenfield ventures. The ratios were reversed for the rest of the world. Geographical distance seems to be an important factor: the closer the investor is to Poland, the more investment takes place via acquisitions, and vice versa. Little investment originates from other East European countries: Russian investment is concentrated in the building of a gas pipeline from Siberia to Western Europe.

Investment projects

According to the Foreign Investment Agency the total financial involvement of the 373 largest foreign investors in Poland (equity and credit) in

Table 6.7 Origin of FDI in Poland, 1988–97 (value of FDI)

LP	Country	31 December 1988		Country	31 December 1993		Country	31 December 1996	
		$mn	%		$mn	%		$mn	%
1	Germany	42.6	22.8	Italy	546.1	30.2	USA	2 399.4	24
2	Sweden	19.7	10.6	USA	347.7	19.2	Multinational	1 467.3	14
3	Norway	18.3	9.8	Germany	214.8	11.9	Germany	1 335.6	13
4	Netherlands	16.8	9.0	Netherlands	143.7	7.9	Italy	953.1	9
5	Multinational	15.4	8.2	France	83.7	4.6	Netherlands	839.1	8
6	West Berlin	13.0	7.0	Sweden	70.1	3.9	France	657.4	6
7	USA	10.3	5.7	Austria	65.9	3.6	UK	393.8	4
8	Italy	10.5	5.6	UK	59.9	3.3	Austria	316.4	3
9	Austria	8.9	4.8	Norway	40.3	2.2	Australia	298.0	3
10	UK	5.7	3.0	Switzerland	40.2	2.2	S. Korea	290.5	3
	% of EU countries	171.5	87.3	% of EU countries	1 572.2	78.8	% of EU countries	8 950.6	56.0
	Total top ten	186.6	91.9	Total top ten	1 809.9	86.9	Total top ten	12 549.1	71.3

Source: Author's own calculations based on data from the Polish State Investment Agency.

mid-1996 amounted to $10.1 billion. The investment commitments of these 373 firms totalled $8.4 billion. Table 6.8 lists the 10 largest foreign investors during the period 1988–96. At end-1988 the Kvaerner Gdynia Shipyard joint venture was the largest investor with a mere $17.5 million (the joint venture was registered but never came to fruition). In 1993 and 1996, a joint venture between Fiat and the Car Factory FSM in Bielsko-Biala topped the league table in terms of actual and committed investments.

In 1988 the top ten foreign investments amounted to $64.7 million and 34.7 per cent of total FDI. This went up to $1 billion in 1993 and $3.3 billion in 1996.

In the period up to 1988, of the top ten firms, three came from the United States, two from Germany, and the others from Norway, Sweden, West Berlin, the Netherlands and Italy. The United States presence increased to six of the top ten firms in both 1993 and 1996.

Legislative changes

The first joint venture law allowing full foreign participation was passed by the Polish Sejm on 23 April 1986. At that time foreign capital participation was restricted to small-scale production and joint ventures with foreign minority interests. These companies were subject to complex authorization procedures that excluded entry into sectors deemed important for social or state interests. Several restrictions also existed on the repatriation of profits and capital invested, which ultimately depended on hard currency availability. In the absence of compensation guarantees against expropriation, with licences usually issued for only ten years, and the restricted transfer of ownership interest even within Poland, it is not surprising that these partnerships usually adopted fast-profit strategies. The average capital investment per firm was low (usually the minimum capital requirement of $50 000).

The foreign investment legislation was liberalized in April 1986: more sectors of the economy were opened up to foreign investors; the full transfer of profits abroad was permitted, and investors acquired greater control over the ventures. A new law introduced on 14 June 1991 abolished the $50 000 minimum investment requirement. In its place, a minimum start-up capital of $1000 was introduced for limited companies, and $26 000 for joint-stock companies. Moreover, the 20 per cent minimum stock-ownership requirement was abandoned, and foreign companies became subject to the same levels of taxation as Polish firms. Special permits were no longer required with the exception of investments in seaports and airports, real estate, defence, the wholesale trade of imported goods, and consulting and legal services. These new regulations providing for full national treatment constituted the most important factor in the second wave of FDI inflows in 1992. Foreign investors increased significantly their stake in established joint ventures both in terms of percentage participation and average capital invested.

Table 6.8   The ten largest foreign investors in Poland, 1988, 1993 and 1996

	31 December 1988		31 December 1993			31 December 1996		
	Foreign investor	$mn	Investor	$mn	$mn future	Investor	$ mn	$mn future
1	Kvaerner Gdynia	17.5	Fiat	180.0	830.0	Fiat	702.1	1581.0
2	Intercell	10.0	Coca-Cola	170.0	50.0	European Bank for Reconstruction and Development	608.3	0.0
3	Hyatt Regency	7.6	International Paper	120.0	175.0	ING Group	343.7	0.0
4	Inter-sport Club	6.6	Warimpex	100.0	80.0	International Paper	340.1	30.0
5	Schooner	6.0	Asea Brown Boveri	100.0	20.0	Polish-American Enterprise Fund	316.3	33.6
6	Polish Cable TV	5.0	Curtis International	100.0	0.0	IFC	277.2	0.0
7	Poloval	4.7	Unilever	96.7	0.0	Coca-Cola	275.3	0.0
8	Sigma	3.8	Polish-American Enterprise Fund	82.3	29.0	Philip Morris	227.2	70.0
9	Polepan	3.5	European Bank for Reconstruction and Development	72.1	0.0	Nestlé	210.0	49.0
10	International	3.2	Procter & Gamble	60.2	130.0	Thompson C.E.	184.5	0.0
	Total 10	64.7		1 021.0	1 314.0		3 299.6	1 714.6
	Total all	186.6		4 248.8	3 467.0		12 549.1	8 467.0
	%	34.7		24.0	37.9		26.3	20.3

Source: Author's own calculations based on data provided by the State Investment Agency.

The 1994–96 period saw a concerted attempt by the government to improve Poland's image as a favourable investment location. Various incentive schemes were introduced to encourage the entry of large investors: these included the creation of special economic areas with preferential treatment (including tax exemptions) to trade and manufacturing industries; the setting-up of barriers for imported products, especially in the car industry; the reduction of corporate income tax; accelerated depreciation and exemption from import duties. These incentives, however, were of the 'hidden' type and tended not to be publicized.

Conclusions

The impact of FDI on Poland's economy has been limited. The first objective of attracting substantial amounts of foreign capital has not been met. Poland's $12.8 billion investment stock constitutes approximately 14 per cent of total FDI in Eastern Europe and only 0.2 per cent of worldwide investment.

The second objective of accelerating privatization has not been achieved either. Approximately $4.0 billion of FDI in privatized Polish companies as of December 1996 amounted to only 42 per cent of all invested capital and a mere 5.3 per cent of state-owned equity, as valued in 1989. The internationalization of Polish enterprises has been a weak contributor to Poland's economic structure and activity.

A third objective – the introduction of modern technologies and management practices – has been partly achieved and only in the case of large firms. Large firms' investments in key industries seem to have contributed to Poland's economic recovery. This recovery was fostered by an increase in domestic automobile production fuelled by foreign investment in the industry (by Fiat and GMC inter alia). Likewise, in brewing – the best performing subsector of the Polish economy – most major breweries are owned by foreign companies.[4] Another important contribution by large transnational firms has been the transfer of modern technology and management practices to Polish affiliates and supplier firms. In the case of International Paper, a series of technology-transfer contracts was signed between headquarters and the Polish subsidiary in Kwidzyn. Furthermore, human-resource developments and local labour-force training aimed at achieving Western quality standards in both manufacturing and services have been a successful outcome of FDI in Poland. For example, Fiat undertakes the training of all its employees in specially designed schools,[5] whilst Citibank spends $400 000 on training annually.[6] Moreover, the transfer of many soft technologies has been complemented by the provision of 'unique' services formerly unavailable (or unknown) in Poland.[7]

The fourth objective – integrating local markets with European markets – was only partially achieved. Large firms have fared better than small ones. Multinationals from Western Europe in particular have helped establish new trade linkages between Eastern Europe and the European Union, sometimes in the framework of regional core network strategies. For example, Asea Brown Boveri's affiliate in Poland now provides electrical engines on a globally integrated basis.[8] As a result, the share of foreign affiliates in foreign trade has risen: they account for 10 per cent of total exports and 12 per cent of imports. To the extent that trade plays an important role in promoting growth and facilitating adjustment, the role of large corporations has been more significant than other indicators regarding the importance of FDI in Poland would suggest.

Smaller firms, on the other hand, have not fulfilled the expectations of strengthening ties with EU markets. Their share in the total sale of goods and services is approximately 10 per cent. Over 40 per cent of small firms with foreign participation are in the trade sector, while most others are in simple food processing, textile production and commodities.

On the whole, FDI in Poland has been fairly small and uneven, but part of this unevenness does suggest that FDI has been relatively important in a number of industries and in key areas to growth and the transition process.

Notes

1 John H. Dunning, 'The Prospects for Foreign Direct Investment in Eastern Europe', in P. Artisien-Maksimenko, M. Rojec and M. Svetlicic (eds) *Foreign Investment in Central and Eastern Europe* (Macmillan, London, 1993).

2 John H. Dunning and R. Narula, *Transpacific Foreign Direct Investment and the Investment Development Path: The Record Assessed* (Maastricht Economic Research Institute on Innovation and Technology, Maastricht, 1993).

3 S. Kubielas, 'Technology Transfer through FDI and Structural Adjustment of the Polish Economy', Department of Economics, Warsaw University, 1996.

4 United Nations Conference on Trade and Development, *World Investment Report: Transnational Corporations, Employment and the Workplace* (New York and Geneva, 1994).

5 Automotive Survey, *Business Central Europe*, 8 February 1994.

6 C. Bobinski in *Financial Times Survey on Poland*, 18 March 1994.

7 R. Lipsey and Z. Zimmy, 'The Impact of Transnational Service Corporations on Developing Countries: Competition, Market Structure and the Provision of Unique Services', in K. Sauvant and P. Mallampally (eds) *Transnational Corporations in Services*(Routledge, London, 1994).

8 A. Robinson in *Financial Times Survey on Poland*, 18 March 1994.

7
Foreign Investment Companies in the Hungarian Economy

Gabor Hunya

Introduction

Hungary has been the most successful East European country in attracting foreign direct investment (FDI), with $13 billion or about 40 per cent of the total cumulative capital invested in the area at the end of 1995. In 1992–95 it was among the first five net capital importing countries in the world per capita. This uniquely high degree of foreign penetration, when compared to the other transition economies of Central and Eastern Europe, is the result of specific economic policy features.

The overall economic performance of Hungary seems to contradict the expectations connected with the penetration of foreign capital: it is characterized by slow economic growth and serious imbalances in the current account and government budget. This chapter examines some of the reasons behind this contradiction. Some lie with the general features of the transformation policy; others are connected with the behaviour of foreign-owned firms. The benefits of foreign investment are more obvious at the microeconomic level, where the fast restructuring of enterprises is taking place. As a result, the increase of labour productivity in Hungarian manufacturing and the shift in export structures towards higher value added commodities have been more rapid than in other transition economies. At the same time a duality can be identified in the performance of the Hungarian economy along the lines of foreign and domestic ownership.

The economic policy environment for FDI

Several features of the Hungarian economy during the transition years benefited the inflow of FDI; these included:

- the early start and positive track record of the market reforms, when Hungary established itself as a stable and reliable partner;

- the cutting of subsidies and strict implementation of a bankruptcy law, under which the assets of state-owned enterprises (SOEs) in financial difficulties were sold off;
- privatization was pursued mainly through direct sales, which permitted foreign investors to outbid domestic ones;
- high foreign debt service obligations necessitated a permanent inflow of foreign capital;
- although privatization and FDI suffered a temporary setback in 1994, severe foreign trade and budget deficits made the sale of more state-owned assets to foreign investors unavoidable in 1995.

During 1990–92, transformation 'shock measures' in the form of import competition, price liberalization and the loss of East European export markets adversely affected Hungarian companies. Hungary's economic policy did not provide relief through hidden subsidies, currency undervaluation or import surcharges, as in the Czech Republic and Poland. The removal of subsidies and the introduction of tough bankruptcy laws and modern accounting regulations were aimed at enforcing hard budget constraints. The rapid restructuring of production, the redirection of sales and the adoption of new technologies were expected to take place on a large scale.

The aforementioned policy measures fell broadly within the parameters of the traditional economic reform thinking prevalent in the 1980s. The socialist economic system described by János Kornai as a 'shortage economy', where enterprises operated under 'soft budget constraints', was to be replaced by a market economy governed by free competition. The economic reforms of the 1980s ushered in the gradual opening of the economy, competitive prices, realistic exchange rates and the tolerance of small-scale private initiative. The reform of the taxation system (1988), the introduction of a two-tier banking system (1987), the authorization of majority foreign-owned companies (1988) and the setting-up of a stock exchange (1990) were all instigated by the last Communist government. The autonomy of state-owned enterprises was guaranteed, allowing for the development of marketing and management skills; spontaneous privatization and asset-stripping also took place before real privatization started in 1990. Thanks to the advance of economic reforms in the early transformation period, privatization could be carried out as an economic process, a 'bargain between buyers and sellers', and the application of voucher schemes practised in less mature transition economies could be avoided.

The changes of the early transformation period came abruptly: 90 per cent of all imports were liberalized in just two years (1990–91) when most subsidies were cut. In addition, the tight monetary policy introduced to curtail inflation with high interest rates was detrimental to companies with large debts. State-owned enterprises, which had borrowed heavily for investment purposes during the 1980s, and their commercial banks ran into financial difficulties. The first transition measures taken by companies were defensive: they curtailed production and employment, cut back capacity and closed down or sold production sites. The bankruptcy law of 1992 speeded up the exit of enterprises in financial distress.

At the same time, extensive foreign takeovers, small investments with high productivity gains and the emergence of new production units added dynamism to the economy. Tens of thousands of new private companies were founded which partly replaced the production of state-owned enterprises and also provided services to them. New enterprises channelled profits from the public to the private sector. The advance of institutional reform and privatization aroused the interest of foreign investors ahead of other transition countries. State-owned enterprises survived mostly by selling assets or inviting foreign investors. The privatization policy, which favoured cash sales to the highest bidder, was advantageous to foreign takeovers as domestic investors lacked the capital to compete.

The chosen policy of privatization stimulated the foreign penetration of Hungarian productive assets and markets. Not only was the sale of companies relatively widespread in Hungary, but the decline of state-owned enterprises, their bankruptcy or closing down also occurred on a fairly large scale. When domestic producers started to curtail production, their market shares were taken over by imported goods and the products of local subsidiaries of foreign firms. The real estate of bankrupt or downsized firms was offered cheaply, and a trained workforce was also available to the incoming owner.

The business sector is relatively free of state intervention; management skills and linguistic abilities are adequate; ownership rights are transparent. Foreign investors have been relatively successful in lobbying for government support, if required. The benefits and tax holidays provided by the government to foreign investment enterprises (FIEs) were often ineffective and subject to frequent changes. However, the liberal legal framework for offshore activities has been a special point of attraction. Most large export-oriented investment projects have received 'free-zone' status, exempting them from Hungarian customs, currency and book-keeping regulations. These foreign-owned companies, mostly greenfield investments, were established without much contact with the local economy. The lack of spill-over effects from such offshore companies is even more noticeable than in the case of other FIEs.

The unexpectedly severe recession, which affected some industrial policy measures in 1993–94, did not change the main rules of the economy. The budget constraints of some major state-owned enterprises and banks were softened in an expensive debt and debtor consolidation programme. The sharp edge of the bankruptcy law was blunted and the automatic trigger for bankruptcy abolished. Privatization policy changed in favour of domestic investors, who received subsidized credit schemes and compensation vouchers. Nevertheless, the mainstream of economic development was still determined by the expansion of foreign and domestic private firms as well as by the further contraction of the larger state-owned companies. A turning point in economic development was reached in mid-1993, when GDP took off and more pronounced investments and growing industrial production put an end to the depression of the early transition years. By 1994 most 'surviving firms' were able to consolidate their position and gather some optimism for the future, whilst macroeconomic imbalances deteriorated. New policies aimed at correcting these imbalances have of late tempered growth expectations.

The high level of inherited foreign debt was one of the unfavourable starting conditions for the Hungarian transformation. Instead of costly rescheduling, subsequent governments carried out debt management by replacing old debt with bonds and new loans with longer maturity. Debt-service obligations remained high with net interest payments reaching 15 per cent of exports, whilst the repayment of principal reached 40 per cent of exports in 1994. The inflow of new credits and FDI facilitated the discharge of payment obligations and the accumulation of reserves, but the situation remained fragile. Revenues from FDI counterbalanced interest payments on the foreign debt but did not result in direct financial gains in net terms. Foreign investment revenues became essential when the current account plummeted to large deficits in 1993 and 1994. The exit of major producers and import-intensive investment projects, in addition to radically changing demand structures, led to a deterioration of the foreign trade balance in 1993 and 1994. The basically successful shift of exports from the former Council for Mutual Economic Assistance to Western markets during 1989–92 was partly based on loss-making production, which could not be indefinitely sustained under hard budget constraints. No transitory protection was afforded to loss-making exporting firms. On the other hand, the closedown of capacities as well as foreign takeovers generated excessive imports of semi-finished goods, machinery and consumer goods. In 1993 exports shrank while imports expanded, and in the following year the pace of import growth exceeded that of exports. The 1994 foreign trade deficit, which reached 36 per cent of exports (customs statistics) was too high for the country's strained foreign financial situation, even if deficits were interpreted as a normal effect of recovering economic growth. As FDI did not add to available resources, it could not give much growth incentive to the economy as a whole. This is the reason for the co-existence of high FDI inflows and slow economic growth.

The central government's budget deficit, which increased to 7.5 per cent of GDP in 1994, was another problem. As the available budgetary means were limited, programmes promoting investment and FDI were weak and short-lived. The government was forced to sell fixed assets in order to reduce outstanding debts and in consequence spend less on debt-servicing.

To avoid any further aggravation of macroeconomic imbalances, an austerity package was announced on 12 March 1995. Measures to curtail the current-account deficit included a one-time 9 per cent devaluation and the introduction of a crawling-peg regime for the next two years. An 8 per cent temporary surcharge on imports was introduced: it excluded energy and allowed refunding for investment-related imports and bought-in components incorporated in export products. The import surcharge is valid for two years and represented an emergency measure under WTO rules. Measures to halve the budget deficit included, first of all, severe cuts in outlays. Under the new system of social spending, universal eligibility was to be replaced by eligibility below a certain per capita income. In addition, wage increases were to be curtailed and fringe benefits cut in the public sector.

Attracting FDI was confirmed as a key element in the government's financial strategy for 1995. The Hungarian National Bank and the government realized that any increase in net debt was hazardous; hence, the current account deficit had to be lowered and FDI revenues increased. The need to reduce the budget deficit gave another stimulus to foreign investors in late 1995. No direct incentive for foreign investors was introduced but an increase in offers for privatization sales was planned. Significant stakes in electricity works, gas distributors and the Hungarian oil company were prepared for sale. In addition, one of the main commercial banks and a pharmaceutical company were offered for privatization and sold to foreign investors. Privatization-related foreign inflows in 1995 surpassed their accumulated value for 1990–94. In privatization contracts, foreign investors in the energy sector committed themselves to further investments in the next few years to the tune of some $3 billion.

FDI inflows outside the privatization process continued at a stable rate in 1995 and the first half of 1996. Hungary has thus become dependent on foreign investment capital and the decisions of transnational enterprises. Its future economic development will, to a large extent, be affected by the behaviour of foreign investors.

The foreign sector at national level

It is not easy to measure the size of the foreign sector, but at national level the data from majority foreign-owned companies can be separated from other sectors in the economy. Companies outside the financial sector which produced 48 per cent of Hungary's GDP in 1993 fell under three categories of ownership: companies with majority public ownership which produced 43 per cent of value added; companies with majority foreign ownership producing 15 per cent of value added; and the remaining domestic private companies (42 per cent) (see Table 7.1). The foreign sector's share was estimated at 9 per cent of total GDP in 1993; this rose to 12 per cent in 1994, about three times as much as in the Czech Republic and Poland, on a par with Austria, but below Spain and Portugal.

Increasing efficiency and profitability can be expected as a result of foreign investment. Calculations of the foreign sector's profitability are based on the national accounts for 1993.[1] The operating surplus (value added minus employees' compensation plus net taxes and subsidies) of all non-financial corporations made up 23 per cent of value added in 1993, but 35 per cent in the case of foreign companies, thus signalling the latter's higher profitability. Foreign companies, producing less than 15 per cent of valued added generated 22 per cent of the operating surplus in the Hungarian economy.

By deducting payments on capital, that is property-related income, from operating surpluses, we arrive at the primary income balance, which can be associated with retained earnings. This amounted to 13 per cent of value added in the case of all companies, and to 19 per cent for foreign firms. Retained earnings are an important source of capital investments. As foreign companies had a relatively high share (21 per cent) of total retained earnings in 1993, the assumption is that they had a higher growth potential than their counterparts in the domestic sector. Foreign companies paid HUF (Hungarian forints) 24 billion in gross dividends to their owners. Assuming that foreign-owned companies repatriated half of their dividends, the income generated for the domestic economy was HUF 58 billion. This corresponds to 23.7 per cent of foreign companies' value added, a higher share than that of the domestic sector (17.5 per cent), which had no registered transfer of dividends abroad. In sum, the Hungarian economy did benefit from the high profitability of the foreign sector in 1993.

Table 7.1 Hungary: Gross value added of companies with double-entry book-keeping, 1992–94

	1992		1993		1994	
	HUF bn	*%*	*HUF bn*	*%*	*HUF bn*	*%*
Public	730.7	57.5	618.2	41.9	–	–
Majority foreign	130.2	10.3	241.9	16.4	–	–
Domestic private	409.0	32.2	615.0	41.7	–	–
Total	1269.9	100.0	1475.1	100.0	1868.8	100.0
FIEs	259.4	20.4	447.5	30.3	732.2	39.2

[1]HUF (Hungarian forints).
Sources: Central Statistical Office (KSH), Budapest, 1994, 1995, 1996.

FDI in foreign investment enterprises (FIEs)

In contrast to the group of foreign companies, which includes only firms with majority foreign ownership, FIEs include all firms with a share of foreign ownership. In FIEs minority foreign owners frequently obtain a controlling position in management: this can lead to improvements in efficiency, particularly if the majority owner is a public company. The state only retains the right to dispose of its share in the company's capital and does not normally participate in managerial decisions.

The economic and financial data of FIEs and their share in the overall economy are analysed below to shed light on the size and behaviour of the foreign sector. A comparison between the performance of foreign and domestic-owned companies is carried out both at the macro and sectoral levels. The analysis differs from other FDI-related investigations, which rely either on case studies or company surveys, which suffer from difficulties in finding the right sample. The set of data analysed below is based on aggregate company balance sheets, which are deemed most representative.

At the end of 1993 the total stock of FDI was reported to be $7400 million while the foreign capital in FIEs covered by our analysis amounted to $6542 million. A year later the total foreign investment stock was $8700 million, of which FIEs amounted to $7480 million. The discrepancy is the result of three main factors:

1 Not all companies have double-entry book-keeping, which forms the basis of the statistical reports;
2 Not all companies registered during the year provided a balance sheet for that year;
3 FDI not registered as capital increase in a company is not included in the FIE data.

Foreign capital penetration in the Hungarian economy rose significantly following the opening of the economy in 1989 (see Table 7.2). In 1994 foreign capital was present in some 23 500 companies (out of a total of 170 000), whilst FIEs accounted for one-third of the nominal capital. Foreign investment made up one-fifth of total nominal capital. Other Central European countries do not come close to Hungary's degree of openness to foreign capital (see Table 7.3). In all four countries foreign capital displays common characteristics: FIEs tend to have higher labour productivity, are more export oriented and have more intensive investment activities than domestic firms.

In the early years of the transformation process, foreign investment was concentrated in joint ventures with state-owned enterprises where foreigners held a minority position. Investors sought maximum security in a predominantly state-owned economy and shared the investment risks with

Table 7.2   Foreign investment enterprises in Hungary, 1989–94 (share in nominal capital and employment)

Year	Nominal capital		FDI in nominal capital		Employment	
	HUF bn	%	HUF bn	%	(thousands)	%
1989	30	2	12	1	–	–
1992	713	20	402	11	360	14
1993	1113	27	663	16	400	20
1994	1398	32	833	19	476	24

Source: Central Statistical Office (KSH), Budapest, 1995, 1996.

the state. Later on, as the state withdrew from the economy, the foreign share started to increase: first, fresh foreign capital was injected in joint ventures which could not be financed by the Hungarian partner; second, unilateral capital increases resulted in foreign dominance in share distribution (in new acquisitions foreign investors targeted majority shares to gain control); third, new ventures were increasingly set up as 100 per cent foreign companies and greenfield investments.

In 1990, as much as 62 per cent of FDI capital and 81 per cent of nominal capital in FIEs was located in joint ventures whilst only 6 per cent of FDI was invested in totally foreign-owned companies. These proportions changed considerably with new projects and capital increases. In 1991 only 34 per cent of FDI was in minority companies, and 18 per cent in wholly

Table 7.3   Share of foreign investment enterprises in the total economy[1] (percentages)

	Czech Republic 1994	Hungary 1994	Poland 1993	Slovak Republic 1994
Nominal capital	7.4	31.9	7.0[2]	5.0
Employed persons	6.0	22.6	5.6	3.8
Output	9.4	38.6	10.8[3]	7.7[4]
Export sales	n.a.	50.6	16.4	n.a.
Investment	16.5	38.0	11.2	11.8

[1]Czech Republic, Slovak Republic: non-financial corporations with at least 25 employees; Hungary, Poland: companies supplying tax declarations.
[2]Estimated
[3]Income from sales and financial operations.
[4]Value added.
Source: Based on national statistical data collected in the framework of the WIIW (Vienna Institute for Comparative Studies) research project on FDI.

foreign-owned firms. In 1994 minority companies had only 16 per cent of the FDI capital, whilst wholly foreign-owned firms made up 41 per cent.

The two economic activities where minority foreign participation dominated in 1994 were the telecom and oil refining sectors. In the first, foreign partners controlled 27 per cent of shares in the national company, MATAV. A management agreement ensured the leading role of the German shareholder in managerial matters. In 1994 the foreign share acquired in the national oil company was marginal.

Foreign penetration by sector

In 1994 foreign investment was negligible in agriculture, as foreigners were not allowed to buy agricultural land. In the energy and public utilities sectors privatization had yet to start. In other activities FIEs had more than a third of the companies' nominal capital.

Mining is mostly in domestic hands, with the exception of stone, sand and gravel mining, where FIEs dominate. The mining of construction materials is dominated by foreign interests. In other construction-related industries, the share of FIEs is about 76 per cent.

The expansion of foreign capital in manufacturing in 1994 was as high as 60 per cent. Above average shares of foreign capital are found in the food industry, and foreign control is almost complete in the beverage and tobacco sectors. In textiles, apparel and leather, the share of FIEs in the total nominal capital was about 45 per cent. The growth of foreign control in 1994 was slow as foreign investors had already selected the most successful companies.

The production of chemical products and rubber are activities with increasingly high foreign penetration, while the crisis-hit steel industry is still mainly in domestic state ownership, with the exception of processed metal goods, where the share of FIEs is above 50 per cent. In some machine-building activities FIEs control more than three-quarters of the nominal capital: namely, office machines, electrical machinery and motor vehicles.

Trade and tourism were among the first targets of foreign investors after the opening up of the economy. In trade, car distribution and wholesale are more foreign owned than the retail sector. Transport and telecommunications are the primary targets of FDI. Hungary was the first of the Central European countries to privatize the national telecom company to foreign strategic investors and open up the mobile telephone business for competition. In financial intermediation, foreign companies control the whole insurance business and have strong interests in banking. High foreign shares in education and health are misleading, because the bulk of these activities are performed by public budgetary institutions not providing tax declarations.

In sum foreign penetration is strongest in branches with a relatively stable or promising domestic market. Some sub-branches of the food industry, including edible oil production, breweries and tobacco factories, are almost exclusively foreign-owned. Household equipment and cars also have good prospects on both the Hungarian and foreign markets. In general, industries with a high level of internalization abroad have been the target of foreign capital, particularly in the machine-building and car industries.

Employment in FIEs

FIEs employed 24 per cent of the total workforce in 1994. The share of FIEs in employment is smaller than that in respect of the amount of invested capital. FIEs are less labour-intensive than domestic firms in all branches of production – with the exception of financial services, and in all sub-branches of manufacturing. The lower labour- and higher capital-intensity of FIEs, when compared with domestic companies, seems to be the result of different company strategies. One may tentatively conclude that foreign firms are faster in restructuring and laying off redundant workers; they also employ more labour-saving technology than domestic firms. Data on investment activity support the view that FIEs have a more recent capital stock than domestic companies.

The employment level of foreign companies increased in all branches of the economy in 1993 and 1994. If we consider that the employment increase took place partly because privatization transferred workers from the public to the private sector, genuine job creation in the foreign sector must have been negligible. Indeed, the years of transformation witnessed a severe depression in the Hungarian economy with rapidly rising unemployment. Structural change enforced by the transformational depression was mainly defensive and labour-shedding. Foreign companies and, to some extent, domestic private companies took over several state-owned enterprises where they speeded up restructuring and lay-offs. Also, in the immediate future, foreign investments will hardly mitigate the problem of unemployment.

Employees in FIEs are better paid on average than those in domestic companies. Per capita annual salaries in the companies surveyed amounted to 374 000 forints, and to 488 000 forints in FIEs, or 30 per cent more than in 1993. In 1994 the difference narrowed and salaries in FIEs reached 552 000 forints, one-quarter more than in the total economy. Salaries were particularly high in full-foreign-owned companies: some 43 per cent higher than the average. It is not known to what extent this result is related to the presence of high-income expatriates in FIEs. Press reports suggest that foreign companies are not generous to local blue-collar workers, and try to economize on wages and demand intensive work.

High capital intensity and efficient use of labour have resulted in higher productivity in the foreign sector. FIEs reported per capita net sales 64 per cent higher than the average of all companies both in 1993 and 1994, whilst wholly foreign-owned firms had two and a half times higher than average labour productivity. These turned out to be a special type of firm, mainly greenfield, equipped and operating with modern technology.

The sales and exports of FIEs

The importance of FIEs has been more pronounced in output than in nominal capital or employment. FIEs contributed 33 per cent to the total *sales* of enterprises in 1993 and more than 38 per cent in 1994. Higher than average sales per unit of invested capital were registered in three branches: financial services, real estate and consulting services, and transport and telecom. FIEs provided 40 per cent in 1993 and 55 per cent in 1994 of sales in manufacturing, with the highest foreign shares in beverages and tobacco.

The export sales of FIEs made up half of the total exports of Hungarian companies in 1993, and 60 per cent in 1994. The share was higher still in the case of the most import export branch, manufacturing, with 65.5 per cent in 1994 (see Tables 7.4 and 7.5). Two-thirds of machinery exports and almost 60 per cent of exports in the food industry originated from FIEs.

Average companies exported 13 per cent of their sales in 1994, somewhat, more than in 1993, but less than in 1992. FIEs exported 20 per cent of their sales in 1993, 21 per cent in 1994 and 22 per cent in 1992. The decline in export shares in 1993 reflects the overall decline in Hungary's exports. The upturn in exports in 1994 was to large extent due to the increasing activities of FIEs.

The highest export shares in 1994 were recorded in manufacturing: 25.4 per cent for all companies and 30.1 per cent for FIEs. Within manufacturing, machine building had an average export share of 35 per cent – 47 per cent for FIEs. The difference was even larger in textiles: 39 per cent on average against 58 per cent for the FIEs. In these sub-branches processing for exports must have been an important motivation for investing in Hungary. The food industry, on the other hand, was highly domestic-oriented. The relatively low export share, 16 per cent in the case of FIEs, reveals that investments in the food industry were motivated by access to the domestic market. Nevertheless, FIEs provided almost 60 per cent of food industry export sales.

Actual trade flows are documented in foreign trade statistics based on customs declarations. An important discrepancy exists between the export sales quoted by companies and *exports leaving the country*. The method of data collection and the range of companies involved make such a difference unavoidable. Indirect exports and exports by companies in duty-free

Table 7.4 Hungary: Share of FIEs in the total economy,[1] by selected industries, 1994 (percentages)

ISIC code:	Industries	Employment	Nominal capital	Sales	Export sales	Investment[2]	FDI[3] (%)
A, B	Agriculture, hunting, forestry, fishing	2.9	6.2	6.2	21.7	10.0	1.2
C	Mining and quarrying	13.4	30.3	24.9	21.5	29.6	1.1
D	Manufacturing	35.3	60.8	54.0	65.5	79.0	48.6
F	Construction	14.4	40.5	28.2	35.7	36.8	4.7
G	Wholesale and retail trade	23.6	40.1	33.5	55.7	53.7	14.1
H	Hotels and restaurants	46.1	50.1	31.6	42.6	40.0	3.6
I	Transport, storage, communications	10.8	36.3	35.1	56.6	47.0	7.9
J	Finance	46.0	47.9	78.5	84.0	37.6	8.9
K	Real estate, renting	13.0	25.9	23.8	58.0	31.2	8.5
	Total	22.6	31.9	36.7	60.0	40.2	100.0

[1] All companies providing tax declarations.
[2] Gross fixed investment.
[3] Distribution of FDI among branches.
Source: Central Statistical Office (KSH), Budapest, 1995.

Table 7.5 Hungary: Share of FIEs in manufacturing, 1994 (percentages)

ISIC-Code	Branches	Employment	Nominal capital	Sales	Export sales	FDI (%)
15–16	Food	38.3	63.4	49.3	70.4	32.7
17–19	Textiles	29.6	43.4	41.0	56.8	4.1
20–22	Paper	24.1	42.7	44.2	54.7	6.4
23–25	Chemicals	53.2	72.5	73.0	67.8	13.4
26	Non-metallic mineral products	40.0	76.2	58.1	70.4	8.2
27–28	Metallurgy	21.7	43.3	35.2	50.5	6.3
29–35	Machinery	38.8	61.0	57.5	77.9	27.6
36–37	Other	23.7	32.2	29.2	55.1	1.3
	Total	35.3	60.8	54.0	65.5	100.0

Source: Central Statistical Office (KSH), Budapest, 1995.

zones are covered in a different way by the two sources. The difference is most significant in the case of FIEs, which reported export sales to exceed actual exports. One reason is that duty-free-zone companies are all foreign-owned: they report their sales outside Hungary as exports in their balances, but do not fill in customs declarations. In fact, Hungarian national foreign trade data do not cover the activity of these important firms (Opel, Suzuki, Philips, etc.).

The export and import shares of FIEs were significantly larger than their contribution to value added, nominal capital or employment. FIEs also tended to import more than they exported, thus exacerbating the foreign trade deficit. In 1993 and 1994, when the country accumulated danger-ously high foreign-trade deficits, FIEs generated 46 per cent and 65 per cent respectively of the deficit (see Table 7.6).

Several specific conclusions can be drawn as to the role of FIEs in foreign trade:

1 The high foreign trade intensity of FIEs suggests that many are engaged as subcontractors in outward processing activities with low domestic value added.
2 Disproportionately high imports can be interpreted as a sign of low levels of integration in the domestic economy. The 'enclave' mentality of some foreign companies, that receive their inputs from abroad but sell their products domestically, begs the question of the extent of spill-over effects and the potential for local sourcing.
3 The high import-intensity of foreign companies is also due to their immature stage of development. During the build-up period, companies import a greater percentage of machinery and components than at a later stage.
4 The smaller decline in FIE exports in the recession year of 1993 may mean that foreign companies rely more extensively on secure foreign markets than domestic companies.
5 FIEs in the trade sector show a higher import-intensity than domestic companies. Some FIEs, especially in wholesale trade and car distribution, were established with the aim of penetrating the Hungarian market with foreign-made products. Foreign-owned retail networks, when operating in the higher price echelons, also show high import ratios.

Gross fixed capital investment and R&D in FIEs

The investment setback in Hungary started bottoming out in 1992 at 84.5 per cent of the 1988 level. In 1993 a real growth rate of 2.7 per cent was recorded, followed by 10.4 per cent in 1994. Thanks to the recovery, 95.8 per cent of pre-recession levels was reached in 1994. (The new setback of investments since the middle of 1995 is not covered here).

Table 7.6 Hungary: foreign trade of FIEs, 1992–94
(HUF bn, current prices)

| | 1992 | | | 1993 | | | 1994 | |
	Total	FIEs	FIE (%)	Total	FIEs	FIE (%)	Total	FIEs	FIE (%)
Export sales	812.5	325.9	40.1	878.2	438.9	50.0	1130.7	684.5	60.5
Exports	843.6	272.9	32.3	819.9	357.1	43.6	–	614.1	54.4
Imports	878.5	323.6	36.8	1162.5	514.7	44.3	–	880.1	57.3
Deficit	34.9	50.7	145.3	342.6	157.6	46.0	–	266.0	65.1

Source: Central Statistical Office, Budapest, 1995.

Recovery was faster in the business sector than in the rest of the economy: economic entities with legal status (all companies plus government, social security and non-profit organizations) invested the same amount in real terms in 1994 as in 1988. The investments of 'organizations without legal status' (households and auxiliary activities and artisans) invested only 82.4 per cent of pre-recession levels. A shift of activities between sectors certainly played a role in the divergence of investments. Also, the composition of investments was uneven: construction investments were more severely hit by the recession and their recovery was slower than in machinery, where 43 per cent of the invested machinery was imported in 1988, rising to 57 per cent in 1994.

Some three-quarters of total investment in 1994 were carried out by companies with double entry book-keeping, of which 262.5 billion forints, or 40 per cent, was done by FIEs. If business investments (excluding budgetary institutions) are taken into account, the share of FIEs is above 50 per cent and increasing. The most rapid increase in investments is among wholly foreign owned enterprises and minority foreign ventures. The shift of Hungarian companies to the foreign investment sector (for example MATAV) seems to have been more important than the increase of investments in older joint ventures. Investments per 100 forints of nominal capital in 1993 amounted to 12 forints for the whole economy, and 16 forints for FIEs; the respective figures for 1994 were 14 and 19. This shows a higher investment propensity for the foreign sector, although the improvements in 1994 took place both in domestic and foreign-related firms.

FIEs invested below average in buildings and above average in machinery, mostly imported. The FIEs' share of machinery investments was between 45 and 50 per cent in 1992–94, and 50 per cent in imported machinery. This suggests that the contribution of FIEs to economic modernization through machinery investments and imports of modern technology is outstanding. On the other hand, the increase of Hungarian imports and the deterioration of the current-account situation must partly be attributed to the investment activity of FIEs.

An important item on the cost side, namely research and development (R&D) expenditure, shows the growing role of FIEs as well. Total outlays on R&D in 1992 amounted to 1284 million forints, of which 37 per cent was spent by FIEs. The sum more than doubled in 1993 to 3507 million forints, of which 41 per cent was spent by FIEs. Most of the yearly increases were due to FIEs, which played a greater than proportional role in the otherwise low-key R&D activities of Hungarian companies. It should be added that foreign investors were interested in investing substantial amounts in acquiring Hungarian companies with significant R&D activity (Ganz, Tungsram and Richter). Access to the domestic R&D potential was clearly an attraction to foreign investors.

The profitability of FIEs

The findings in this chapter have been aggregated from FIEs' tax declarations, but have not been converted into the national accounts methodology, and thus show somewhat different trends from those outlined previously. Post-tax profits in the Hungarian economy were negative in 1993. FIEs recorded one-quarter of total losses (30 billion forints), only slightly less than their share in invested capital. Losses in 1993 were half of the losses in 1992 for both domestic companies and FIEs. In 1994 the financial results of companies improved as losses were halved compared to the previous year at current prices. FIEs recorded losses of only 5 billion forints, or 11 per cent of the total. Manufacturing turned into the black for both foreign and domestic companies, whilst trade remained the major loss-maker. Losses incurred during these two years were caused by two sets of factors, besides profit-hiding: first, the Hungarian economy was in a state of general depression until 1994. Fixed costs and employment did not decrease as rapidly as sales. Unit costs increased more than sales revenues. Some foreign investors overestimated the expansion of the domestic market and suffered from under-utilized capacity. The downsizing and selling-off of assets reduced fixed costs and generated revenues for domestic companies, but not fast enough to compensate for operational losses. Second, new investments had a launching period during which no profit was made. Foreign investors usually provided their Hungarian subsidiaries with a grace period of 2–5 years before expecting profits. Subsidiaries even increased their capacity during periods of negative profitability to achieve an optimum size of operations and the best product range.

Losses in manufacturing amounted to 40 billion forints in 1993, of which 7 billion forints were recorded by FIEs: both sets of figures were higher in nominal terms than in the previous year. Some sub-branches, however, were exceptions: in the chemical industry both domestic and foreign companies made profits. This was the result of a very selective privatization process affecting healthy subsectors. The food, beverages and tobacco sector was profitable among FIEs, but losses were recorded among domestic firms, as the best enterprises were allowed into the privatization process. The greatest losses occurred in metallurgy and machine-building. In the latter the foreign sector's losses were higher than those of the domestic sector. Old industries were being streamlined whilst new ones were being built up (such as the car industry), resulting in temporary losses in anticipation of future profitable operations.

In 1994 manufacturing FIEs had net profits of 27 billion forints, primarily because machine-building, textiles and clothing stopped generating losses. The chemical industry continued to be the most profitable sector.

In 1993 FIEs showed a slightly higher return on total capital (1.4 per cent) than all companies (1.1 per cent). The gap widened in 1994 but both groups of companies showed improvement (2.71 per cent for FIEs and 1.62 per cent for all companies). Foreign companies operated with higher capital costs and lower wage costs per unit of output than their domestic counterparts. All companies, including FIEs, reported low profits, suggesting that repatriated dividends must have been low. However, the suspicion of transfer pricing and other ways of unrecorded transfers subsisted.

Lessons from international comparisons and case studies

The features characterizing FIEs in Hungary are in line with worldwide trends:[2] FDI is more pronounced in capital- and technology-intensive branches than in labour-intensive sectors. The higher the technological level in an FIE, the higher the foreign partner's share. Telecommunications and utilities are common exceptions.

The development of manufacturing enterprises under foreign ownership has become dependent on decisions in multinational corporations. The fast tempo of restructuring in Hungarian manufacturing is the result of large-scale foreign penetration, which has also made the development of whole industries foreign-dependent. By comparison, in the Czech Republic and Poland, most companies have tried to preserve their independence even at the cost of slower restructuring, but in the hope of being able to pursue advantageous strategies.

In respect of microeconomic restructuring, the Hungarian transformation process for 1990–94 has differed from the Czech approach. Hungary's industrial labour productivity in 1995 was 34 per cent above 1989 levels, contrasting favourably with the Czech Republic, where it was 4 per cent lower. The Czech economy is characterized by 'capital hoarding, postponed bankruptcies and missing financial capital for restructuring'.[3] Under such conditions the chances of preserving old structures are higher, while restructuring is slower but less painful. Czech privatization was mainly effected through vouchers and not capital investment, hence capital costs remained low in firms with amortized assets. Export revenues were increased through the sales of products with a low unit-value. As the pressure to invest was not very strong, most firms survived in domestic hands.

The current research supports the global developments of the past few decades, namely that intra-industry and intra-multinational company trade leads to more successful and dynamic specialization, as in the Hungarian case. If the changes are too abrupt, however, this may increase the need for imports and external financial resources. This was instrumental in retarding dynamic economic growth in Hungary.

Successful initial restructuring by foreign investment is no safeguard for future success. It is still premature to judge whether Hungarian subsidies will be carefully integrated into the global networks of multinationals and succeed in raising their technological know-how.

Foreign ownership, though beneficial at the initial stage of restructuring, limits the choice of future company strategies. Incorporation into global sourcing implies a narrower assortment, competition for higher-standard products inside the multinational network and sets limits on R&D activity. Import dependence on other members of the multinational group may increase without a test of alternative supplies. This increases imports and may remove traditional domestic suppliers. Market access is also restricted by the multinational owner. A study of the car industry in Hungary reveals the difficulties experienced by local companies in becoming subcontractors to multinational car producers. While Suzuki aims to increase local sourcing, European investors (such as GM, Audi and Ford) operate as islands with marginal local sourcing.

Some conclusions

Based on aggregate company data, a high level of foreign penetration can be identified in the Hungarian economy. The foreign sector shows higher productivity and is more export-oriented than the domestic sector. It also plays a primary role in capital investment as well as in research and development. Differences between FIEs can be identified according to branches of economic activity and investing country. Expanding and export-oriented enterprises exist alongside stagnating and rent-seeking ones.

FIEs have been the most dynamic part of the Hungarian economy. In 1993 they accounted for about half of all investments and exports whilst their share in industrial production reached one-third. According to some estimates, the FIEs' share in exports reached 70 per cent in 1995.

Hungary has now embarked on a more *mature stage of FDI-penetration*. Among newly established firms greenfield investment has become increasingly important. Capital investment into existing ventures and reinvestment of profits have taken on an increasing share of FDI. In December 1995 a new stage of privatization was kick-started with the partial sale of the gas and electricity distribution companies.

Relatively high and increasing foreign penetration has become a specific feature of the Hungarian economy. FIEs have had a high impact on microeconomic development (subordinated to the global strategy of multinational enterprises) and are likely to influence future economic development (rapidly increasing openness).

Given the success to date in attracting foreign capital, the Hungarian authorities have been under little pressure to grant special incentives to foreign investors. There is scope, however, for improving the *investment climate*: first, in order to reduce investment risks, legal and institutional transparency and stability must improve. Second, taxation, social security contributions and other cost-related items should be fixed for longer periods of time and not depend on annual state budget requirements.

Third, incentives must also be more lasting and easily calculable: the time horizons of government action (one year) and company-level investment decisions (ten to fifteen years) should move closer to each other.

A problem related to FDI in Hungary is the large part of the *current account deficit* associated with the activities of FIEs. This was larger than the inflow of new and reinvested FDI in 1992–94.

Strong foreign penetration of the Hungarian economy brought about a serious *dichotomy between the foreign and domestic sectors*. Foreign engagement concentrates on specific industries, is located in a few privileged regions and attracts mainly the younger and more educated part of the workforce. Areas with a long industrial tradition located in the west of the country have benefited more than the eastern regions. Education policy has been pushed into training elites with foreign language skills, while general public education has suffered from organization and financial shortcomings. The low proportion of the workforce benefiting from relatively high salaries in FIEs has limited their popularity.

Closer integration by the foreign sector in the domestic economy should receive priority in policy-making, as it would lead to a wider choice of favourable investment locations and help preserve and develop human capital. The dichotomy might be partly overcome by *spill-over effects* in the wake of economic growth. In addition, regional and labour policy measures seem to be necessary. Infrastructure investment and regional policy instruments must be implemented. Action stimulating labour mobility towards the more affluent regions should also be considered. The budgetary means for such expenditures seem to be neither abundant nor well-placed; improvements in this respect would benefit economic growth and simultaneously promote FDI.

Notes

1   Central Statistical Office (KSH), National Accounts, Hungary 1991–93, Budapest 1995.
2   M. Rojec, *Foreign Direct Investment and Privatization in Central and Eastern Europe* (ACE Project, Ljubljana, 1995).
3   For details, see A. Zemplinerova and V. Benacek, 'Foreign Direct Investment – East and West: The Experience of The Czech Republic', ACE Project Workshop, Prague, 6–8 April 1995; and A. Zemplinerova, R. Lastovicka and A. Marcincin, 'The Restructuring of Czech Manufacturing Enterprises: an Empirical Study', CERGE-EI Working Paper 74, Prague.

8
Foreign Capital and Privatization in Hungary
Maria Illes

Macro- and microeconomic background

Foreign debt

Hungary is an open economy, where the foreign trade balance has had a significant influence in guiding macroeconomic processes. This function has been satisfactorily performed for decades by using a methodology continually adjusted to changing circumstances. Debts accumulated before 1973 did not exceed 1 billion dollars.

The onerous indebtedness of the country came about as a result of three waves of debt accumulation.

The first wave began around 1983 and was caused by two main factors. In part, a change in economic attitudes justified growing indebtedness to accelerate progress. Favourable credit supply conditions supported that course of action. The other cause was the first hike in energy prices at the time, or more accurately the erroneous economic policy used to handle it. As a consequence almost $7 billion of gross debt accumulated over a short period.

The second wave of debt accumulation took place between 1985 and 1987. In three years the gross debt went up by nearly $10 billion, reaching a peak of $17 billion.

The third wave, which lasted longer than the previous two, can be interpreted as a legacy of the change in economic regime. From the threshold of the change of regime in 1989, the $20-billion debt increased to $32 billion by early 1995.

In the years leading up to the transition, the debt of $20 billion needed to be addressed. Some attempts were made, unofficially. A private meeting of experts in London was reported in the Hungarian press. It dealt not only with the handling of debts but also with the privatization strategy to follow. The idea of a 'debt equity swap' was put forward. This technique, however, could only have been partly used because of the wide scope of mixed creditors. As for the many thousands of bondholders, this method was entirely impractical.

Given the mass of information continuously reported in the daily press, it can be assumed that the Hungarian Communist Party played a subordinate role in the conceptual guidance of economic stabilization, debt handling and privatization. Even before the change of regime, the IMF had kept an eye on the Hungarian economy and made the granting of further loans dependent on the acceptance of its various proposals for economic regulation and budgeting. However, these agreements were not announced publicly at the time.

Cumulative disinvestment in enterprises

A considerable amount of disinvestment took place as early as the mid-1980s. Among the most prevalent channels of disinvestment were the following:

1 Economic regulations between 1985 and 1987 attached amortization, the revenues from sales of property and after-tax profits to a fund, which was used to finance various taxes (wage tax, income tax, property tax, fixed assets acquisition tax), as well as to pay premiums and bonuses and cover welfare expenses. Property was allow to leak out of companies either directly or through amortization – in the form of current expenditure. This ensured that a large section of the property sector became part of the budget.

2 The possibilities for letting property 'escape' were increased by the Business Association Act of 1988 and the Conversion Act.

3 As the state-owned companies were set up with little capital strength, they all commenced operations with sizeable loans. Disinvesment created a demand for even more loans. Under these forced loan conditions, companies suffered from the sudden increase in credit interest in 1990. While, on average, there was nearly zero profitability, the credit interest exceeded the average producer price index (of 10–30 per cent) of industry by some 15–20 per cent. In this way, a large part of capital income vanished into credit interest.

4 The Hungarian accounting system was not familiar with the concept of inflation profit. Deductible amortization reflects the price conditions at the time of acquisition. Consequently, the difference between the original and inflation-added prices of fixed assets utilization deducted as amortization can only be recovered in the form of profit. That amount would also be necessary for reacquisitions. Amortization makes it more difficult to cover the reacquisition of assets. Inflation, which started to accelerate from 1990, would have necessitated the reinvestment of an increasing part of inflation profits. However, if some profits could be achieved in spite of high credit interests, they were burdened by a large

profit tax. The cumulative growth of inflation profit and its withdrawal into credit interests and profit tax can also be interpreted as a major disinvestment channel.

The reduction of money in circulation, at a time when the number of business ventures multiplied, broadened the possibilities for disinvestment and had its own independent destructive effect on the economy. The break-up of large companies into several enterprises in itself increased the volume of funds necessary for turnover transactions. The financial administration, however, ignored all these factors and pursued a severely restrictive monetary policy. This had a decisive role in reducing the availability of funds within the Hungarian economy. Insolvency was also frequent among companies performing well. The majority of bankruptcies led to liquidation. This was intended to accelerate privatization and, through the relatively low price of assets of liquidated companies, to encourage domestic investors. However, this expectation was only partially fulfilled.

The combined effect of these factors meant that companies not privatized (or more precisely, those not privatized with foreign capital) struggled with a lack of resources. As a result of unreasonably high credit interest rates, these companies could only be rescued through the involvement of foreign capital.

In Hungary the process of intensive disinvestment proved to be an effective motivating factor for companies to search for a foreign privatization business partner and show a receptive attitude to interested parties.

Although the system of both intensive disinvestment and tax allowances indicated that privatization through the involvement of foreign capital was a desirable path to follow, it cannot be said that there was an entirely uniform intention on the part of the companies to go in that direction.

Lack of capital market knowledge

In the two decades preceding the change of regime, Hungarian enterprises had a relatively wide degree of economic 'freedom' which required a knowledge of market economics. This was assisted by direct foreign trade relationships with foreign companies. However, experts in economic management were lacking the most fundamental microeconomic knowledge: this was illustrated by the vast number of economic regulations that were harmful to companies.

Not only was capital market knowledge lacking but also fundamental knowledge on how to operate a company. Frequently, the persons in charge of privatization decisions had a very poor grasp of matters they were negotiating.

One of these publicized cases involved the State Property Agency (SPA) selling a company for DM 48 million which it claimed would be profitable as early as 1992; failure to meet this profitability target would have resulted in the asking price being reduced by DM 10 million. Clearly, the seller's representatives should have known how easy it was to 'produce losses' in any given year even if profitability was good. It is not incidental that the audited balance sheet of this company was prepared only in August 1993 due to 'bookkeeping difficulties'. Moreover, the executive manager denied that it was in the company's interest to depreciate its stocks.

The lack of effective capital market knowledge and the vast number of urgent tasks required for the implementation of privatization implied the involvement of foreign experts with special skills. As a result, the number of foreign auditors, asset evaluators and privatizing agents increased. The number of Hungarian consulting firms also started to grow rapidly.

Foreign consulting firms played an indispensable role in the search for foreign investors and in providing a proper system of information. In general, Hungarian managers were successful in introducing their companies and conducting negotiations. Their economic expertise became perceptible. The professional attitude emanating from these forums encouraged the arrival of foreign investors in Hungary.

Foreign capital and privatization

Legal regulations have allowed the involvement of foreign working capital into the Hungarian economy since 1982. Until 1988, these regulations only permitted the establishment of joint ventures with Hungarian majority shares, and prescribed a complex legislation procedure. As a result, the inflow of foreign capital during that period remained small. Since 1988 the investments of foreigners in Hungary have been legally regulated. Enterprises with foreign participation can be established in most business activities. The ratio of property shares is no longer restricted and the former compulsory permission procedure has given way to simple court registration.

The law stipulates that foreign investments in Hungary will enjoy full protection and safety. Asset contributions are duty-free and profits can be repatriated.

Until the end of 1993, tax allowances were granted to promote foreign investment. In this period enterprises were granted a 60 per cent tax allowance for the first five years from establishment and a 40 per cent allowance for the second five-year period, provided that the company's capital stock reached 5 million Hungarian forints (HUF) and more than half of annual revenues came from the manufacturing of products or the operation of a hotel built by the enterprise. In special priority sectors the allowance was 100 per cent for the first five years and 60 per cent for the next five years. The reinvestment of profits in Hungary by foreign investors also qualified for tax allowances. These tax allowances ceased to apply on 1 January 1994; from this date, they could be granted on the basis of individual judgement.

Hungary entered into international contracts with several important foreign partners. These contracts stipulated that the participants would mutually protect the safety of the foreign investment of their country's citizens; regulations were also introduced to avoid double taxation.

The direct purchase of assets by foreigners was not hindered in any way, with the exception of real estate purchases, which required a legal permit. The Business Associations Act stipulates that public limited companies (plcs) with exclusive or majority foreign ownership should not obtain majority shares in other plcs.

In contrast to capital imports, Hungarian regulations require a permit for capital export. By 1994 nearly 1500 enterprises with Hungarian investment had been established abroad, with Western Europe a major destination of capital outflows. Most of these foreign investments are production enterprises. Since the mid-1990s the East European countries, mainly the Ukraine, Russia, Romania, Slovakia and the Czech Republic, have come to the forefront. Hungarian companies have also favoured commercial and service investments abroad with a short pay-back period. Mainly small and medium-sized enterprises are taking part in capital exports.

Foreign investors fall under the same regulations as all other investors taking part in privatization. Privatization laws stipulate that assets, state-owned securities or property shares may be purchased primarily by way of tenders. Anyone with the required financial background may apply for the purchase, which is publicly announced in most cases. The bidder with the best offer wins the tender.

However, when equal conditions are offered, the legislation of 1992 stipulates the following order of priority:

1 Business associations or cooperatives operating with the participation of the workforce (if at least 25 per cent of the workers take part);
2 Those participating in employees' share ownership programmes of the association;
3 The worker of the association as an individual entrepreneur;
4 The property manager.

Privatization and corruption

The vary nature of privatization seems to attract corruption, the primary reason being that the buyer's highly dominant price-oriented interests may conflict with the community's interests, which are often blunted by the interests of mediators.

The simultaneous presence of several problems unique to Hungary has offered an ideal hotbed for corruption. The main causes have included:

• the lack of effective knowledge of the capital market;
• chaotic economic conditions;

- the acceptance by the political leadership of the process of 'original capital accumulation';
- the value crisis connected with the change of regime.

Although specific cases of bribery are very seldom publicized, a widely held opinion is that transactions proceed with difficulty unless 'illegal payments' are made. Rumours circulate that few transactions of privatization can be completed without buying-off the appropriate officials or without the substantial support of foundations close to governmental circles.

Main periods of privatization

The conditions and legal regulations of Hungarian privatization have been changed several times. Consequently, Hungarian companies have been privatized with great diversity according to different sets of rules.

Spontaneous privatization (1986–90)

Privatization was not a product of the change of regime. The first attempts were made in 1986 with the lease of small commercial and catering units. Later on, its scope was expanded. A larger volume of privatization was made possible by the early transformation of some enterprises. These were companies whose internal units could be made economically independent. The premises and internal units were made independent by their conversion to business associations. This enabled both foreign and Hungarian investors to acquire property in companies formerly in exclusive state ownership.

The smoother transformation of the ownership system required the establishment of a legal background. Significant steps were made in this respect with the passing of the Business Associations Act in 1988 and the Transformation Act in 1989. The former determined the forms of corporate enterprise applicable in the economy, and the latter required the transformation of government corporations into business associations (while ensuring a fulfilment period of several years for the process).

In 1989 there was also a major modification of the Constitution, which recognized private property and state property as equal. In this period the control and handling of privatization by the state was extremely uncertain. This resulted partly from the premise that transferring property to private ownership would be in the hands of company managers. In these legal conditions there was doubt about who had the right to sell the property. During this early period company managers could convert state property into their own private property almost at will.

Public outcry against spontaneous privatization enforced the control and monitoring of privatization by the state. The State Property Agency was established on 1 March 1990, prior to the change of regime.

Business privatization – mainly for cash (1990–92)

Privatization was led primarily by political factors following the change of regime. One major concern was to ensure the irreversibility of the change of political regime, particularly from the property standpoint.

Privatization was considered acceptable only on a business basis, and even within this scope priority was given to spot sales. A clause stipulated that privatization income should be used for decreasing the public debt.

As there was little domestic purchasing power, openings had to be made towards foreign investors. A popular slogan at the time was that property was worth as much as investors were willing to pay. Significant losses threatened where interest was lacking. In most cases, the deals were signed when there was only one bidder.

By the mid-1990s the government had worked out the package plan of the First Privatization Programme in conjunction with foreign advisers. It comprised the privatization of 20 viable and profitable large companies working in the fields of industry, hotel trade, commerce, tourism and transport. Their total property was worth nearly $400 million. Shortly afterwards, the Second Privatization Programme was initiated for companies that had transferred at least 50 per cent of their property into business associations and thus operated as property management centres. There was also a conception that privatization should be carried out by means of package sales for the purpose of better organization, control and transparency. Potential foreign purchasers were offered the option of buying companies included in the first, then the second, package, but they seemed to be interested in other companies. As a result, these programmes, and then the idea itself, died off.

In March 1991, the Existence Credit was introduced, which offered repayable financial resources to Hungarian private individuals for purchases of state property. However, little interest was generated due to the strict terms of credit. During this period, privatization could be initiated by the state companies or investors.

The acquisition of property by Hungarian citizens (1992–94)

A total of 79 per cent of privatizations in 1990 and 78 per cent in 1991 consisted of sales to foreigners. The prevalence of sales to foreigners had to be eliminated for several reasons. The best companies were already sold, which reduced foreign interest. The increasing privatization offers of former socialist countries strengthened this tendency even further. The collapse of the East European market made its effect felt as a risk factor as early as the middle of 1991. As a result, the focus of the privatization process had to be changed. Privatization opportunities for Hungarian citizens had to be expanded.

From 1992 the terms of the Existence Credit and the Instalment Benefit were mitigated. The Employees' Stock Purchase Programme was enacted in

June 1992. Privatization leasing also broadened the opportunity for Hungarians to acquire property. The Small Investors' Stock Purchase Programme (similar to the credit plan) was enacted in 1994. Compensation notes also produced a considerable effective demand.

With the expansion of credit opportunities, two new institutions were created: the Kisvállalkozói Garancia Alap (Small Entrepreneurs' Guarantee Fund) and the Hitelgarancia Rt (Credit Guarantee plc), which helped entrepreneurs establish the guarantees required for taking up loans.

The new strategy recognized the necessity of an industrial policy. It was intended to give specialized departments greater freedom of movement and to encourage them to reinvest part of their revenues into the economy.

A new objective was to ensure that companies be made viable before being privatized in order to realize a much higher selling price. Criteria of calling, and especially those of judging, privatization tenders were significantly modified. As a result of the above factors, the proportion of sales to foreigners decreased: compared to the 80 per cent value of the first two years, it was cut down to 55 per cent by 1992 and to 33 per cent by 1993. The decrease, however, did not imply a reduction in absolute volumes of sales, which kept on increasing.

New directions for privatization in the post-1995 period

The change of government in 1994 was preceded by criticisms of privatization activity. It is estimated that a loss of $5–7 billion of state property resulted from the property depletion of firms not privatized and liquidation procedures.

The new privatization act changed the organization of privatization: the separate holding company and privatizing agency were reunited under the State Privatization and Holding Company.

The scope of companies not to be privatized was thoroughly narrowed, as was the scope of those which should remain in majority state ownership. Whilst the previous government had treated $15 billion of state property in 850 companies as property to be kept in permanent state ownership, the new government narrowed down the number of companies to 161 and $2 billion.

Foreign capital is primarily expected to come into those sectors which produce surplus exports. Since there is a growing need for privatization revenues, 20 to 22 public service companies, chemical and pharmaceutical companies of high value worth a combined $10 billion are expected to bring major sales revenues. Deficiencies in knowledge and corruption make it a high risk strategy to hand over the majority ownership of large public service companies to foreign strategic investors.

Trends in foreign direct investment

The early 1990s were characterized by rapid privatization. However, some would argue that even this pace was too slow when the continuous loss of property by companies not privatized was taken into consideration.

It was mentioned earlier that sales to foreigners were predominant (nearly 80 per cent) in the first two years of Hungarian privatization and that this percentage fell to 55 per cent and 33 per cent in subsequent years. Annual inflows of working capital in cash recorded through the banking system are listed below ($mn).

1988	1989	1990	1991	1992	1993	1994
23	192	311	1459	1471	2339	1146

Since 1972 a total of nearly $7 billion of working capital was invested in this way. If the value of asset contributions is also taken into account, the sum of working capital inflows goes up to $9 billion for the same period.

FDI figures in Table 8.1 include investment in intellectual property and assets besides cash contributions. After the change of political regime the number of business organizations involving FDI also started to grow rapidly. While there were 1350 economic organizations with foreign ownership in Hungary at the end of 1989, their number reached approximately 25 000 by the end of 1994.

Little competitive effort was required of foreign partners to enter the underdeveloped Hungarian market, as new market segments could be obtained cheaply and dominant market positions could be inherited on purchase.

Table 8.1 Business organizations with FDI in Hungary, 1989–93

Date	Number of organizations	Subscribed capital (million $)	FDI	Foreign Ownership (%)
End 1989	1350	2105	508	24
End 1990	5963	4475	1508	34
End 1991	9117	7167	3136	44
End 1992	17 182	10 173	5501	54
End 1993	20 999	14 528	8373	58
Newly registered business organizations involving FDI				
1994	4431	398	301	76

Source: Central Statistical Office of Hungary.

Equity structure

The stepping-up of privatization plans and the increase of foreign income led to the spreading of a particular type of equity. In the daily practice of privatization policy, it became more common to offer a majority ownership (50 per cent + 1 vote) share for sale; alternatively, the foreign strategic investor could obtain majority ownership through a capital increase soon after the purchase. Between 1989 and 1992 the foreign ownership share in the registered capital of business organizations with FDI grew yearly by 10 per cent.

The increase of foreign capital shares in Hungarian firms is illustrated in Table 8.2. While foreign ownership had a minority share in 87 per cent of business organizations with FDI in 1989 (and 78 per cent of FDI functioned as minority capital), by 1993 the proportion of joint ventures with minority foreign ownership decreased to 37 per cent (and contained only 19 per cent of FDI).

In the process of transformation, the proportion of companies with 100 per cent foreign ownership increased to 35 per cent, and the proportion of companies with majority ownership increased to 27 per cent. The latter group of companies operated 50 per cent of all FDI.

FDI in economic sectors

The distribution of FDI among economic sectors has been uneven. In the early period of transition, foreign owners took over large segments of the

Table 8.2   Capital and ownership structure of business organizations with FDI in Hungary, 1989–93

	1989	1990	1991 %	1992	1993
By number of organizations					
100% foreign ownership	1.9	4.1	13.0	27.0	35.1
Majority foreign shares	11.5	11.2	22.0	25.0	27.5
Minority foreign shares	86.7	84.7	65.0	48.0	37.4
Total	100.0	100.0	100.0	100.0	100.0
By subscribed capital					
100% foreign ownership	0.3	2.0	8.1	16.6	18.2
Majority foreign shares	8.1	16.6	31.2	38.7	38.3
Minority foreign shares	91.6	81.4	60.7	44.7	43.5
Total	100.0	100.0	100.0	100.0	100.0
By amount of foreign ownership					
100% foreign ownership	1.4	5.8	17.8	29.4	30.6
Majority foreign shares	20.1	31.7	48.5	50.4	50.1
Minority foreign shares	78.4	62.6	33.7	20.2	19.3
Total	100.0	100.0	100.0	100.0	100.0

Source: Central Statistical Office of Hungary.

food industry, as well as most of the construction and the building material industries and commercial and hotel chains. They also acquired ownership shares in several manufacturing sectors.

Tables 8.3 and 8.4 show the proportional distribution of FDI in different sectors in 1991, 1992 and 1993. By the end of 1993, as much as 50 per cent of all foreign working capital flowed into the manufacturing industry. About 20 per cent of all FDI within the manufacturing industry was in the food and tobacco industry, implying that 43 per cent of all registered capital in this subsector came from foreign countries. The proportion of foreign capital was above average in mining (19 per cent), construction (26 per cent) as well as in hotel and catering (28 per cent). It was insignificant in the electricity, gas and water supply sectors (0.5 per cent) and agriculture (2.5 per cent).

The difference between the number of companies and their share in the registered capital shows that companies with 100 per cent foreign ownership are smaller than average, and that those with majority foreign ownership are larger than average size. This is particularly true of manufacturing, where more than half of FDI is concentrated, and the catering industry. Most foreign capital to date has been in the manufacturing industry. Its

Table 8.3   Sectoral distribution of FDI in Hungary, 1991–93

Sector	FDI distribution (%)		
	1991	*1992*	*1993*
Agriculture	0.5	0.7	1.2
Mining	1.0	1.8	1.3
Manufacturing	55.9	54.1	49.9
Electricity, gas and water	0.1	0.6	0.8
Construction	4.3	4.1	3.9
Wholesale and retail trade, repair of motor vehicles, motorcycles and personal and household goods	12.5	14.3	13.6
Hotels and restaurants	3.3	3.2	3.9
Transport and communications	2.0	2.0	8.7
Financial intermediation	11.4	9.5	7.3
Real estate, renting and business activities	8.2	8.8	8.5
Education	0.0	0.0	0.1
Health and social work	0.4	0.1	0.2
Other community, social and personal service activities	0.4	0.8	0.6
Total	100	100	100

Source: Central Statistical Office of Hungary.

Table 8.4   Foreign ownership of shares in all subscribed capital, Hungary, 1991–93

Sector	Foreign shares (%)		
	1991	*1992*	*1993*
Agriculture	0.4	0.9	2.5
Mining	4.9	17.1	19.0
Manufacturing	13.5	22.2	31.2
Food, beverage & tobacco	17.2	33.8	43.0
Textile, wearing apparel & leather	12.8	16.2	23.1
Wood, paper products, printing & publishing	15.6	21.1	27.8
Chemicals	6.0	11.5	14.8
Non-metallic mineral products	19.4	30.8	48.2
Basic metal industries	9.7	17.5	24.9
Machinery	17.9	24.4	37.7
Other	11.4	13.6	23.4
Electricity, gas and water	0.1	0.3	0.5
Construction	11.7	17.1	25.8
Wholesale and retail trade, repair of motor vehicles, motorcycles and personal and household goods	8.7	15.2	22.1
Hotels and restaurants	12.9	15.5	28.3
Transport and communications	1.9	3.1	13.8
Financial intermediation	15.2	21.7	14.9
Real estate, renting and business activities	8.8	5.7	16.7
Education	6.7	5.2	12.5
Health and social work	42.9	29.4	31.8
Other community, social and personal service activities	3.0	7.3	3.9
Total	8.8	10.6	15.9

Source: Central Statistical Office of Hungary.

share, however, has been decreasing as telecommunication, mail services, shipping and storage are taking on a larger part of FDI. The privatization of MATAV, the Hungarian Telecommunications Company is a case in point: in 1993 alone, $875 million of FDI flowed into Hungary.

Regional distribution

Over half of business organizations with FDI in 1994 were situated in Budapest, with 70 per cent of total capital stock. Many of these companies were formed in the counties of Bács-Kiskun, Gyôr-Moson-Sopron and Pest (see Table 8.5).

Countries of origin of foreign direct investment

Most FDI into Hungary originates in the United States, Germany, France and Italy. Table 8.6 shows the number of new companies founded with foreign capital in 1992 and 1993.

Table 8.5 Regional distribution of FDI in Hungary, 1990–93

Capital, county	By the number of organizations (in %)		By the value of invested foreign capital (in %)	
	1990	1993	1990	1993
Budapest	58.1	52.2	58.8	62.1
Baranya	2.7	3.4	2.2	2.2
Bács-Kiskun	3.5	4.8	1.9	2.1
Békés	1.1	1.3	0.8	1.4
Borsod-Abauj-Zemplén	1.9	1.7	4.2	2.1
Csongrád	2.4	5.3	0.8	1.1
Fejér	2.3	2.1	5.8	3.9
Gyor-Moson-Sopron	4.1	4.4	3.7	3.6
Hajdú-Bihar	2.0	1.7	0.9	1.4
Heves	0.7	0.8	0.1	1.3
Komárom-Esztergom	2.4	2.1	2.7	3.2
Nógrád	0.8	0.7	0.4	0.8
Pest	7.9	6.2	9.0	6.3
Somogy	1.8	2.0	1.4	0.8
Szabolcs-Szatmár-Bereg	1.2	1.3	2.9	0.9
Jász-Nagykun-Szolnok	1.0	1.0	1.2	0.8
Tolna	1.2	1.1	0.2	0.5
Vas	1.5	2.5	1.1	2.9
Veszprém	1.9	2.8	0.9	1.1
Zala	1.5	2.6	1.0	1.5
Total	100.0	100.0	100.0	100.0

Source: Central Statistical Office of Hungary.

American investors, ranked first according to the total amount of capital brought in, usually prefer greenfield investments and therefore would not top a league table based on privatization revenue. German investors, ranked second by amount of capital brought in, tend to acquire property through privatization. A list of investing countries published monthly by privatization organizations is reproduced in Table 8.7.

Size of foreign direct investment

Table 8.1 above showed that nearly 25 000 enterprises with foreign participation were operating in Hungary at the end of 1994.

The *Financial Times* (17 November 1993) listed the top 50 foreign companies operating in Hungary as well as the main characteristics of their investments (Table 8.8). According to this table, the top 50 FDI importers brought in $5993 million by mid-November 1993. Jointly with the $875 million brought in by the privatization of MATAV at the end of 1993, this totalled $6.8 billion or 95 per cent of the total inflow of $7.2 billion at end 1993.

Table 8.6 Hungary: new business organizations set up with foreign capital, 1992–93

Country	Organizations				FDI			
	Number		Share (%)		Value ($ mn)		Share (%)	
	1992	1993	1992	1993	1992	1993	1992	1993
Austria	580	613	14.1	14.3	117.2	40.2	21.6	8.0
Germany	937	1065	22.8	24.9	61.8	109.4	11.3	21.8
USA	269	256	6.6	6.0	24.2	23.4	4.4	4.7
Italy	239	246	5.8	5.7	10.0	21.0	1.8	4.2
Netherlands	100	104	2.4	2.4	26.3	54.1	4.8	10.8
UK	112	131	2.7	3.1	10.3	54.8	1.9	10.9
France	81	94	2.0	2.2	25.5	78.8	4.7	15.7
Belgium	46	39	1.1	0.9	119.4	10.3	22.0	2.1
Sweden	59	49	1.4	1.1	2.0	1.9	0.4	0.4
Finland	17	20	0.4	0.5	0.4	7.5	0.1	1.5
Denmark	13	14	0.3	0.3	0.1	8.6	0.0	1.7
Switzerland	156	143	3.8	3.3	35.9	9.7	6.6	1.9
Spain	20	14	0.5	0.3	0.5	0.4	0.1	0.1
South-America	11	8	0.3	0.2	0.8	3.9	0.1	0.8
Canada	57	73	1.4	1.7	7.2	3.2	1.3	0.6
Japan	11	12	0.3	0.3	2.5	4.2	0.5	0.8
China	271	407	6.6	9.5	5.4	12.4	1.0	2.5
Korea	4	5	0.1	0.1	0.5	0.0	0.1	0.0
CIS	195	288	4.8	6.7	19.7	14.2	3.6	2.8
Yugoslavia	130	215	3.2	5.0	2.1	8.8	0.4	1.8
Croatia	32	28	0.8	0.7	0.3	0.4	0.1	0.1
Slovenia	9	13	0.2	0.3	0.5	0.1	0.1	0.0
Czech Republic	**	14	**	0.3	**	0.1	**	0.0
Slovakia	32**	36	08**	0.8	05**	0.7	01**	0.1
Poland	8	15	0.2	0.4	0.1	0.2	0.0	0.0
Romania	24	34	0.6	0.8	0.2	1.0	0.0	0.2
Egypt	9	15	0.2	0.4	0.3	0.2	0.1	0.0
Others	233	335	5.7	8.8	13.4	32.8	2.5	6.5
No marking	446	–	10.9	–	56.4	–	10.4	–
Total	4101	4286	100.0	100.0	543.5	502.3	100.0	100.0

** Czechoslovakia.
Source: Central Statistical Office of Hungary.

In mid-1995, 35 of the 50 largest multinational firms worldwide had an investment base in Hungary.

Efficiency of foreign direct investment

Judging the efficiency of economic units on the basis of index numbers is extremely difficult even if adequate numerical information is available. In the case of companies privatized with foreign capital, very few data are available, and where they are, they often suggest a biased approach.

Table 8.7   Hungary: FDI stock, April 1995

| | State holding co. | | SPA | | | Total | |
	No.	($mn)	No.	($mn)	No.	($mn)	Share (%)
Germany	3	379	79	408	82	787	25
United States	2	375	28	356	30	731	23
Austria	–	–	106	420	106	420	14
Great Britain	3	84	30	129	33	213	7
France	1	23	35	191	36	214	7
Netherlands	–	–	12	229	12	229	7
Belgium	–	–	8	133	8	133	4
Sweden	–	–	9	94	9	94	3
Switzerland	–	–	14	73	14	73	2
Italy	2	26	21	37	23	63	2
CIS	–	–	13	49	13	49	2
Others	3	28	37	94	40	122	4
Total	14	915	392	2213	406	3128	100

Source: SPA and State Holding Company.

In 1992 and 1993 the lowest profitability was produced by companies in foreign ownership. In fact, foreign and domestic companies were both showing a deficit, and the greatest average deficit was incurred by those in foreign ownership. (see Table 8.9). In 1990, that group of companies was the most profitable. Profits projected to equity capital and the value of assets exceeded those of companies in Hungarian ownership. But the presence of foreign capital in Hungary was minimal at the time.

Table 8.8 Hungary: top 50 foreign investments, 1993

Rank	Investor	Nationality	Type*	Year	Size of major shareholding (%)	Investment in $ million
1	General Electric	US	P	1990	100	550
2	Volkswagen-Audi	Germany	G	1993	100	420
3	US West International	US	JV, G	1990 1993	49 51	330
4	General Motors	US-Germany	JVG	1990	67	300
5	Suzuki, C Itoh, International Finance Corporation	Japan, International	JV, G	1991	60	250
6	PTT Netherlands, Telecom Denmark and other Scandinavian operators	Various	JV, G	1993		250
7	Allianz	Germany	JV	1990	67	220
8	Transroute International, Banque Nationale de Paris, Caisse des Dépôts, Strabag	France Austria	O	1993		200
9	Alcoa	US	JV	1992	51	165
10	Ferruzzi, Unilever	Italy, Netherlands-UK	P	1992	90	160
11	Prinzhom Group	Austria	JV	1990	40	160
12	Ansaldo, subsidiary of IRI	Italy	P	1990	75	130
13	PepsiCo International	US	P	1993	79	115
14	Guardian Glass	US	JV	1989	100	110
15	Alitalia, Simest	Italy	P	1992	35	100
16	Hungarian Investment Company	UK	O	1990		100
17	Sanofi	France	P	1990	51	100
18	Ford	US	G	1991	100	100
19	Sara Lee – Douwe Egberts	US	P	1991	100	100
20	Coca-Cola Amatil	Australia	P	1991	100	100
21	Kempinski, Dresdner Bank	Germany	G	1987	85	95
22	Nestle	Switzerland	P	1991	97	94

Table 8.8 Hungary: top 50 foreign investments, 1993 (continued)

Rank	Investor	Nationality	Type*	Year	Size of major shareholding (%)	Investment in $ million
23	Siemens	Germany	P	1991	100	94
24	Banca Commerciale Italiana, Bayerische Vereinsbank, the Long-Term Credit Bank of Japan, The Sakura Bank, Société Générale	Italy, Germany, Japan, France	JV	1979	64	87
25	First Hungary Fund	US	O	1990		80
26	Stollwerck	Germany	P		70	80
27	Marriott, GiroCredit, others	US, Austria	P	1992	90	77
28	Agrana	Austria	P	1990	53	70
29	Hoechst-Messer Gr	Germany	P	1991	97	70
30	Voest-Alpine	Austria	P	1992	50	70
31	Ferruzzi Beghin Say	Italy (France)	P	1991	40	70
32	Reemtsma	Germany	P	1992	85	68
33	Electrolux	Sweden	P	1991	100	65
34	Total	France	G,P			65
35	British-American Tobacco	UK	P	1991	51	60
36	Hungarian-American Enterprise Fund	US	O	1990		60
37	Sarp Industries	France	P	1993	52	60
38	Philip Morris	US	P	1991	80	69
39	Amylum	Belgium	P	1991	99	60
40	Julius Meinl	Austria	P	1991	51	59
41	Aral	France	G			57
42	Skanska	Sweden	G			56
43	European Bank for Reconstruction & Development	Financial Insti.	O	1992		55
44	Columbian Chemicals	US	JV	1993	60	55
45	Institutional investors	US	O	1991	32	54

Table 8.8 Hungary: top 50 foreign investments, 1993 *(continued)*

Rank	Investor	Nationality	Type*	Year	Size of major shareholding (%)	Investment in $ million
46	Accor	France	P	1993	51	52
47	Tengelmann	Germany	P	1989–92		50
48	Primagaz, Calor Gas (in JV Pamgas)	France, UK	P	1992	51	50
49	Tetra-Pak	Sweden	G	1992	100	50
50	Atex	CIS	P	1991	30	50

* P = privatization, G = greenfield, JV = joint venture, O = other
Source: Financial Times, 17 November 1993.

Table 8.9   Profitability of enterprises in Hungary

(a)   Based on the $\frac{\text{after tax profit}}{\text{value of assets}} \times 100$ ratio

Type of enterprise		Profitability	
	1990	*1992*	*1993*
Enterprises with FDI	4.39	(4.23)	(3.38)
Private enterprises with			
domestic owners	2.60	(4.35)	(2.58)
State-owned enterprises	2.77	(1.90)	(2.47)

(b)   Based on the $\frac{\text{after tax profit}}{\text{equity}} \times 100$ ratio

Type of enterprise		Profitability	
	1990	*1992*	*1993*
Enterprises with FDI	9.4	(11.5)	(9.8)
Private enterprises with			
domestic owners	4.8	(9.0)	(6.1)
State-owned enterprises	4.1	(6.1)	(6.2)

9
The Problems of Foreign Capital Participation in Russia's Privatization

*Yuri Adjubei**

Introduction

Privatization has been, so far, one of the most visible achievements of market economic reforms in Russia. Along with economic stabilization and institution-building, privatization creates prerequisites of structural transformation and economic efficiency gains in the future. This opportunity is generated by the emergence of new private enterprise owners, changes in managerial elites and improved corporate governance.

In all transition economies, decision-makers attribute to foreign investment an important role in the privatization process. Companies from abroad are expected to bring in the investment capital required to restructure the former state-owned enterprises (SOEs), as well as technological and financial expertise and managerial know-how, with the objective of transforming the inefficient 'giants of socialist industry' into modern competitive entities.

Despite invariably welcoming government declarations with regard to foreign participation in economic transformation, so far the role of foreign companies in Russian privatization has been limited. Cumulative foreign investment in privatization was estimated not to exceed 10 per cent of FDI stock in 1996. This compares unfavourably with the more advanced economies of Central Europe. In Hungary, for example, some 48 per cent of accumulated FDI was estimated to have gone to privatized SOEs in 1996.

This chapter analyses the progress of privatization in Russia; it highlights the legal basis of foreign participation in privatization and explores the obstacles to a more active role by foreign companies in this process.

---

* The author works for the Secretariat of the United Nations Economic Commission for Europe. The views expressed here are his own and do not necessarily reflect those of the Secretariat.

Objectives, stages and institutions

In Russia, privatization has been viewed by reformers as a means of creating an efficient economic sector and a class of owners and managers which would crowd out the old state managers. The latter goal of laying down the social foundation for a market economy has been of paramount importance. The acting State Programme of Privatization claims as its first objective the formation of a broad stratum of private owners as an economic basis of market relations.[1]

The Programme does not explicitly refer to the increase of fiscal revenues as an objective of privatization. In practice, however, the replenishment of the budget has been its most important aim, often determining the speed and methods of privatization.

As in several other transition economies, privatization in Russia has been conducted in two stages. The first phase (1992–94) consisted of the free distribution of state property to the population through vouchers and direct sales of small enterprises to individuals (the so-called 'small' privatization). At the second 'commercial' or 'cash' stage of privatization, which started in 1995, large enterprises (the 'jewels of industry') were privatized through conversions into joint stock companies and subsequent sales of blocks of shares through auctions and tenders.

In institutional terms, the main government body supervising the privatization is the State Committee on Managing State Property (Goskomimuschestvo or GKI) which inherited its function from the USSR's GKI. This body is in charge of drawing up privatization programmes and schedules and has its counterparts at regional and municipal levels. Being responsible for implementing privatization, the GKI is not the formal owner of SOEs. Instead, a parallel body of property funds at federal, regional and local levels was created to serve as the seller of state property. While the Federal Property Fund often supports powerful industrial ministries, Goskomimuschestvo is intended to neutralize the resistance to privatization of vested interests.

The first stage of privatization

In its first stage, privatization consisted mostly of an exchange of vouchers freely distributed to the population against a fixed part of state property. In parallel, 'small' privatization, which accompanied voucher privatization, resulted in the de-etatization (through employee buy-outs and direct sales) of municipal property – stores, small shops, restaurants and repair shops.

At the end of the first stage of privatization as many as 47 per cent of SOEs were privatized (end 1994)[2] and by mid-1995 almost half (117 000 or 49 per cent) of 240 500 SOEs found themselves at varying stages of privatization. As many as 16 462 enterprises with the aggregated statutory capital of RUR 1421 billion were put on sale at voucher auctions. During 1992–94, government revenues from privatization made up RUR 1100 billion.[3]

In the context of 'small' privatization, the proportion of municipal enterprises privatized increased from 25 per cent at the end of 1992 to 68 per cent one year later. Most enterprises privatized during 1992–94 (about 60 per cent) had a total number of employees not exceeding 200. In sectoral terms, mass privatization focused on trade intermediation, public catering and consumer services enterprises.[4]

Along with small-scale privatization, conversion into joint-stock companies or corporatization, as a preliminary stage of privatizing larger units, was effected in industry. According to the industrial 'ministries' data, by September 1995, out of 1575 engineering enterprises only 159 or 10 per cent remained in state ownership. As many as 80 of those remaining were slated for privatization in 1995 and 1996.[5] By the end of 1995, in the timber sector, as many as 90 per cent of timber-processing plants and 98 per cent of pulp and paper combines had been converted into joint-stock companies.[6]

According to Russia's Institute of Economic Analysis, as a result of voucher privatization, in 1995 the number of workers in the private sector amounted to 36 per cent of the total workforce, as compared with only 18 per cent in 1992.[7]

Current stage of commercial privatization

The transition to the commercial phase has brought to the forefront such privatization methods as auctions, tenders and buy-outs of leased property.[8] While the last of these is applicable mostly to domestic investors, the former two are relevant to foreign investors as well. The major difference between auctions and tenders is that under auction, the property is acquired by the bidder offering the highest price. In the case of tenders, large blocks of shares are offered at below market prices. At the same time, the winner must propose the most attractive investment programme and fulfil several other conditions specified by the organizers.

In 1995, federal property was sold at 4131 cash auctions and 555 investment tenders. In the same year, out of 261 tenders of enterprises with statutory capital exceeding RUR 50 million, 122 or almost half did not take place because of insufficient demand (lack of applications).[9]

After the end of the non-cash stage, the number of privatized SOEs continued to grow at a much slower rate. When compared with the previous year, in 1995 the number of privatized enterprises dropped almost four-fold and did not exceed 6172. In cumulative terms, by the end of 1995 as many as 118 800 former SOEs were privatized in Russia, representing 56.7 per cent of their total number (official estimate).[10]

At the beginning of the cash privatization phase, the structure of privatized enterprises remained very similar to that prevalent during mass privatization. As much as 88 per cent of enterprises privatized in 1995 were small (with the number of employees not exceeding 200), of which 56 per cent belonged to trade and services.[11] At the same time, the privatization of large enterprises in mining, engineering, transport and communications had started.

In 1995, the 2770 newly established corporations issued 854 million shares. Of these, about one-third was distributed among the enterprise workers and less than a third (272 million) was earmarked for unrestricted circulation. About 8.9 million of these shares were sold at investment tenders to domestic and foreign investors, and 110 million (40 per cent) at auctions.[12]

In that same year, the share prices of new joint-stock companies were relatively low due to the lack of demand and favourable conditions for alternative financial investments. At the same time, the government was forced to agree to low price offerings because of the acute need of budgetary resources. As a result, large blocks of shares of 900 corporatized former SOEs were sold for RUR 911 billion (or $200 000 per block). Even the attractive stock of the United Energy Systems of Russia was offered at a minimal price, some 40 per cent below market quotations.[13]

Despite the efforts of privatizers, in 1995 over half of the newly issued stock earmarked for unrestricted circulation remained undistributed.[14] As a result, the state revenues from privatization (RUR 7200 billion) fell short of the targeted RUR 8700 billion, and this gap would have been much wider had the shares-for-loans auctions not saved the privatization budget from complete collapse (see below).[15] That year, budgets at various levels received 71 per cent of all privatization revenues from those auctions (including the repaid tax indebtedness of companies thus privatized).[16]

In 1996, the number of privatized enterprises grew to 126 800 or 60.5 per cent of the total number of enterprises. The cumulative receipts of the budget had reached about RUR 3200 billion by the end of 1996.[17] However, in that year the exchequer received only 14 per cent of targeted privatization revenue.[18]

The privatization revenue target for 1997 was reduced to RUR 5000 billion. This figure already includes the RUR 1330 billion raised from the sale of an 8.5 per cent stake in the power grid operator United Energy System.[19]

Thus, the cash stage experience has attested to the slowing down of privatization and, at the same time, to the increasing difficulty encountered by the state in collecting the targeted privatization incomes.

Privatization-related efficiency gains

The empirical evidence to date suggests that privatization has resulted in enterprises' enhanced efficiency. A survey of 266 state-owned and privatized enterprises in 8 branches of industry in 13 regions of Russia conducted by the International Centre of Social and Economic Studies (Leontiev Centre) showed that, in 1993–94, privatized firms had significantly higher efficiency indicators than state enterprises. The efficiency indicators of enterprises with a state share of capital of less than 25 per cent were higher than those of SOEs by 42 per cent. The percentage for enterprises more than 25 per cent state-owned was 21. The financial stability and solvency of enterprises were also positively related to the degree of privatization. In 1994, the production volume of privatized enterprises increased by 2.3 per cent as compared with 1993, while that of state-owned enterprises declined by 12 per cent. A more limited survey covering 40 machine-building and consumer goods-producing enterprises in St Petersburg in 1995 showed that the efficiency of privatized enterprises that year increased by 10 per cent while that of state enterprises dropped by 15 per cent.[20]

Privatization may also have positively influenced the performance of individual industrial sectors. The timber industry, for example, experienced a sustained recovery in 1995, the year which followed massive privatization; by the end of that year foreign companies had invested in this sector as much as $500 million.[21]

Legal basis of foreign participation

The legal basis of foreign participation in privatization was established in the Laws on Foreign Investment and Privatization which were enacted in 1991.[22] The Foreign Investment Law laid down the legal basis for foreign investment in privatization, allowing all types of partnerships as well as foreign participation in the stock of existing national firms. The Privatization Law, however, severely restricted foreign investment in SOEs. In practice, foreign investors could participate in the voucher privatization in several indirect ways: through an intermediary, by buying vouchers on the secondary market and through joint ventures with the local companies.

Subsequently, the Privatization Programmes which spelled out concrete privatization rules, liberalized the conditions of foreign participation in privatization. In particular, the Privatization Programme adopted at the end of 1993 introduced fewer restrictions on foreign participation: foreign investors were allowed to take part in auctions, commercial and investment tenders, even if they were the only participant.

Government approval is required for foreign participation in the privatization of defence-related enterprises, as well as in transport, communications, oil and gas extraction and the processing of strategic ores, precious stones ad radioactive minerals. Foreign investment is forbidden in enterprises located in restricted areas. Finally, the Federal Counter-Intelligence Service has the right, within one month of the auction or tender won by foreign investors, to advise the government that the privatization deal should be stopped.

At the regional level, the participation of foreigners in trade and service enterprises, as well as in small industrial, construction and transport enterprises, requires the authorization of local authorities.

The Privatization Programme also stipulates that no further restrictions on foreign participation in privatization should be added.[23] While there are few legal limitations on the participation of foreigners in privatization, the latter can be handicapped in practice by both the prohibitive interpretation of those restrictions and administrative impediments contradicting the law. In particular, the privatization of large SOEs requires approval and support of the government at both federal and local levels.

Additional restrictions are likely to appear when foreign investment contradicts the interests of industrial ministries, which have lobbied to acquire special conditions of privatization often beneficial to insiders. Simultaneously, due to developing autonomist tendencies in Russia, foreign investment in privatization increasingly depends on the attitude of regional and local authorities. As a rule, the latter try to obtain additional commitments from foreign companies, in particular by seeking their investment in local infrastructure.[24]

Understandably, large investments are more easily implemented in regions under the political control of reformers. Thus, one of the largest foreign investments in privatization – the purchase of 90 per cent of the stock (and commitment of further investment worth $150 million) of the Balakhna paper mills by Germany's Herlitz International Trading in co-operation with the IFC – occurred in the Nizhni Novgorod region which pioneered economic reform.[25]

Magnitude of foreign participation

In the absence of official statistics, the available data referring to foreign investment in privatization are sketchy and often contradictory.

According to estimates by Russian observers, up to 10–12 per cent of shares offered for vouchers during the first stage of privatization were bought by non-residents through intermediaries. In many cases, however, these non-residents represented the managers of state enterprises, which used illegal capital outflows to finance the purchase of stock with the aim of increasing control over their enterprises.[26]

The Russian Fund of State Property estimated the volume of foreign contributions to privatization at about $2 billion in September 1993.[27] By 1995, non-residents made 1.5 per cent of applications at privatization specialized auctions. At the same time, non-resident investors were the source of 23 per cent of capital paid for shares.[28]

According to information made public during the privatization hearings in the State Duma in April–May 1996, as many as 125 commercial and investment tenders in which foreigners could take part were organized during 1993–95. Of those tenders, 21 were won by foreign investors (foreign companies and joint ventures with foreign participation). Foreign winners' commitments amounted in sum to about $230 million (RUR 468 billion plus $144 million), and their share in total RUR and $-denominated committed investment (worth RUR 2600 billion plus $2.4 billion) made up 18 and 6 per cent respectively.[29]

While foreigners have not been eligible to participate in a large part of privatization auctions and tenders, the budgetary deficit has worked as a powerful argument in favour of broadening foreign participation. Thus, at the end of 1995 when it became clear that the targeted revenue from privatization could not be collected, Goskomimuschestvo organized auctions of the shares of 136 profitable enterprises in fuels, chemicals, sea and air transport, gas, timber and wood-processing industries. While only Russian nationals were eligible for participation in some of these auctions, groups of financial investors from the United Kingdom and Cyprus acquired packages of shares in the Sidanko Oil Company (worth RUR 100 billion or $20 million) and the defence-related enterprise Avionika (60 per cent of shares). Smaller packages of shares were sold to foreigners by Yuvelirprom (a jewellery enterprise) and the Novorossiysk Sea Shipping Company.[30]

In the absence of official statistics, information collected from press reports partly fills in the data gaps. This information confirms that, by the end of 1996, the amount of foreign investment in privatization remained small. By that date, foreigners had acquired 19 relatively large equity stakes (exceeding $10 million each) in former SOEs (including takeovers) (see Table 9.1). The aggregated initial foreign investment (that is investment to be effected during the first four years of the project's life) in these enterprises was estimated at $585 million. At the end of 1995, the indicated value of initial foreign investment in large privatization projects was equivalent to about 9 per cent of the cumulative mid-year value of foreign investment, as reported by the State Committee on Statistics.

In 6 of the 19 projects for which the information is available, foreign investors came from the United States and the European Union. This suggests that foreign investment in privatization is highly concentrated in terms of source countries, while investors from the transition economies and developing countries have so far not acquired large equity stakes.

In terms of industrial distribution, the bulk (83 per cent) of foreign investment to be effected during the first 4 years of the project's life went to 16 manufacturing enterprises. The rest was distributed among mining, telecommunications and banking. Within manufacturing, foreign investment focused on chemicals, paper and food industries and, to a lesser extent, on tobacco processing and several branches of engineering.

While the quoted information is by no means complete, it does suggest that foreign investors have tended to buy more stakes in manufacturing

Table 9.1 Large privatization-related foreign investment projects in the Russian Federation, by year
(takeovers and equity stakes)

| | Initial foreign investment[a] | | Total foreign investment[b] | |
| | *Value* | *Number* | *Value of projects* | *Number of projects* |
	(mn US$)		*(mn US$)*	
1991	–	–	300.0	1
1992	25.0	1	–	–
1993	136.2	4	23.6	1
1994	92.9	5	151.0	3
1995	195.0	7	128.0	1
1996	136.0	2	–	–
Total	585.1	19	602.6	6

[a]Foreign investment to be effected during the first one to four years of project life.
[b]Foreign investment to be effected over the whole project life.
Note: Data refer to projects which have initial or total foreign investment equal to or exceeding USD 10 million. Figures may not add to totals due to rounding.
Source: UN/ECE Secretariat.

and less in mining. The investment intentions of sample foreign investors reveal rather a contradictory picture. In the second half of 1995, under conditions of moderate inflation, companies from abroad were prepared to direct over a quarter of their investment (26 per cent) to oil companies and almost one-fifth (19 per cent) to related 'energy' producers.[31] This foreign interest in the stock of energy-extracting and processing companies (45 per cent of total foreign investment) attests to the considerable potential of foreign investment in privatized SOEs in this sector, on the one hand, and to existing restrictions with regards to such investment, on the other.

It is worth noting that, despite strict government controls, some cases of 'creeping' foreign acquisitions may have remained unknown to the public. For example, press reports suggested that, by 1997, most aluminium smelters in Russia (Bratsk, Sayany, Novokuznetsk, Krasnoyarsk and Novolipetsk) had an important, often controlling foreign stake. The British Trans World Group has acquired considerable interests in these enterprises, mostly through deliveries of raw materials, which after the break-up of the Soviet Union needed to be imported.[32]

In sum, while the available information is by no means complete, it is unlikely that the volume of actual foreign investment in privatization by the end of 1996 had exceeded $0.8–1.0 billion, testifying to a rather limited foreign participation. The main impediments were economic, political and regulatory.

Major problems

Economic impediments are faced by both domestic and foreign investors, and refer to the absence of a clear perspective due to the economic slump and inflationary expectations. The impact of these factors has been quite strong. The above-mentioned survey of various investor groups conducted in the second half of 1995 showed that, under restricted inflation, foreign companies may have contributed up to two-fifths of the demand for the former SOEs' stock.[33]

Political risk considerations may have been even more important for foreign investors than macroeconomic factors. In the first half of 1996, for instance, when the outcome of the forthcoming presidential election was unclear, the proportion of foreign to total investment demand was assessed by the Russian marketing association at less than one-tenth of a per cent. In the first half of 1996, of 150 foreign investors with whom Goskomimuschestvo maintained privileged relations, only 2 were ready to take on investment risks.[34]

At the micro-level, problems relating to foreign participation often involve existing regulations, valuation methods and technical privatization rules. Among these, the most important include:

1 *The inadequate regulatory framework for privatization*: foreign participation in the secondary trading of shares is particularly vulnerable. Buying into domestic enterprises through the local financial market is hampered by insufficient regulations and the lack of institutions servicing this market. In particular, after the initial public offering, the former SOEs have often denied foreign investors access to share registers, which has resulted in error and fraud. Press reports indicate that foreign investors have found their shares crossed out of registers. The lack of a centralized system of registration of ownership changes has also restricted the liquidity of the market. The experience thus far shows that facilitating foreign investment in privatization would require making security markets more transparent. In particular, the availability of price and volumes of transactions information through a unified stock quotation system should be ensured; further, enterprises offering their shares should be legally obliged to make their financial statements public.

Some of these hurdles have been or are being overcome with the help of foreign investors and international organizations. The Bank of New York, with the participation of the EBRD and the IFC, has set up a new Russian Registry Company as an independent share registration service. The new company, whose central office will be linked with nine regional branch offices, is intended to stop the proliferation of local registries. The EBRD has also taken steps to establish a Depository Clearing

Corporation, which is intended as a clearing organization for the various stock exchanges.[35]

2 *Problems relating to the valuation of SOEs' assets:* In many cases the latter are undervalued as compared with those of similar enterprises in the West. According to official data, the assets of the 500 largest companies privatized in Russia during the first round of privatization were valued at only $7.3 billion. Of these, only 92 companies were valued at more than $10 million. The voucher auction prices of the largest companies were 2–4 times lower than the subsequent secondary market valuation, and in the case of several oil and gas enterprises this difference went up by 10–15 times.[36]

The undervaluation of assets is also characteristic of industries which are to be privatized at the commercial phase. In the mid-1990s, the shares of an average Russian oil company were valued at between 10 to 40 cents per barrel of proven reserves as compared with $7 in the United States.[37] In the United States, manufacturing companies had an average market value of about $100 000 per employee, while in Russia this indi-cator was one hundred times lower.[38] In telecommunications, the assets/product ratio amounted to 70 in Russia, 1637 in the United States and 848 in Western Europe.[39]

As much as 40 per cent of the United Energy Systems' stock distrib-uted in the first half of 1995 was equivalent to 8 per cent of that company's capital ($1 billion and 12.5 billion, respectively). The value of one Megawatt of sold capacity was equivalent to $780; in the devel-oped market economies one Megawatt cost at least $300 000.[40]

On the one hand, the undervaluation created the potential for intense secondary trading and, other factors being equal, for enhanced foreign involvement in privatization. On the other hand, it sharpened public sentiment of a sell-out of the 'family jewels', and encouraged protection-ist lobbying by domestic competitors.

While the assets of many large SOEs remain undervalued, the inade-quate domestic valuation methods create a strong disincentive for foreign companies to buy into small and medium-sized enterprises. Western investors trust the asset evaluation effected by foreign experts or licensed local consultancies trained in Western methods of valuation. Because of the costs involved, only large SOEs can afford such a service. Consequently, the lack of correct asset value impedes SMEs to offer themselves for sale to foreign investors.[41]

3 *Technical barriers to foreign participation in privatization auctions and tenders:* These barriers include the lack of coherent information on enter-prises to be privatized, the timing and conditions of auctions and

tenders, an insignificant proportion of stocks offered for sale (10–15 per cent in 1995) and short time periods during which RUR-denominated claims need be settled. Sometimes, in order to avoid undesirable takeovers, the managers of SOEs do not hesitate openly to break the rule established by Goskomimuschestvo, by halting the collection of bidders' applications earlier than scheduled or conducting a tender in an area where foreign access is restricted.

The lack of detailed instructions and the breach of the existing rules facilitate the challenging of privatization results in courts. According to press reports, the capital committed in investment tenders is often not implemented because the results of the tenders are contested in arbitration courts by unsuccessful bidders.[42]

Despite undeniable progress, the underdeveloped market institutions remained a major problem in transferring assets to private hands in the second half of the 1990s. Among related aspects, the officials of Goskomimuschestvo have mentioned ineffective capital structures due to insider (SOEs staff) privileges, lack of legal safety for equity holders, the absence of market-oriented land legislation and inadequate control of investment programme implementation.[43] The objective of creating an adequate institutional background is further complicated by the fact that the stock market, the protection of shareholders' rights and management of privatized companies need to be developed simultaneously.

Host country policy

The Russian Federation's policy toward foreign participation in privatization is determined by an intricate interplay of interests. Politically, privatization has been a central programme issue for liberal reformers. At the same time, its principles, methods and results have been the preferred objective of attacks from neo-communist and nationalist opponents.

During the voucher stage, the speed of de-etatization was in fact the only privatization policy objective. Even the goal of raising additional budgetary receipts played a subordinate role. Consistency in this privatization policy during the first half of the 1990s was backed up by the strong personal impact of reformers involved in decision-making, and this personality factor continued to influence both government policy and investors' attitudes toward privatization also throughout the second half of the decade.[44] The objectives of the voucher phase left foreign investment attraction at the margin, and the participation by foreigners in the primary distribution of property was legally restricted.

In 1995 and 1996, budgetary deficits pushed the government towards using privatization as a source of fiscal revenues. At the same time, experience to date confirmed that the hasty de-etatization was not an efficient tool of replenishing the state budget. In particular, the lack of normative acts governing the privatization techniques and the lack of agreed valuation methods have contributed to failures in individual deals and to decreasing budgetary receipts. As was indicated earlier, while in 1995 the Exchequer acquired about 83 per cent of the targeted privatization revenues (mostly due to shares-for-loans auctions), in 1996 this percentage dropped to 14.

Increasingly, the privatization officials have advocated the slowing-down of privatization and the enhancement of its role as a development and structural policy tool.[45] The heart of the emerging new policy is the so-called selective approach, according to which the privatization of individual large SOEs, first of all in natural resource development and defence-related industries, should proceed on a case-by-case basis. Simultaneously, increased attention should be paid to enhanced private ownership efficiency. To this end, the new Privatization Programme under preparation at the beginning of 1997 advocated the elimination of preferences to the workers of SOEs in the form of guaranteed and/or cheaper stock. Higher efficiency would also be sought through conceding state ownership in trust management of private entities.[46]

The changing policy stance, coupled with political uncertainties and inadequate legal background, have considerably delayed the state of the new commercial stage of privatization. While officially the cash stage was introduced by a presidential decree on 22 July 1994, no specialized auctions were held that year.[47] *De facto*, this phase commenced almost one year later, when the lists of SOEs to be privatized in 1995 were published. Of 7186 SOEs which were put on sale in early 1995, none belonged to the defence industry, oil sector or could be considered 'strategically important'.[48]

The turn of focus from the rapid conversion of enterprises into private hands towards the enhanced efficiency of former SOEs implies finding an effective owner as a primary objective. This altered policy stance, in principle, creates new opportunities for foreign investors. The latter, often having technological, managerial and financial advantages over local competitors, can play a useful part in establishing effective corporate governance. At the same time, by the mid-1990s new obstacles to foreign participation in privatization had emerged. By that time, a number of relatively large domestic private companies had stood on their feet and rejected the role of junior partners to their Western counterparts. These domestic enterprise groups, which are led by a number of rapidly growing banks and petrochemical companies, actively lobby the government to ascertain their privileged position *vis-à-vis* foreign competitors. In the privatization area, this lobbying has found its practical outcome in the so called share-for-loans proposal made to the government by several leading commercial banks.

Shares-for-loans schemes

According to the shares-for-loans schemes, the successful bidder acquires shares of selected state-owned enterprises at an auction, manages these blocks of shares during periods ranging from six months to three years, and has the right to sell them thereafter. In exchange, the banks offer loans to the government to cover the budgetary deficit.

In the second half of 1995, the government accepted the bankers' proposal, and Goskomimuschestvo chose for its auctions over 20 elite enterprises, comprising several leading oil- and metal-producers and shipping companies.[49] The shares of most of those enterprises are quoted on stock exchanges, and the new managers could expect to increase the stock value significantly through conducting a reliable audit, trimming the shareholders' registers and guaranteeing their rights. As a result of share price rises, the resale of this stock will have enabled the participating banks to receive both an interest on loan[50] and a commission fee (the loan-givers are entitled to get 30 per cent of capital gains when the shares are resold).

In practical terms, as many as 12 auctions were known to have taken place by the beginning of 1996. For example, at the end of 1995 the Menatep Bank agreed to lend the government $159 million in return for the right to manage a 45 per cent stake share-holding in Yukos – the second largest oil company – for about a year. The bank expected to secure full ownership of the share block thereafter. Simultaneously, Menatep acquired a further 33 per cent of Yukos' shares through an investment tender in which it pledged to invest some $150 million in that company.[51] In the same way, Oneksimbank won the auction for a 38 per cent block of shares of Norilskii Nikel – a nickel producing combine – committing to provide a loan to the government worth $170.1 million. It made a commitment to consolidate an investment worth $1 billion over 1996–97.

While giving privileged domestic financial groups unique opportunities of raising profits and expanding their control, the shares-for-loans schemes have also permitted the government to improve its budgetary situation. Goskomimuschestvo has counted the loans received from the banks as privatization revenue, and in 1995 only, this was equivalent to over $1 billion.[52] It is less certain whether these schemes have contributed to upgrading the corporate governance of the former SOEs. The rules of the shares-for-loans auctions are contradictory in this respect. In particular, the banks managing the shares cannot restructure companies under their control through management changes or sale of subsidiaries.[53]

At the same time, these schemes have clearly demonstrated a strengthened protectionist bias in privatization policy. On the one hand, the government has given the green light for the largest domestic banks to secure control over the most lucrative companies at bargain prices, first of all in the primary sector (the Goskomimuschestvo officials do not hesitate to call the shares-for-loans scheme a 'delayed sale with pre-payment').[54] On the other, foreign companies are often not allowed to participate in loans-for-equity auctions. In 7 of 16 shares-for-loans auctions declared in 1995, only Russian legal persons were eligible.[55] At the time of writing (beginning of 1997), no foreign winners of shares-for-loans schemes were known from the press.

The growing domestic capital orientation of decision-makers erodes the national treatment principle stipulated by the foreign investment law and questions the inflow of foreign direct investment in industries with the best potential for such inflows.

Outlook

While all through 1996 the Privatization Programme was virtually stalled, at the beginning of 1997 signs of its restarting appeared. The most attractive assets on offer from the state were a 15 per cent stake in Lukoil, Russia's biggest oil company, and a 2 per cent stake in United Energy Systems, the electricity generator. The government was also committed to selling 50 per cent of Rosgosstrakh, Russia's biggest insurance company, as well as about 20 per cent of Slavneft, a Russian-Belarus oil concern, and a 5.34 per cent stake in Novorossiysk Sea Shipping, one of the largest shipping companies.[56]

At the time of writing (1997), it was not clear, however, what the conditions of foreign investors' participation in future privatization sales would be. As indicated above, the loans-for-shares schemes give domestic investors the first option, often via opaque insider deals. It is also obvious that the government will closely monitor and restrict the foreign share in the largest and most lucrative companies. As an example, only 9 per cent of Gazprom stock will be open to foreigners.

In general terms, by the second half of the 1990s foreign investors had acquired a relatively modest stake of state assets being privatized. While some of the deals increasing foreign participation probably were not yet made public at the time of writing, it is certain that despite a generally favourable legal basis, the situation in the mid-1990s was not conducive to foreign participation in privatization. This situation was characterized by a combination of general investment crises and barriers to foreign investment in SOEs. The persistence of the latter is explained by the struggle of the SOEs' insiders (workers and directors) to preserve their priority of ownership rights. Increasingly, domestic groups of large private banks are seeking to control the most profitable segments of the Russian economy. In the second half of the 1990s these financial groups maintained privileged relationships with the authorities and succeeded in deterring foreign participation in privatization in sectors where investor interest was strongest – oil, gas and metal mining.

Powerful regional interests, which often contradict those of the Federal centre, add uncertainty to the future course and the prospective role of foreign investors in privatization. It is almost certain that a prolonged period of property redistribution will follow 'official' privatization. At that stage, the role of foreign investors might strengthen considerably.

In sectoral terms, Russia has welcomed foreign investors in oligopolistic industries, which require major injections of capital and technology. As elsewhere in transition economies, large parts of telecommunications, for example, are likely to be taken over by foreign companies. The food and consumer goods sectors have been undercapitalized for decades and have few chances of delivering competitive products without externally financed modernization. Major world companies invest in these industries in order to strengthen their presence in newly opening markets. Foreign investment is likely to increase in the privatized food processing, beverages and tobacco manufacturing industries, in the production of textiles and garments, domestic chemicals and appliances and cars.

At the other end of the spectrum, there are enterprises and sectors in which foreign participation in privatization will encounter strong opposition from domestic interests and be strictly monitored by the government. High technology and defence-related industries will seek cooperation with foreign companies in order to improve their access to financing and marketing. At the same time, the foreign equity participation and takeovers of such enterprises on a massive scale are unlikely.

The perspectives of foreign participation in privatization in the extraction of hydrocarbons (oil and gas) and mineral mining will depend on the behaviour of the major players involved. On the one hand, portfolio investment by foreign financiers (e.g. investment funds) will be welcomed by oil and mining companies and encouraged by the government. On the other, domestic financial groups will be trying to prevent foreign control in mineral development and will be lobbying the Federal government to win its support. Regional and local authorities, by contrast, might look auspiciously at foreign direct investment in the mining enterprises located on their territories, if prospective investors guarantee local participation in export revenues and commit themselves to upgrade the local infrastructure and maintain employment.

In general terms, the Russian decision-makers will need to find a balance between the various interests involved, and ensure that economic efficiency and host country benefits should not be surrendered to short-term political considerations and lobbying efforts.

Notes

1 *Ekonomika i Zhizn'*, 2 (January 1994).
2 *Ekonomika i Zhizn'*, 19 (May 1996).
3 *Moskovskiye Novosti*, 25 June–2 July 1995.

4 CIS Statistical Committee, *Statisticheskii Byulleten'*, 21 (June 1995), p. 49.

5 *Finansovye Izvestiya*, 7 September 1995

6 BBC Summary of World Broadcasts, Weekly Economic Report, SU/W 0411, 4 November 1995, p. WC/3.

7 *Finansovye Izvestiya*, 26 October 1995; V. Gimpel'son, 'Chastnyi sektor v Rossii: zaniatost' I oplata truda' (Russia's private sector's employment and labour remuneration), *Mirovaya Ekonomika i Mezhdunarodnye Otnosheniya*, 2 (1997), p. 84.

8 The Privatization Programme enacted in 1994 singles out the following methods:
   • sale of the stock of incorporated enterprises;
   • auctioning of non-incorporated enterprises;
   • commercial tenders of non-incorporated enterprises (including those with a limited number of participants);
   • sale of the stock of incorporated enterprises through investment tenders;
   • auctions and tenders of enterprises under liquidation, and of unfinished construction;
   • buying out of leased property;
   • sale of state and municipal shares and parts through auctions and commercial tenders (*Ekonomika i Zhizn'*, 2 (January 1994).

9 *Ekonomika i Zhizn'*, 47 (November 1996).

10 *Ekonomika i Zhizn'*, 19 (May 1996).

11 *Ekonomika i Zhizn'*, 10 (March 1996).

12 Ibid.

13 *Kommersant*, 3, 6 February 1996.

14 *Ekonomika i Zhizn'*, 10 March 1996.

15 Of the revenues received, about RUR 4700 billion (or 54 per cent) came from 12 shares-for-loans auctions, about RUR 1500 billions from the direct sale of shares and another 1000 billion from the sale of convertible bonds issued by the oil company Lukoil (BBC Summary of World Broadcasts, Weekly Economic Report, SU/W 0416, 5 January 1996, p. WP/2).

16 *Ekonomika i Zhizn'*, 19 (May 1996).

17 BBC Summary of World Broadcasts, Weekly Economic Report, SU/W 0476, 7 March 1997, p. WA/3,

18 This gap was formed by the failure to sell off the Svyazinvest telecommunications holding company to the Italian telecommunications group Stet. This sale would have produced 33 per cent of the targeted revenue; the failed sale of shares of Rosneft's oil company, which should have given 4 per cent of the projected revenues, had the same results.

19 BBC Summary of World Broadcasts, Weekly Economic Report, SU/W 0470, 24 January 1997, p. WB/3.

20 *Ekonomika i Zhizn'*, 49 (December 1995); 19 (May 1996); *Izvestiya*, 5 December 1995.

21 BBC Summary of World Broadcasts, Weekly Economic Report, SU/W 0411, 4 November 1995, p. WC/3.

22 See Y. Adjubei, 'Russia: A largely Untapped Potential' in P. Artisien-Maksimenko and Y. Adjubei (eds) *Foreign Investment in Russia and Other Soviet Successor States*, Macmillan, Basingstoke and London, 1996.

23 *Ekonomika i Zhizn'*, 2 (January 1994).

24 Darrell Slider, 'Privatization in Russia's Regions', *Post-Soviet Affairs*, 4, October–December (1994), p. 387.

25 *Business Eastern Europe*, 27 February 1995; *Izvestiya*, 3 March 1995.

26 *Finansovye Izvestiya*, 3 August 1995.

27 *Ekonomika i Zhizn'*, 36 (September 1995).
28 *Ekonomika i Zhizn'*, 19 (May 1996).
29 *BIKI* 13 June 1996.
30 Ibid.
31 Calculated from *Kommersant*, 20 June 1995, p. 14.
32 *Kommersant*, 18 March 1997, pp. 42–43.
33 Calculated from *Kommersant*, 20 June 1995, p. 14.
34 *Izvestiya*, 24 February 1996.
35 Finance Eastern Europe, 21 April 1995, p. 14.
36 *The Economist*, 5 November 1994, p. 74.
37 *Financial Times*, 28 November, 1994.
38 *The Economist*, 5 November 1994, p. 74.
39 *Finansovye Izvestiya*, 3 August 1995.
40 *Finansovye Izvestiya*, 5 September 1995.
41 The lack of appropriate audit and valuation of assets may block the privatization not only of small but also large enterprises. As an example, these circumstances contributed to the failure of the takeover of the telecommunication operator Svyazinvest by the Italian company Stet (*Kommersant*, 23 January 1996, pp. 34–5).
42 *Kommersant*, 6 February 1996, p. 16.
43 *Finansovye Izvestiya*, 10 September 1996.
44 In particular, the head of the GKI, Anatoli Chubais, was the driving force behind the first voucher stage of privatization, overcoming the resistance of industrial ministries and the corps of enterprise directors. By contrast, the xenophobic declarations of his successor, coupled with the start of military intervention in Chechnya, contributed to a virtual standstill of privatization-related investment in late 1994–early 1995.
45 It remains to be seen, however, how practical the idea of not using privatization as a source of government revenues is. The demand for fiscal receipts did not decline in 1996–98. The government's agreement with the IMF required the budgetary deficit to decrease each year from 4 per cent in 1996 to 1 per cent in 1998, while no new sources of financing could be quickly found.
46 *Finansovye Izvestiya*, 7 March 1996.
47 *Ekonomika i Zhizn'*, 22 (June 1995).
48 BBC Summary of World Broadcasts, Weekly Economic Report, SU/W 0380, 21 April 1995, p. WB/1.
49 Noril'skii Nikel', for example, produces about one-fifth of the world's nickel and cobalt, and 42 per cent of the global platinum supply; in 1994, its sales reached $2.8 billion and earnings almost $700 million (*Business Central Europe*, February 1996, p. 16).
50 It is not clear, however, how high such an interest might be. One source indicates that the loans obtained by the government in exchange for shares are interest-free (*BIKI*, 8 August 1996).
51 *Financial Times*, 9/10 December 1995.
52 *Ekonomika i Zhizn'*, 19 (May 1996).
53 *Business Central Europe*, February 1996, p. 16.
54 *Ekonomika i Zhizn'*, 44 (November 1995).
55 *Ekonomika i Zhizn'*, 19 (May 1996).
56 *Financial Times*, 10 February 1997.

10
Foreign Investment and Privatization in Slovenia

Matija Rojec

Introduction

The ultimate aim of privatization in the countries of Central and Eastern Europe (CEE) is to create the basis for increasing economic efficiency. The transfer of ownership from the state or social sector (in the case of Slovenia) into private hands will help achieve this aim only in the long term: only when the major opportunities for cheap acquisitions and resulting substantial earnings are exhausted, will privatization bring about 'responsible' owners whose objectives are to improve company performance, efficiency and long-term development.

Foreign direct investment (FDI) is unlikely ever to become the major mode of privatization in CEE. However, FDI from strategic foreign investors can make an immediate contribution to the host economy by raising company efficiency.

This chapter is based on two premises:

1 Privatization and FDI in their mutual interlinkage are important for the transformation of the CEE economies: first, privatization earmarks the transformation process of CEE countries, including Slovenia; second, the ultimate objective of privatization is to raise efficiency in the CEE economies; third, inward FDI as a mode of privatization can contribute to building up a national competitive position through reductions in natural entry barriers to Western markets; and fourth, acquisitions will be a predominant type of FDI in the area in the medium term.
2 Nationwide privatization schemes in their early 'distribution' phase have not normally contributed to the economic efficiency of the CEE economies. By contrast, privatization through strategic foreign investors offers more encouraging possibilities.

Given the recent opening up of CEE countries to inward FDI, their policy in this field is still rudimentary. The absence of macro-organizational policies is compounded by a lack of well-defined micro policies (Dunning, 1993). This has resulted in a dichotomous and emotionally charged perception of inward FDI, particularly in terms of foreign privatizations, that is acquisitions of non-privatized local companies by strategic foreign investors: on the one hand, naïve expectations that FDI could bring an instant panacea; on the other, lingering fears of a 'sell-out' of national assets to profit-motivated outsiders.

The objective of this chapter is to analyse Slovenia's concept of and experience with privatization through FDI and define the country's policy framework on foreign privatizations.

Due to the lack of reliable and systematic official data on privatization, the research was based mostly on primary empirical sources. These included

(a) three case studies of foreign privatizations in Slovenia;
(b) interviews with staff at the Agency for Restructuring and Privatization and the Development Fund (since renamed (1998) the Development Corporation of Slovenia).

Legal and institutional framework

The legal and institutional framework for FDI in Slovenia is governed by the national treatment principle. Foreign investment enjoys full 'national treatment', that is, companies with foreign capital participation and wholly foreign-owned subsidiaries have the status of Slovene legal entities and operate in accordance with Slovene regulations. They are treated in the same manner as domestic companies. A foreign investor may either purchase the shares or assets of an existing Slovene company directly, or form a new company and, through it, purchase the shares or assets of the target company. If this company was at least partially socially owned, the acquiring company had to comply with the privatization regulations.

During the privatization process, foreign investors had to distinguish among different groups of companies in order to identify appropriate partners for negotiations:

1 The first and largest group were socially owned companies (social capital stock without a defined owner), which were the subject of the Law on Ownership Transformation. The negotiating partner in this case was the company's management, which was also responsible for preparing the ownership transformation programme to be approved by the Agency for Privatization.

2 The second group consisted of companies providing special public services (railways, telecommunications, airports). The status of these companies is regulated by the Law on Public Service Companies; they were

exempted from the provisions of the privatization law and decisions on their privatization have yet to be taken. Banks, insurance companies, enterprises engaged in gambling and companies undergoing bankruptcy procedures were also exempted from the Law on Ownership Transformation;

3 The third group consisted of companies within the portfolio of the Development Fund, which held a controlling stake in more than 60 companies. After undertaking the necessary restructuring measures, such as the implementation of corporate governance, the reduction of over-employment and rescheduling of debts, the Fund had a mandate to privatize its portfolio as quickly as possible. From the standpoint of the foreign investor, the main advantage of acquiring a company owned by the Development Fund was the possibility of starting immediate negotiations; there was no need to participate in transformation programmes required by the privatization law;

4 A fourth group consisted of bankrupt companies and firms in the process of liquidation. The foreign investor was able to buy a company from this group at auctions without obligations to its employees (whose employment with the company was terminated on the day of the beginning of the bankruptcy or liquidation procedure) or liabilities. The buyer was free to decide the legal form in which the company is to operate.

Two government institutions were established in December 1990 with the purpose of supervising, structuring and assisting the privatization process in Slovenia: the Agency for Restructuring and Privatization, which had a monitoring and control function, sets guidelines and approves privatization programmes; and the Development Fund which was involved in selling socially owned companies and financial restructuring.

Up to the end of 1992 Slovenia did not have a comprehensive privatization law. However, the absence of such a law did not prevent transactions, including foreign privatizations.[1] Socially owned companies themselves (workers' councils and managers) were in a position to decide whether to initiate privatization or not. No government agency was able to force a company into privatization. However, the Agency for Privatization was empowered to approve any privatization transactions, including joint ventures, where local socially owned companies contributed their existing assets to the new (joint venture) company. In privatization transactions involving the sale of shares of existing capital stock of socially owned companies, the Fund had the authority to negotiate the transaction, sign the sales contract and be in charge of proceeds from the sale. The preparation of the complex privatization law lasted almost two years, during which the Agency and the Fund controlled all foreign privatization transactions on the basis of the principles of competitive and transparent procedures and business valuation.

In November 1992 the Law on Ownership Transformation was adopted. Its main characteristics included a combination of free share distribution and commercial privatization; a flexible and multi-track approach; the immediate transformation of all enterprises into companies with known owners, to be followed by gradual real privatization; the decentralization and supervision of transformation programmes; an active role by specialized government institutions in commercial privatizations; and competitive and transparent procedures when a commercial technique of privatization (such as the public offering of shares, public auctions and tenders) was used.

The initiative to commence the privatization of a company had to originate from its management and employees. When completed, the transformation programme had to be adopted by the company's governing body. On receiving pre-approval from the Agency, the company could begin the programme's implementation.

The privatization law imposed some restrictions on the immediate resale of shares acquired through free distribution or with a discount. The law, therefore, regulated both commercial privatizations and the initial 'free' allocation of shares.

Slovenia's privatization law provided several methods of transformation:

1 The free transfer of 40 per cent of ordinary shares to institutions in the following proportions: 10 per cent to the Compensation/Restitution Fund; another 10 per cent to the Pension Fund and 20 per cent to the Development Fund. The latter subsequently sold this portfolio to special investment funds in return for shares with ownership certificates gathered from Slovene citizens, who were granted ownership certificates according to their age to a nominal value ranging from DM 4000 to 6000.

2 The internal distribution of shares to employees in exchange for ownership certificates (this was limited to 20 per cent of the company's shares).

3 The internal buy-out of shares was limited to 40 per cent of shares in the social capital. This favourable scheme enabled employees and others to acquire an ownership stake gradually (at 50 per cent discount) in four yearly instalments. Before an internal buy-out could take place, a free transfer of 40 per cent of shares to the relevant institutions, as well as an internal distribution of shares, had to be carried out.

4 The sale of the company's shares (existing and newly issued) had to be carried out in the forms of a public offering of shares, a public auction or a public (restricted) tender. Guidelines for these were determined by the Agency.

5 The sale of the company's assets combined with liquidation was contracted by the Development Fund. The latter took over all liabilities, which were subsequently repaid from the proceeds arising from the sale of assets.

Companies were free to opt for a method, or combination of methods, of their choice, but the overall transformation programme had to be approved by the Agency. Each company was required by law to prepare an opening balance sheet and transformation programme.

Foreign investors could participate in the privatization programmes as minority or controlling partners. The programme itself could be structured as a complete share or asset sale to the foreign investor.

Although the privatization law had no explicit stipulations on joint ventures or sales of subsidiaries from the portfolio of socially owned holding companies, such 'partial' privatization transactions, including asset acquisitions, were possible, subject to the Agency's approval.

The general principles applied by the Agency for Privatization and the Development Fund in foreign privatizations are listed below.

1 Business valuation was carried out through a system of qualified appraisers, who had obtained a valuation licence by passing the required exams. The most usual approach of seeking the most suitable buyer was the public invitation for bids or restricted tenders via letters of invitation. Competitive bidding and transparent procedures were applied whenever possible.
2 Foreign investors usually insisted on managerial control over the company. This is commonly achieved through the acquisition of at least 51 per cent of the company's shares.
   In such cases, the domestic partner had to be provided with specific minority rights relating to changes in statute and capital, dividend policy, liquidation and the sale of a substantial proportion of assets.
3 The purchase price of share acquisitions was usually paid in cash. The Fund, when acting as seller, might accept financial instruments from the buyer for a small percentage of the purchase price.

Privatization via foreign investment

Although any kind of FDI involvement in or with a non-privatized Slovene company implied privatization, we need to distinguish between:

(*a*) 'Direct FDI privatization', where the existing local non-private ownership was transformed into private foreign ownership (the direct sale is in the form of a 'share deal' or 'asset deal'); and
(*b*) 'Indirect FDI privatization', where the existing local non-private ownership was not transformed but merely combined with the new private foreign (majority) ownership ('joint venture acquisition' in a 'share deal' recapitalization or 'asset deal' form).

The major characteristic of 'direct FDI privatization' is the definite privatization of the acquired company with a possible immediate impact on efficiency improvement. In the case of 'indirect FDI privatization', the socially/state-owned part of the company has yet to be privatized.

Direct sales – also referred to as trade or negotiated sales – as a privatization method have some other advantages: first, they can be applied in conditions of undeveloped capital markets. Second, they do not require extensive and costly governmental administration. Third, the lack of adequate and reliable accountancy information (financial audits) does not prevent transactions of this kind from being completed; yet it does, to a certain extent, have a restraining impact by delaying their completion. Finally, direct sales can act as a relatively uncomplicated way of attracting strategic investors (buyers), who are usually existing partners of the target company seeking to acquire a controlling share in it. From this perspective, direct sales may be viewed as an effective means of acquiring fresh infusions of capital, technology and management expertise.

For companies undergoing privatization and new company owners in the post-privatization period, direct sales to strategic foreign investors are particularly suitable where new technology, markets, know-how and input supplies from a strategic investor are essential for the firm's survival and further development. Direct sales are also attractive where capital infusions by strategic domestic or foreign investors can improve the target company's operations. In the privatization process, direct sales are relevant mostly to medium and large-sized companies.[2]

The complexity of each direct sale transaction, however, has two important consequences:

1 The process itself is not very transparent to outsiders because many details of the transaction have to be kept confidential for competitive reasons. It is necessary to expect some public scepticism when such transactions are completed, especially if strategic investors/buyers are from overseas.

2 Because of a lack of expertise, experience and adequate staff, target companies are not capable of adequately executing the transaction, hence favouring the strategic buyer.

As Slovenia is a relatively small economy which, during privatization, faced a chronic shortage of capital, it was almost impossible to find domestic strategic investors, especially in the case of large target companies. Therefore direct privatization sales of medium and large-scale companies were mostly linked to foreign strategic investors. All large trade sale privatizations in the non-financial corporate sector (the Tobacco Factory of Ljubljana, the Paper Mills at Količevo and Vevče) were realized with foreign strategic investors. This made direct sales implicitly a politically sensitive issue.

Direct sales can take the form of share or asset deals. In the former, the strategic investor acquires a majority (control) equity share. A similar goal can be achieved through an asset deal, that is, by buying the target company's assets, which are then used by the strategic investor/buyer to conduct business in the new wholly foreign owned or joint company. Under Slovenia's privatization law, the sales of a company's shares or assets were specifically defined as possible methods of ownership transformation.

The asset deal has a number of advantages for the foreign investor:

- The object of the purchase is to obtain only those assets that are necessary for a certain activity; the remainder stays in the existing company.
- The employees remain on the books of the old company; therefore, the new owner does not encounter over-employment problems.
- The transaction by-passes the possibility of taking on hidden responsibilities (including environmental) and losses, especially in the absence of a proper financial audit or revision of the company's legal status.
- The assets purchased are newly evaluated: this results in a higher depreciation rate and has tax implications.
- In the case of a joint venture acquisition, if the local assets make up the domestic partner's equity contribution to a joint venture, the newly invested foreign capital ('purchasing money') does not go to the appropriate state agency, as in the case of a straightforward acquisition, but stays within the newly formed company (Business International, 1991).

From a foreign investor's viewpoint, the joint venture acquisition (hereafter JV acquisition) realizes exactly the same purposes as the asset deal. The JV acquisition is a joint venture (with the status of a new legal person) formed by an existing local company (its assets) and new capital invested by a strategic foreign investor.

Table 10.1 shows that JV acquisitions were the most popular form of FDI in Slovenia during the privatization period. Apart from the aforementioned advantages of asset deals for strategic foreign investors, which also hold true for JV acquisitions, executives of sample firms specifically mentioned the relevance of the Slovene legislation, which they described as best suited

Table 10.1 Types of FDI in Slovenia (sample of 47 firms)

Type of foreign investment	Percentage distribution
JV acquisition	66
Partial or entire acquisition	4
Greenfield joint venture	30
Total	100% (= 47 firms)

Source: Rojec, M., 1993.

to the JV acquisition form; until mid-1993 JV acquisitions were also seen as the least risky solution in the Slovene environment. Prior to 1994, the liberal character of Slovene company law established a firm legal basis for asset deals and JV acquisitions, which enabled foreign investors to deal exclusively with preferred assets and local partners to retain the proceeds arising from sales to foreign investors.

A major concern of foreign investors involved in JV acquisitions is to prevent the unprivatized local partner of a joint venture (holding company) from being acquired by a competitor. This concern is usually resolved in a contractual clause giving foreign investors a pre-emptive right on the local partner's share in the joint venture.

From the target company's viewpoint, the major problem with asset deals and JV acquisitions is that, frequently, only the best parts of the company are privatized by strategic (foreign) investors, while issues of over-employment and dubious claims rest to a large extent with the unprivatized partner.

General trends in foreign investment and privatization

The new, more liberal FDI legislation adopted at the end of 1988, together with a favourable attitude towards FDI and market-oriented economic reforms, brought about a breakthrough in FDI to Slovenia. At end 1988, only 28 joint ventures were in existence with $114.3 million of invested foreign capital; by the end of 1997, the number of foreign investment enterprises (enterprises with a 10 per cent or higher foreign equity share) had increased to 1044 and the value of invested foreign capital to $2194 million.

We outline below the main features of FDI in Slovenia:

- Most FDI to Slovenia comes from Austria (30.7 per cent of stock at end 1997), Germany (13.5 per cent), Italy (13.6 per cent) and France (8.3 per cent). The high ranking of Croatia (13.8 per cent) is mainly the consequence of inherited investments in the former Yugoslav Federation, while France's high ranking is almost exclusively due to Renault's investment in car manufacturing. The aforementioned countries account for more than 74 per cent of FDI stock in Slovenia (see Table 10.3).
- Manufacturing industry, with a 45 per cent share of total FDI stock at end 1997, is by far the most important recipient of FDI in Slovenia, followed by financial and business services and trade. In the manufacturing sector, FDI is concentrated in chemical products, electricity supply, automobiles, paper and machinery and equipment (see Table 10.4).
- A typical foreign investor in Slovenia is a small-to-medium sized company from one of the neighbouring European Union countries. The FDI stock is concentrated in a relatively small number of large FDI pro-

Table 10.2 Flows, stocks and changes in stocks of inward FDI[1] in Slovenia in 1993–98

	1993	1994	1995	1996	1997	1998
Values in US$ million						
End-year stock						
Total value[2]	954.3	1 331.0	1 744.7	1 934.3	2 194.0	n.a.
Equity and reinvested profits	709.7	965.7	1 200.1	1 261.8	1 551.5	n.a.
Net liabilities to foreign investor	244.4	365.3	544.6	672.5	642.5	n.a.
Change of end-year stock						
Total value	n.a.	376.6	413.7	189.6	259.7	n.a.
Equity and reinvested profits	n.a.	256.0	234.4	61.7	289.7	n.a.
Net liabilities to foreign investor	n.a.	120.9	179.3	127.9	−30.0	n.a.
Annual inflow	112.6	128.1	176.0	185.5	320.8	165.0
Growth rates in %						
End-year stock: total value	n.a.	39.5	31.1	10.9	13.4	n.a.
Annual inflow	1.4	13.8	37.4	5.4	72.9	−48.6

[1]FDI = 10% or higher foreign equity share (According to OECD benchmark definition of FDI).
[2]Total value = equity + liabilities to foreign investor – claims to foreign investor.
n.a. = not available
Source: Bank of Slovenia

Table 10.3 Distribution of end-year stocks of inward FDI in Slovenia by investing countries in 1997 (US$ million and %)

| | 1997 | | Change of share | |
	Value	Share	1997/93	1997/96
Total	2194.0	100.0		
Austria	673.1	30.7	+11.7	−3.6
Croatia	302.9	13.8	−19.0	−4.7
Germany	296.5	13.5	−3.6	−0.6
France	181.6	8.3	−4.8	+0.8
Italy	170.9	7.8	−2.4	+0.4
UK	117.4	5.4	+5.0	+0.7
USA	107.0	4.9	+4.5	+3.6
Netherlands	85.9	3.9	+3.3	+1.9
Switzerland	82.8	3.8	−0.2	+0.3
Spain	56.2	2.6	+2.6	0.0
Denmark	38.1	1.7	+0.6	+0.6
Gibraltar	21.6	1.0	+1.0	+1.0
Czech Republic	10.0	0.5	+0.5	−0.6
Other countries	50.0	2.3	+0.8	+0.3

Source: Bank of Slovenia.

jects with European multinationals.[3] Among foreign acquisitions, some of the largest have included acquisitions of the Ljubljana Tobacco Factory by Reemtsma (Germany) and Seita (France), the insulating construction materials producer Novoterm by Pfleiderer (Germany), the car producing factory Revoz by Renault (France), the electro-thermal apparatus producer ETA Cerkno by EGO (Switzerland), two paper mills, Vevče by Brigl & Bergmeister (Austria) and Količevo by Saffa (Italy) and the car tyre manufacturer Sava Kranj by Goodyear (US).

• Most significant FDI projects have been realized by foreign investors with a long experience of doing business in Slovenia (see Rojec, M. 1993).

Case studies of foreign privatizations

In the absence of a systematic database on foreign privatizations in Slovenia, and given the small number of realized foreign privatizations, the only relevant analytical method is the case study. For the purpose of our analysis we selected three cases of direct sales on the following premises:

• The evidence presented in the case studies is intended to help Slovene officials, managers and consultants deal with strategic foreign investors. Hence, the case studies express predominantly the seller's perspective;

Table 10.4 Distribution of end-year stocks of inward FDI in Slovenia by industries in 1997 (US\$ million and %)

NACE industries	1997 Value	1997 Share	Change of share 97/94	Change of share 97/96
Total	2 194.0	100.0		
15 Food and beverages	53.2	2.4	+1.3	+0.5
16 Tobacco products	40.0	1.8	n.a.	n.a.
17 Textiles	35.2	1.6	+1.0	+1.1
21 Pulp, paper & paper products	127.0	5.8	−3.2	−1.6
24 Chemicals & chemical products	167.4	7.6	+1.7	+1.8
25 Rubber & plastic products	40.7	1.9	+0.8	+0.7
26 Other non-metal mineral products	66.2	3.0	+0.9	+0.5
27 Basic metals	29.2	1.3	+0.7	+0.3
29 Machinery & equipment	120.0	5.5	−0.5	+0.1
31 Electrical machinery & appliances	41.9	1.9	+0.3	+0.5
32 Radio, television & equipment	25.2	1.1	0.0	−0.3
33 Medical & precision instruments	26.8	1.2	+0.6	+0.1
34 Motor vehicles and trailers	137.1	6.2	−4.5	−1.0
40 Electricity, gas, steam	225.1	10.3	−12.0	−3.4
50 Sale & repair of motor vehicles	90.3	4.1	−0.2	+0.3
51 Wholesale trade	202.0	9.2	+1.8	+0.4
52 Retail trade and other repairs	69.0	3.1	+0.6	+0.6
63 Supporting & auxiliary transport	39.6	1.8	+1.1	+1.2
65 Financial intermediation	296.8	13.5	+5.7	−3.6
74 Other business activities	230.1	10.5	+3.6	+1.4
92 Recreation, culture & sport	21.6	1.0	+1.0	−0.1

Source: Bank of Slovenia.

they are based on the experience and views of the managers who actively participated in the transactions on the sellers' side.

• The cases concentrate on the preparatory, negotiating and contracting phases of the transactions. The post-privatization phase and longer-term restructuring impact of the transactions on the acquired companies and host country are only partially addressed.

• The case studies are not methodologically integrated. The basic objective was to give interviewees scope and discretion to ensure that all relevant aspects of the transactions were covered.

The three case studies differ in many respects and cover a variety of direct sale modalities:

1 Case studies A and B are from the paper industry, whilst case study C is in the manufacturing of insulating construction materials (glass–wool).

2 Strategic foreign investors are from Germany, Austria and Italy, the major investing countries in Slovenia.

3 In cases A and B the major 'local' motivation for a direct sale was to gain access via strategic foreign investors to fresh capital, knowledge and markets, to help target companies improve their viability and to restructure and increase development potential. In case C, the major motivation of the domestic parent company was to sell off its subsidiary in order to restructure and strengthen its mainstream activities.

4 Case studies B and C are share deals; Case Study A is an asset deal.

5 The roles of the Agency for Privatization and the Development Fund differed in all three cases:

- In Case A, both the Agency and the Fund had yet to be established and no institutional framework for foreign privatizations was in place at the time.
- In Case B, prior to the transaction, the Fund took over the ownership position in the target company.
- In Case C, the Agency and the Fund provided financial and legal assistance to the domestic seller company.

Case study A: Privatization through a joint venture company – asset acquisition of a Slovene paper mill by an Austrian strategic investor

Abbreviations:

PMApo:	target company/socially-owned paper mill
PMALtd:	new joint venture company
FIA:	strategic investor from Austria
LBA:	local bank/PMA's major creditor
VU:	value unit

PMApo is one of the oldest and largest companies operating in the Slovene paper industry.

PMApo had faced problems since 1987. In 1988, the company purchased its second coating machine. This investment directed its activities in the production of high quality papers: yet, at the same time, it put the company in a very difficult financial position. Other factors also contributed to PMApo's unfavourable performance: Slovenia's worsening economic situation, rising disproportions between input and output prices, a drastic fall in sales, over-employment and the management's inability to adjust the company's business policy to prevailing financial and market conditions.

PMApo was restructured through a joint venture set up with an Austrian strategic foreign investor (FIA), who acquired a majority share (51 per cent) in the newly created company. The specific feature of this 'asset drop down' transaction was the simultaneous financial restructuring (debt to equity) conducted by the Slovene bank (LBA), itself a major creditor of the target company.

The end result of the deal was the creation in 1990 of the joint venture company PMALtd jointly owned by the foreign investor FIA, the leading creditor LBA and the socially owned company PMApo (whose only asset on the balance sheet was its share in the joint venture with the foreign investor).

Ownership restructuring of PMApo

The structure of the target company's liabilities and equity prior to the acquisition showed a very unstable financial situation; only half of the company's fixed assets were financed by equity capital, whilst its current liabilities greatly exceeded the level of its current assets. Because of a lack of working capital, the company was under serious threat of going bankrupt.

In 1989 another potential foreign investor made a preliminary financial review of PMApo's operation, but an in-depth study of measures for its financial recovery was not prepared until 1990 by a British consultancy firm.

The main characteristics of the approach to the company's financial and ownership restructuring included:

1 LBA took the initiative and control over the implementation of the privatization programme.
2 As the target company and its workers' council did not see any other alternatives to bankruptcy, the decision-making process of the company's workers' council was carried out promptly.
3 The backbone of the privatization programme was the involvement of FIA, a paper-producing company from Austria, as a guarantee for the successful implementation of the proposed programme.

The objective of the restructuring programme was to establish a new joint venture company, PMALtd, in which the socially-owned PMApo would participate with its business assets. Other investors in the new company would include the strategic foreign investor, FIA, as majority shareholder and the bank, LBA.

Preparatory steps

Before entering into the joint venture agreement, the target company PMApo was required to establish a desired asset structure, that is to clear its balance sheet of all non-business assets.

For this purpose, PMApo created two additional limited liability companies, PMa and PMb (they were established out of PMApo's existing non-core-business production programmes). This provided a first step in preparing the desired balance sheet. In the next step PMApo transferred part of its assets and liabilities, including all non-business assets, to the newly established companies. Over VU 19.7 worth of PMApo's assets were assigned to the two newly established companies, together with capital stock of VU 6.7 and VU 12.9 of its liabilities.

After this operation, PMApo's capital stock (equity) decreased from a book value of VU 51.2 to VU 44.5, and its liabilities from VU 122.1 to VU 118.2. When all PMApo's non-business assets (apartments, holiday homes, etc) had been transferred to the newly established companies PMa and PMb, the book value of PMApo's social capital stock decreased further by VU 15.8 in the preparatory stage.

There is little doubt that such restructuring was necessary as it enabled better comparability of the foreign investor's contributions with the value of core-business assets of the target company.

The efficiency of the two additional established companies PMa and PMb, burdened with non-business assets, is questionable. Of more than 200 employees involved in these non-core-business production activities, the newly created companies kept only 140. A full assessment of the efficiency of both companies will only be possible after the privatization of the social capital stock.

Motives behind the foreign investor's entry

Prior to the establishment of the joint venture company PMALtd, PMApo and FIA had no cooperation links. This is unusual for Slovenia, where the majority of FDI projects are based on previous trade cooperation. The first contact between PMApo and FIA took place at a London seminar attended by their respective managers.

FIA chose to invest in PMApo mainly because of the perceived investment opportunity. It was estimated that PMApo's equipment met FIA's requirements and that the acquisition would be cheaper than establishing a new paper mill at home. One important factor in FIA's decision was PMApo's share in the markets of the former Yugoslavia, Germany and Italy.

The establishment of the joint venture company PMALtd

The second step in the implementation of the privatization programme was the establishment of the new joint venture company PMALtd by the following shareholders: the target company PMApo itself, FIA and LBA. The target company PMApo contributed its total assets to the new joint venture while the new company PMALtd took over all of PMApo's liabilities.

In calculating FIA's necessary cash contribution for the acquisition of a 51 per cent share in the joint venture, the net asset value of target business assets was taken into account. PMApo's share in the new company was calculated on the basis of the new book value of its business assets, stated in the balance sheet before the formation of the joint venture.

	(in VU)
Book value of PMApo's assets	162.7
less losses	−15.5
	146.2
less liabilities	−118.2
Net value of PMApo's assets	28.0

The stated capital of the newly created PMALtd was VU 91.4. The target company PMApo invested the book value of its assets and acquired a 30.6 per cent share. FIA contributed VU 46.6 in cash and acquired a 51 per cent share, while LBA invested VU 16.8 and acquired an 18.4 per cent share. From the foreign investor's view point, the transfer of a substantial portion of PMApo's liabilities into the joint venture company was merely a technical operation.

By transferring most of PMApo's liabilities to the new joint venture company, the bank LBA protected its outstanding claims. LBA swapped its outstanding claims in the amount of VU 16.8 into equity. Part of the outstanding loan claims of LBA and other creditors were fully settled by cash contributions paid in by the foreign investor.

The original target company PMApo has since become a shell company, holding a share of VU 28 in PMALtd. The remaining social capital stock in the target (holding) company PMApo has yet to be privatized.

PMALtd's business performance

Since the elimination of non-core-business assets through the establishment of PMa and PMb, PMALtd has concentrated its business activities on producing the same product range as the strategic foreign investor FIA. To optimize and specialize production, PMALtd and FIA have split up their production activities according to market and types of production. The joint venture PMALtd is therefore an integral part of its Austrian parent company.

In the process of restructuring, PMa and PMb took over 140 workers and PMALtd the remaining 1172. Today PMALtd employs less than 500 people. Over-employment in the target company resulted in drastic reductions in the workforce following the acquisition.

The stated capital of PMALtd (VU 91.4) generated VU 190.5 of total revenue in the first year after the acquisition. The gross operating profit was VU 18.1, while earnings before interest and taxes amounted to VU 7.4.

The company's business performance seems to meet the expectations of FIA. The efficiency of PMALtd almost equals that of the foreign parent company and exceeds that of its Hungarian subsidiary.

Export and import structure of PMALtd

In the first year of operations, PMALtd exported 60 per cent of its total production. The following year, this share increased to 72 per cent, thus exceeding the projected 70 per cent target.

More than 90 per cent of PMALtd's exports are to Western markets: 34.5 per cent are destined for Italy, 27.4 per cent for Germany, 5.4 per cent for Great Britain, 4.8 per cent for India and 3.1 per cent for Austria. FIA does not impose any export restrictions on PMALtd. PMALtd has exclusive selling rights in Slovenia and other parts of the former Yugoslavia, as well as in CEE and some developing countries (India, Cyprus, Malaysia and Egypt).

As much as 90 per cent of inputs needed in PMALtd's production are imported (but not supplied by FIA). Such a high share of imported inputs is due to the lack and high prices of appropriate inputs on the domestic market.

Summary

The strategic foreign investor's entry through a typical joint venture transaction allowed PMApo, which faced bankruptcy, to survive. The sale of the majority share in the target company to the strategic (foreign) partner also facilitated its further development. PMALtd's performance improved as a result.

In initiating the transaction, the LBA bank as main creditor of the troubled socially owned company PMApo played an important role.

The basis for determining the ownership structure in the newly established joint venture company PMALtd was the book value and not the business valuation of PMApo. Data included in income statements, especially those that have yet to be audited, cannot be considered as a reliable indicator of the company's market value. The use of the balance sheet before acquisition as a basis for the transaction price for determining PMApo's share in PMALtd shows that there were practically no negotiations about the price of the assets contributed by PMApo.

Case study B: Acquisition and recapitalization of a Slovene cardboard-producing mill by an Italian strategic investor

Abbreviations:

PMB: target company/cardboard producing paper mill
FII: potential buyer/strategic investor from Italy
FIA: potential buyer/strategic investor from Austria
LBB: local bank/PMB's major creditor
VU: value unit

Case study B is an example of a direct sale in which PMB elected to attract a strategic majority foreign investor through the acquisition of existing social capital and immediate additional investment. This was one of the first cases in which the Development Fund assumed the ownership position in the target company prior to the transaction. In other words, from a legal point of view, the Fund acted as seller of PMB's equity capital.

This acquisition was characterized by complex transactions involving the acquisition of part of the social capital transferred to the Fund, additional investment in (recapitalization of) PMB and an attempt to (partially) rehabilitate the local bank, which was jeopardized by the concentration of its portfolio in PMB.

Pre-privatization

PMB was established in 1928 and nationalized in 1947. At the time of privatization, the company was a medium-sized producer of cardboard, with 640 employees, 90 000–100 000 tonnes of annual production and annual sales of between VU 70 and VU 84. Thirty per cent of cardboard production was sold in Slovenia and the remainder was exported

A major increase in PMB's production capacities occurred in 1979, when newly installed capacity raised the daily cardboard production from 100 to 400 tons. The investment in new capacities was almost entirely financed by foreign credits and a contractual joint venture with a foreign partner. The amount of foreign liabilities originating from this investment was approximately VU 120. These liabilities were regularly serviced until 1982. From then on, the repayment became an increasingly heavy burden for PMB. Before the acquisition, PMB's liabilities amounted to VU 70.

Before privatization, PMB faced severe problems, including undercapitalization and indebtedness.

- Given the unfavourable financial situation at the time, little investment or production modernization took place in PMB in the last years before privatization: all efforts were concentrated on resolving the financial problems (servicing of debts and financing of current operations). PMB was no longer able to service its foreign liabilities.
- This situation worsened in the aftermath of the loss of the former Yugoslav market. The 'forced' reorientation to Western markets would, given the intensive competition in the cardboard industry, have to be linked to additional investments and intensified contacts with potential buyers abroad. PMB was unable to implement this new orientation.
- During the general rescheduling of foreign credits in 1982, a major part of PMB's foreign credits was transferred to the local bank LBB. As a result, LBB had a considerable part of its total credit potential in PMB. This weakened LBB's portfolio structure/diversification.

In this situation, the management of PMB turned to strategic foreign investors with a view to recapitalizing the company with a majority foreign share.

Potential buyers and their motives

The cardboard industry has shown characteristics of growth and stability. In the past few years European cardboard consumption has grown at 3 per cent annually.

Two trends have emerged which favour cardboard producers:

- the substitution within the packaging industry of non-recyclable materials (plastics) with recyclable 'environmentally friendly' forms of packaging, such as cardboard;
- within the cardboard industry, a shift from the virgin-fibre-based grades towards recycled-fibre-based grades (waste paper);
- increasing pressure from environmentalists and legislators to reduce the absolute volume of packaging used.

With a forecast 2.6 per cent average annual growth rate in European cardboard consumption between 1990 and 2000, the industry is expected to experience a consolidation phase over the next few years, which will provide considerable opportunities for low-cost efficient producers.

The European cardboard industry is dominated by four major manufacturers, two of which were bidders for PMB; FII from Italy, who won the bid, is the second largest European cardboard producer; the unsuccessful bidder from Austria, FIA, is Europe's largest.

The Italian firm is a diversified industrial holding company operating in five sectors. In the cardboard sector, it concentrates on the production of coated cardboard based on recycled paper. Besides Italy, it has cardboard production capacities in Spain and Tunisia (as a minority shareholder) and in Slovenia. FII's main objectives include a broader presence on international markets as a leading company in the cardboard and packaging sector with the accent on environmentally friendly materials and products.

The bidder's motivation was driven by strategic considerations:

- With the acquisition of PMB, both potential buyers would increase their market shares, enter new markets and manage paper mills in new geographical areas, with resulting improvements in the efficiency of distribution and the quality of services.
- The cardboard industry was experiencing stable growth and had good prospects.
- 'Oligopolistic reaction': the two bidders are leading companies in the European cardboard industry and follow 'each other's footsteps' to retain (FIA) or conquer (FII) the position of market leader.

Background to privatization

As early as May 1990, PMB signed a letter of intent with FII about recapitalization; discussions with FIA were intensified in early 1991.

In September 1991, at the request of the Agency for Privatization, PMB announced a public tender in which interested buyers were invited to submit offers for the company's recapitalization. Only FIA reacted with a concrete proposal.

During negotiations, FIA offered to acquire a 76 per cent equity share in PMB through recapitalization, that is through additional (immediate and future) investments in PMB.

The agency, upon whose approval the transaction depended, viewed the offer as unacceptable for two reasons:

1 First, although the offer took into account the assessment of the company's value made by the licensed appraiser (VU 58.8), the implicit value contained in the offer was much lower (only VU 27.9);
2 Second, the transaction was deemed unacceptable from a legal point of view: for each instalment of credit repayment, a write-off of social capital was envisaged.

Negotiations

PMB's management asked the Agency to participate actively in the realization of the transaction. At the same time, an additional valuation was carried out as the premise on which the previous valuation had been based had changed. The new valuation reduced the fair market value of PMB from VU 58.8 to VU 50.

In its new offer, FIA changed the structure of the transaction whereby 76 per cent ownership would result from the acquisition of 51 per cent of the social capital of PMB and immediate recapitalization amounting to VU 42.8. FIA was also prepared to grant special rights to minority shareholders (including priority shares and the nomination of a minority shareholders' representative on the supervisory board) and invest in fixed assets not less than VU 56 over the next five years. The offer was rejected because PMB's implicit value arising from the restructuring would only have been VU 41.2 or VU 44.1 (a 76 per cent ownership share would be achieved through the acquisition of VU 23.9, a 54.3 per cent share in the ownership and the immediate recapitalization of VU 39.9), while other elements of the offer remained unchanged. FIA finally rejected the Agency's restructuring package.

Denationalization and restitution

One important reason for putting an end to the public collection of offers was the adoption of the Denationalization Law in early 1992. The new law allowed the preliminary restitution of an ownership share in PMB to its former owner, who had been expropriated in 1947. Negotiations with the former owner's successors resulted in their acquiring a 28 per cent equity share in PMB.

The following criteria were used in calculating the former owner's share in PMB:

(*a*) The ratio between production volumes in 1940–46 and 1991: assessed at 6.08–7.00 per cent;

(*b*)   The ratio between the number of employees in 1940–46 and 1991: assessed at 41.03–54.45 per cent;

(*c*)   The ratio between the values of the nationalized property in 1947 and of the net assets in 1991: assessed at 28.19–33.32 per cent.

The former owner's weighted average share ranged between 25.10 and 31.59 per cent. The final decision of 28 per cent was the outcome of negotiations.

To enable the direct sale of PMB to a strategic foreign investor, two transfers of PMB's social capital took place prior to the transaction:

- In accordance with the Denationalization Law, 28 per cent of company's social capital was transferred into the ownership of the successors of PMB's former owner.
- PMB's Workers' Council elected to transfer 72 per cent of PMB's social capital to the Fund. Of that, the Fund put aside 14.4 per cent for free distribution among employees in line with the forthcoming privatization legislation, while the remainder was put up for sale to a strategic foreign investor.

Through these transfers the Fund became the 100 per cent owner of PMB. In other words, from a legal point of view, the Fund acted as seller of PMB's equity capital. From a legal view point this was the only way to conduct the transaction, as the law requested the Fund to act as seller of the social capital.

Letters of invitation

The reopened bidding process for the acquisition of PMB – based on a restricted tender via letters of invitation – was prepared and managed by the Agency and the Fund. Letters of invitation for 'proposals of acquisition' of PMB were sent to FII and FIA, and to the other Italian company, whose offer had interrupted the first round of negotiations with FIA. Only FII and FIA submitted offers.

The invitation letter structured the proposed transaction in detail and requested that the offers be presented in a single document to increase comparability. Potential bidders were told that the submitted proposals should cover:

1   The financial and commercial arrangements through which a bidder would take a stake in PMB. Potential buyers were requested to structure the transaction according to the following guidelines:

- Purchasing up to 57.6 per cent, but not less than 50 per cent of the total capital from the Fund; a 14.4 per cent share of capital would remain temporarily within the Fund for subsequent distribution to employees in line with the forthcoming privatization law;

- Raising additional capital of an amount not less than VU 28. Investors were also encouraged to put forward proposals about immediate investment in fixed assets and repayment of PMB's liabilities before maturity;
- The final ownership share of the foreign partner should not be less than 76 per cent.

2 Bidders were requested to identify steps to be taken to modernize PMB's plant and equipment as well as guarantees for the implementation of these plans. They were also asked to quantify their proposed level of capital investment over the next five years and its potential impact on PMB's financial structure.

3 Plans for employment and training. PMB's management, the Agency and the Fund were aware of the needs to reduce PMB's employment in some areas and establish a modern organizational structure. The invitation letter asked the bidders to address those issues, including indemnities for redundancies. The invitation letter stressed that proposals which would create new jobs in Slovenia would be particularly welcomed.

A continued commitment to the development of staff, the maintenance of employment and the improvement of employees' standards were another important area. Potential investors were also required to address training issues.

4 A scheme for minority shareholders' rights. The invitation letters contained specific requests about minority shareholders' rights:

- The minority share should be dominated in DM or other hard currencies and be fully transferable, upon proper notification, to PMB;
- The minority shares should be entitled to a minimum 5 per cent fixed dividend out of the company's declared net profit in a given year, before any distribution of dividends to ordinary shareholders took place;
- The minority shares should have a proportional right to profits and net worth, as well as voting rights at shareholders' meetings;
- The holders of minority shares should have the option to sell their shares back to the company at any time within one year of the acquisition. The company should have an irrevocable obligation to buy back minority shares for cash, provided a written notification was issued 90 days in advance.

Selection of the winning bidder

The bidding committee, consisting of representatives of PMB, the Agency, the Fund and the local bank LBB, made the following assessment of submitted offers:

Criteria	Maximum possible no. of points	No. of points attributed to	
		FII	*FIA*
Price offered	30	30	0
Immediate additional equity investment (recapitalization)	20	0	20
Medium and long-term investments in fixed assets	10	10	0
Employment policy[1]	10	10	10
Protection of minority shareholders	10	10	10
Financial, market and production status of buyer	5	5	5
Premature repayments or assuming credit liabilities of PMB	5	not applicable	
Other criteria up to the committee's discretion	10	not defined	
Total no. of points	100	65	45

[1]Additional employment; retaining existing levels of employment; reduction of employment (indemnities).

On signing the final contract, FII became the 76 per cent owner of PMB. The major elements of the final contract included:

- the implicit value of PMB at VU 114.8;
- the immediate purchase of 57.6 per cent of the equity capital;
- the immediate increase in equity capital (recapitalization) by the additional investment of VU 28;
- over the next 4 years following the conclusion of the final contract, the investment of VU 78.4 in fixed assets.

Summary

The overall assessment of the domestic actors involved in the sale of PMB – PMB's management and employees, the Agency and the Fund – is generally positive thanks mainly to the competitive bidding approach. The alliance with a strategic foreign investor has considerably improved PMB's development and business potential. The Agency and the Fund's involvement addressed the broader host-country perspective, namely the issue of PMB's privatization and financial restructuring linked up with the partial rehabilitation of LBB. From a financial viewpoint, the sale of PMB meant the acquisition of its equity capital as well as its recapitalization. From a strategic point of view, the sale included a development and investment plan to accelerate the company's restructuring. In the first phase, this plan envisaged investments which would increase PMB's production capacity to 150 000 tons annually. The plan also envisaged training programmes for local staff and company executives.

For the Fund, the transaction meant the inflow of additional foreign capital. The employees obtained an ownership share in accordance with the privatization law and special minority shareholders' rights. The state 'revived' an operational enterprise which can fulfill its tax and other obligations and contribute to the development of the local community. The management team retained their positions and have the option of additional training. The former owners received compensation for their nationalized assets.

Case Study C: Acquisition of a Slovene glass-wool producing company by a foreign strategic investor

Abbreviations

MCC: local parent company/the seller
GWC: glass-wool producing target company
FI1: first potential buyer/strategic foreign investor
FI2: second potential buyer/strategic foreign investor
VU: value unit

Case study C consists of a direct sale in which a local socially owned parent company, MCC, sold an 80 per cent share in its subsidiary GWC to the strategic foreign investor FI1. The agency and the Fund provided financial and legal assistance in an advisory capacity. In all other previous cases, the Fund had assumed ownership prior to the transaction by taking over the socially owned capital of a target company.

Reasons behind the sale to a strategic foreign investor

The parent company MCC is one of the two pharmaceutical companies in Slovenia which, besides pharmaceuticals, has also developed spas, cosmetics, herbs and glass-wool insulation materials. The glass-wool producing company GWC was set up as a limited liability company, 100 per cent owned by MCC.

MCC's major motivation for selling GWC was to strengthen its mainstream pharmaceutical programme.

It was thought that the foreign investor would provide GWC with:

- new technologies;
- increased output capacity via additional investments;
- access to European markets through its sales network.

On the whole, GWC was in a sound financial condition and well managed. The company's major production and marketing characteristics are listed below.

Strengths

- An adequate technological level for coping with international quality requirements and ecology standards. Key production lines were controlled and operated by a computer system. Modern technology and qualified management and technical structures conducted the production process with minimal interruptions.
- The proximity of a major raw material base. The main production inputs were provided locally.
- Favourable projections of market growth. GWC had no competitor on the local market and there were strong indications of rising demand abroad, particularly in Germany. The potential increase in demand for insulation materials was projected at 5–10 per cent annually.

Weaknesses

- The target company's operations were well below optimal standard capacity.
- The high sensitivity of production costs to electrical energy prices.
- A low technological development potential to keep pace with new techniques in the production process.
- A high dependence on markets in a restricted geographical radius from the company's headquarters (given the voluminous nature of the product).

Pre-privatization activities

Corporatization of the target company

The first step undertaken by MCC after the strategic decision was made to attract a foreign investor was the corporatization of MCC's non-core business activities; three limited liability companies (Spas, Cosmetics and GWC) were set up. All production programmes related to pharmaceuticals remained within the domain of the holding company MCC, enabling it to concentrate on the development of core business (pharmaceuticals). GWC was created via the asset drop-down technique, whereby the new company took over all employees engaged in glass-wool production and all related assets and liabilities.

Assessment of the target company

GWC was assessed by an independent licensed appraiser, using international valuation standards and principles. The objective was to assess the value of the business as a going concern, which would serve as a basis for negotiations with a potential foreign buyer. Two valuation methods were applied: net asset value under the assumption of a going concern and discounted future cash flow. According to the net asset method, the fair market value was determined at VU 49.6 while the discounted future cash flow method resulted in a slightly higher figure of VU 52.6. Both values were also suggested by the appraisers as a minimal acceptable price (VU 49.6) and the highest expected price (VU 52.6) were put forward.

Instead of submitting a memorandum of the main business, financial and legal aspects of the company, the seller, MCC sent the valuation report to potential buyers. This 'cemented' the ceiling price of GWC.

The early disclosure of the valuation report to potential buyers clearly weakened MCC's negotiating position.

Privatization plan and identification of potential buyers

Both parent and subsidiary viewed the potential buyer FI1 as a more favourable partner, particularly in terms of potential technological inputs. Potential buyer FI2, a large multinational enterprise, was considered more 'unpredictable'.

The company's desire to retain a more flexible position and greater degree of autonomy, if the acquisition was made by a buyer of similar size, was the prevailing perception.

The privatization plan prepared by advisers to the Agency and the Fund was accepted by MCC's management. The key issues included:

- a formal, transparent and competitive bidding procedure with at least two potential bidders;
- MCC would offer for sale not less than 80 per cent of its holdings in GWC;
- the evaluation committee (members from MCC, GWC and the Agency/Fund) would select the winning bidder on the basis of bidding criteria set forth;
- a competitive bidding procedure would determine the transaction price;
- the timing of the acquisition process would be dictated by the seller.

Potential buyers

No public announcement for invitations to bid was made. When the Agency and the Fund stepped in as coordinators of the bidding process, a detailed acquisition discussion with FI1 was already in place. The advisory team's objective was to introduce at least one additional potential buyer before serious negotiations with all interested partners began.

FI1 is a company with annual sales of VU 2100. Its main production range consists of prefabricated building materials and insulation materials. Its market strategy is to gain a significant market share in construction materials, particularly in glass–wool in the CEE countries.

FI2 is an industrial group with annual sales of VU 31 000 with extensive international experience. FI2 concentrates on products derived from or using glass fibres. The insulation industry contributes 13 per cent to FI2's total sales. In the insulation industry and in a number of other products, it ranks as a world market leader.

Both bidders were driven primarily by the newly emerging German building construction market. The demand for construction materials was expected to rise by 10 per cent annually, that is approximately 6 percentage points above the normal average annual increase. The location of GWC in Slovenia offered additional advantages: glass–wool, as a voluminous good, reduces the transport radius. From Slovenia, both the German and Balkan markets could be easily accessed.

Negotiations

The first round of discussions with both bidders was devoted to clarifying their proposals and explaining the seller's priorities. The core question related to the ceiling price that FI1 and FI2 were willing to pay for GWC. Information that a new factory of similar size in the potential buyers' home countries would cost up to VU 140 was a valuable but not completely reliable indicator. A complementary indicator consisted of financial projections of the target company put forward by the bidders in their offers. Discounted future cash flows from FI1's projections over the next five years suggested a transaction price between VU 70 and VU 75.6.

Both bidders were informed that the seller intended to complete the transactions as soon as possible and that a decision would be based on the bidders' first written improvements of their offers. This was intended to prompt the bidders to disclose their upper price limits before the second round of negotiations.

During the second round of negotiations both bidders only marginally improved their offers. The decision to choose FI1 was reached unanimously.

Summary

First, the parent company MCC originally intended to enter into a joint venture by retaining a substantial minority share. This complied with the widely used practice of foreign investors to offer, in the first instance, the joint venture formula to an acquisition candidate. The advisory team from the Agency and the Fund proposed a different approach to MCC, namely the direct sale of an 80 per cent share in GWC. The arguments against the joint venture concept were twofold: first, there would be no immediate cash proceeds from the divestment; second, being locked in with a large minority share with questionable potential returns might not be an attractive proposition for the seller.

The only reason why MCC remained a 20 per cent shareholder in GWC was related to the issue of potential ownership participation of GWC's employees in the company. Second, the basic philosophy of the transaction was the divestment of non-core-business of the parent company, which is now concentrating on the development of its core pharmaceutical activities. Third, targeting two serious bidders was crucial for the successful completion of the transaction. If one of the key criteria for the assessment of the transaction was the implicit price of the target company, then the difference between the initial and final prices was a positive outcome. Fourth, the direct sale of GWC was critically dependent on the cooperation of its management, who paid particular attention to keeping the target company's workforce informed of post-transaction employment conditions. The privatization of GWC was not linked to any lay-offs, which certainly contributed to the smooth completion of the deal.

Conclusions

The privatization process of trade and industry in Slovenia has been completed. Around 1500 socially owned companies were reorganized into public limited companies or limited liability companies and subsequently privatized. At the end of 1998, the social capital of a smaller number of companies (less than 2 per cent of total social capital), which did not undergo ownership restructuring by themselves, was transferred to the Development Corporation of Slovenia, which will either privatize or liquidate them. What remains to be privatized are the financial institutions (banks and insurance companies) and public utilities.

This is a new situation which puts the possible lessons of the case studies into a different perspective. The lessons are no longer relevant for the government agencies faced with a need to manage a mass privatization process embracing hundreds of companies. The lessons are, however, still relevant for new private owners/companies facing the need to attract strategic foreign investors, and the government privatizing a small number of (relatively) large financial institutions and public utilities.

Notes

1 The management of socially owned companies often had little incentive to initiate the sale of the company's shares or assets.
2 See Jašovic 1993; Korže and Simoneti 1992; K. Szabo 1992.
3 The principal exception is Goodyear's acquisition of the car tyre manufacturer Sava Kranj.

11
Foreign Investment in Estonia

*Philip Hanson**

Introduction

'Generally speaking, F[oreign] D[irect] I[nvestment] continues to follow natural resources – where these are abundant – and progress in transition.' Thus the authors of the European Bank for Reconstruction and Development (EBRD)'s *Transition Report 1997* (p. 125) comment on FDI flows to ex-communist countries. Estonia has little in the way of natural resources. Moreover, the country's economic circumstances, when communist rule collapsed and it regained its independence, were unfavourable in the extreme. By Central European standards, however, it has been extremely successful in attracting foreign investment. This has been attributable largely to its 'success in transition'.

At mid-1997, according to the central bank's bulletin (Eesti Pank 1997) Estonia had a stock of foreign direct investment (FDI) of 14.8 billion Estonian kroons (EEK). At the average exchange rate of first-half 1997 that is equivalent to about $1.1 billion, or some $731 per head of population. At the start of the year, Estonia's FDI stock per head of population was the third highest, after Hungary and the Czech Republic, of any of the 25 ex-communist countries monitored by the EBRD (EBRD 1997, p. 122–6). True, Estonia, with its population of just over 1.5 million, is the smallest of the 25; and the total inward FDI involved was, by world standards, puny. True, too, the per capita amount is a reminder of how modest foreign investment in all the so-called transition economies has been. None the less, this lead was more than an arithmetical quirk. It reflected an excellent economic-policy performance against the odds.

---

* The author is indebted to Kitty Ussher of the Economist Intelligence Unit and Joe Palacin of Daiwa Bank for some useful background information.

The Estonian authorities have created a strong currency, brought inflation under control, created an institutional environment that is hospitable to investors, both foreign and domestic, proceeded resolutely in liberalizing and opening the economy, and conducted privatization in ways that facilitated the entry of foreign firms as strategic investors.

In 1997 the thoroughgoing nature of Estonian reforms received clear international recognition. The country was included in the shortlist of five potential 'first-wave' ex-communist EU entrants, with whom accession negotiations would begin in 1998. And Estonia received an improved, investment-grade sovereign credit rating from Standard & Poor's of BBB+ on 11 December (*Eastern Europe Daily Brief*, 17 December 1997).[1]

In this chapter the development of this favourable environment will first be reviewed, under the headings of financial stabilization, the building of market institutions and liberalization. Then the growth and composition of foreign investment will be described.

In 1996–97 private sector capital inflows have extended well beyond FDI, to include substantial amounts (by the standards of very small ex-communist economies) of foreign portfolio investment (FPI) and other foreign investment (chiefly bank loans). The mid-1997 stock of these, EEK 7.12 billion, and EEK 17.31 billion, respectively, actually exceeded the FDI stock. This diversification of types of capital inflow is problematic. On the one hand, it reflects Estonia's increased integration into global markets and provides additional financing. On the other hand, FPI and loans are more volatile and much more easily reversed than FDI; they introduce a new element of potential instability into Estonia's development. This increased potential volatility will also be considered.

After that, the factors that may be influencing foreign investment will be reviewed. Surveys of the motivations of foreign investors in the ex-communist countries tend to show them asserting that it is these countries' domestic markets that are the main magnet. If that were true in the case of Estonia, the stock of foreign-owned capital there would soon reach a modest ceiling.[2]

Clearly, the future growth of foreign investment in this tiny country will depend on its own continued openness and, even more, on the likelihood, and likely timing, of its accession to the European Union. This point is emphasized in the final section, on prospects.

Financial stabilization

In June 1992, contrary to the advice of the International Monetary Fund (IMF), the Estonian government broke completely with the ex-Soviet rouble area and established its own currency, the kroon. Until that time, all fifteen ex-Soviet states had continued to rely on the rouble both in settlements between themselves and internally. Various surrogate and parallel currencies were already circulating in the former Soviet Union alongside the rouble, including the US dollar and, in Estonia, the Finnish mark. But none of them was an exclusive legal tender replacing the rouble and endowed with all the properties of money.

Kroon emission is based on a currency board system. The currency is pegged at 8 kroon (EEK 8) to the Deutschmark. It is a legal requirement that the monetary base (in this case, all kroon currency in circulation plus the reserves, both obligatory and excess, of commercial banks with the Bank of Estonia (Eesti Pank) be at least 100 per cent backed by foreign currency, and freely convertible into DM at the pegged rate.

The central bank may not lend to the government or normally to the commercial banks. If the public finances (central plus local government budgets plus off-budget funds such as the social insurance and health insurance funds) are in deficit, this can be financed by borrowing from the commercial banks, but not from the Eesti Pank. The central authorities have only limited scope for discretionary monetary policy (in so far as reserves at any time exceed the obligatory backing for the kroon): the money supply adjusts automatically to changes in international reserves, inflation should in principle be curbed by the consequent changes in imports, exports and other external transactions.

Estonia's experience with its currency board has so far been favourable.[3] Inflation, measured by December–December changes in the consumer price index, was 95 per cent in 1992 and 29 per cent in 1995; in 1997 it was down to about 11 per cent; and it was expected to be of the order of 8 per cent in 1998 (EBRD 1995; Eesti Pank 1996a; Eesti Pank 1997; *Eastern Europe Daily Brief*, 17 Dec. 1997). In general, the kroon has come quite quickly to be seen as a strong currency. As well as being freely convertible within Estonia, it is now held and traded offshore, mainly in Scandinavian countries.

Financial stability in general is helpful for foreign investors. There is another advantage for foreign investors that is specific to a currency board. The kroon is a very close substitute indeed for its reserve currency, the Deutschmark. For foreign companies – and this includes banks as well as non-financial corporations – there is very little currency risk attached to activities in Estonia. To be precise: the kroon may change in value against the pound, dollar or other currencies in line with the DM (the kroon appreciated nearly 10 per cent against the dollar between 1994 average and 1995 average, and depreciated against the dollar in 1997); its value against the DM can change only if, by new legislation, the Estonian currency board regime is seriously modified or abandoned. That possibility can never be ruled out, but the Estonian authorities have so far been able to maintain confidence in the currency-board system. Doubts arose on the financial markets for a time in late 1997, after the 'Asian flu' market turmoil associated with East Asian financial collapses; but the kroon had at the time of writing (end-1997) overcome them.

The credibility of the present regime is indicated by the close tie that can be observed between DM and EEK interest rates. In 1995 inter-bank deposit rates in the two countries, for example, moved closely together, with the EEK rate typically showing a margin of about 0.6 per cent on the DM rate (Eesti Pank 1996a). The margin had been reduced by late 1997.

The determination with which Estonian policy-makers have pursued financial discipline began to be rewarded by a recovery of output that started in the course of 1995. EBRD assessments put GDP growth at 6 per cent in each of the two years, 1994 and 1995. Eesti Pank estimates, and those of the Estonian statistical office, are less favourable. But Eesti Pank economist Urmas Sepp has acknowledged that the official figures effectively track the decline in the state sector better than they do the overall performance of the economy (Sepp 1995b). Eesti Pank figures for growth in 1996 and 1997, even so, are 4.0 per cent and about 8 per cent (the latter an early estimate). The EBRD figures suggest that GDP in 1995 was 73 per cent of its 1988 level, 1988 being the last year of officially recorded growth. Extrapolating with Eesti Pank figures from this EBRD measure, one arrives at a 1997 figure of 81 per cent. By contrast, the Russian officially measured GDP was little more than 50 per cent of its 1989 level and, in 1997, only just flattening out from a seven-year fall.

Thus, Estonia, like Poland, the Czech Republic, Slovakia and Slovenia, has exhibited a strong and relatively early output recovery following a brisk and tough-minded application of stabilization policies.

The building of market institutions

In their 1995 *Transition Report*, EBRD economists devised scores on an array of 'transition indicators' for the 25 countries in which the bank operates. The scores are expert ratings on a scale from 1 to 4 of each country's status (not its rate of progress) in large-scale privatization, small-scale privatization, enterprise restructuring, price liberalization, trade and foreign-exchange liberalization, banking reform, development of security markets and other non-bank financial institutions, and the extent and effectiveness of legal rules on investment (EBRD 1995, p. 11).

Estonia's overall score worked out at 29 out of a possible 36. For comparison the Czech Republic and Hungary scored 31 each, Poland 30, Slovenia 28, Russia 23, and Ukraine 20; Turkmenistan, bringing up the rear, scored 10. Subsequent, more differentiated, assessments by the EBRD, as well as by the IMF and, in 1997, the EU Commission, in its *Agenda 2000* assessment of candidates for accession, continue to place Estonia amongst the leaders in market reform.

These comparative assessments would, I think, be supported by most businessmen, journalists and academics familiar with the region as a whole. The reshaping of economic institutions has been more rapid and purposeful in Estonia than in most other ex-communist countries.

Of particular importance for foreign investment, in this reshaping of institutions, is the approach to large-scale privatization, the liberalization of prices and external transactions, the development of securities and other financial markets and the legislation affecting investment.

Large-scale privatization has relied heavily on a German Treuhand-like approach of preparing and selling off batches of state enterprises to strategic investors, with no special advantages received – generally speaking – to domestic investors. This was supplemented by a voucher programme of mass privatization, to secure popular consent to privatization as a whole and facilitate restitution to pre-communist owners and their descendants; but in the domain of large-scale privatization vouchers have been used chiefly to acquire minority stakes, initially in dispensed holdings (Purja 1994; Sepp 1995b).

The main channel for initial privatization of large state enterprises to strategic investors was a series of six offers for sale of Estonian enterprises, beginning in 1992 and ending in early 1995, and resulting in the sale of over 250 enterprises. There was some criticism of this privatization strategy on the grounds that the business of preparing and then offering enterprises for sale, with specific conditions laid down in each case, necessarily involved substantial state activity, and tended to be slow and bureaucratic (*Financial Times*, 13 December 1994, p. 2). However, the back of the large-scale privatization task was broken in less than four years from Estonia's achievement of independence, and less than three years from the start of the programme; there were on average six bidders for each of the last batch of 43 enterprises (*OMRI Daily Digest*, 10 February 1995), suggesting a successful marketing exercise and competition amongst bidders; and the upshot is a predominance of strategic, 'outsider' ownership for large Estonian companies, as distinct from dispersed ownership or a dominance of pre-privatization workers and managers, as in Russia. These circumstances augur well for effective corporate governance and company restructuring; and foreign investors were able to participate in privatization from the start.

The EBRD estimated that by mid-1997 about 67 per cent of GDP was being generated by the private sector. Some analysts put the figure somewhat higher, at 75 per cent. Small-scale non-farm privatization developed quite swiftly, as has been the case in all ex-communist countries where governments did not impede it. Large-scale privatization, always a more tricky reform to carry through, was largely complete in 1997 except for utilities. At the end of 1997 plans for the privatization of telecommunications, energy and (in part) railways were well advanced. Land privatization, as elsewhere, has been slower. It has been complicated by questions of restitution to former owners and by delays in the development of land registration (EBRD 1997, p. 167).

The development of financial markets has been strongest in the banking sector, and somewhat late, but sound, in securities markets. That is the logical outcome of a transformation process in which priority has been given to achieving a strong currency and a rapid transfer of assets to strategic investors. The regulation of banking has been tough and effective. By early 1996 there were 16 licensed banks, down from 42 in 1992. One of the 16 was a branch of the Finnish Merita Bank. Capital adequacy and liquidity measures in 1995–96 were well above those required by the central bank, and the volume of overdue loans was small (Eesti Pank 1996b, pp. 58–9). There was a further tightening of requirements in 1997 (Eesti Pank 1997; *Eastern Europe Daily Brief*, 17 Dec. 1997). Thus, up to mid-1996, most flows of funds within the Estonian economy went through the banks, and the general state of the banking system was good, for a transforming economy. At mid-1997, when the securities market was already developing strongly, the volume of domestic credit outstanding was equivalent to 22 per cent of GDP (EBRD 1997, p. 168). That suggests a healthy development of the banking system.

For foreign investment to continue to play a major role in future, the development of securities markets was desirable. Markets for corporate control need, for the sake of corporate governance, to be contestable, and therefore liquid and transparent. The character of Estonian privatization did not at first facilitate this, since large companies were privatized chiefly to strategic investors. However, over-the-counter trading in corporate securities developed in 1995. The Ministry of Finance has set up the Central Register of Securities, which is operated by the private (bank-owned) Estonian Central Depository (EVK in its Estonian acronym).

The Tallinn Stock Exchange (TSE), founded in April 1995, opened for business at the end of May 1996 (*Moscow Times*, 1 June 1996, p. 11), with an initial list of five publicly quoted companies, in the form of five leading Estonian banks. By 9 August 1997 there were 10 companies on the TSE Main List, six on the Secondary List and another eight on the 'Free Markets' – a transitional arrangement allowing a company's shares to be traded ahead of its expected listing. The TSE's market capitalization, turnover and prices (as measured by the TALSE index) all rose very strongly in its first two years of operation. Market capitalization at mid-1997 was equivalent to about 26 per cent of GDP (EBRD 1997, p. 168). Stock market turnover at that time was around 40 per cent of GDP: that suggests a high level of liquidity for a new stock market in an ex-communist country.[4]

A review of the organization and regulation of the TSE (Lustsik 1997) also suggests that the stock market is well regulated and transparent, as well as comparatively liquid, for an ex-communist country. Its rapid growth has been assisted by a rapid growth of foreign portfolio investment (FPI). Lustsik cites an assessment, probably for mid-1997, that a third of shares listed on the TSE are held by non-residents. It should be stressed, also, that the TSE is primarily a market for private-sector securities; because of the working of the currency board, there is only a very small market for government paper. Finally, there has been some integration of Baltic states' securities markets, in part by Estonian acquisitions of Latvian and Lithuanian brokerage houses. That enhances the TSE's attractiveness to foreign investors.

The Estonian economy is therefore hospitable to both foreign direct investment and foreign portfolio investment. In 1995 net foreign portfolio investment was negative, and the gross inflow small (Eesti Pank 1996a, p. 33). As the securities market has developed, at a time when international financial markets were greedy for emerging market securities (1996 and the first eight months of 1997), this situation has turned around. The net inflow in 1996 and the first half of 1997 was of the order of $200 million (Eesti Pank 1997). The gross inflow was substantially larger.

Legislation relevant to investment is in general well developed. Laws regulating the issue of securities and the activities of investment funds are in place. Companies and land can be owned by foreigners (though land privatization is not yet complete), and profits can be freely repatriated. In 1997, on EBRD estimates, 30–40 per cent of assets in the industry and services sectors were owned by non-residents – mostly Finnish, Swedish and Russian. Most foreign investment does not require government approval. Companies can be created in less than two months. Records of share transactions are available with a lag of a month. The texts of laws are published in full, and there is access to the details of important court decisions. Public officials are considered to be appointed on merit, and to be accessible. Investment disputes can be got to court within a year. A law on commercial pledges came into effect in 1997, filling one of the few serious remaining gaps in commercial legislation (EBRD 1995, pp. 110–11; EBRD 1997, pp. 167–8).

To sum up this section: the institutional framework for a well-functioning market economy in general, and in particular for a well-functioning capital market, is largely in place.

Liberalization: prices, trade and competition

In a very small economy, such as that of Estonia, decontrol of domestic prices and outputs will achieve relatively little without a matching liberalization of external transactions. If the economy remains largely closed, monopoly will be widespread, impeding improvements in efficiency. Barriers to imports of goods and services would, in addition, limit export performance. All in all, such a setting would be unattractive to foreign investment.

In fact, Estonian policy-makers adopted from the start a policy of openness. They dismantled tariffs and quotas, relying on an undervalued exchange rate for the kroon to provide initial protection for domestic producers. At the same time, prices were, with a few exceptions, swiftly decontrolled.

The result is that most of the Estonian economy is subject to competition, while a relatively low-wage and moderately high-skill workforce makes the country potentially attractive as a base for production. The average wage in May 1997 was $250 a month at the exchange rate. (In local purchasing power it was probably more of the order of $500.) The Estonian statistical authorities distinguish between the open and sheltered sectors of the economy – roughly, between tradable and non-tradable production. Some prices in the sheltered sector, such as housing rents and public transport, have continued to be regulated. On the whole, however, some three-quarters of the economy seems to have prices governed by international competition (or the threat of it). Prices in the sheltered sector are influenced indirectly by international market forces, through competition for inputs with the open sector.

Inflation continues to be well above West European levels, despite the generally stabilizing effect of the currency board. This is because the initial undervaluation of the kroon, plus the fixing of the kroon–Deutschmark exchange rate, led to a shift of kroon prices in the open sector towards world levels (accompanied by improvements in product quality that may be inadequately captured in price indices, entailing some underestimation of 'real' output growth). This is, in principle, a once-for-all adjustment, after which inflation should be low.

However, Estonian economists have argued that productivity rises in the open sector, exceeding those in the sheltered sector, tend to raise the real supply price of labour, and thus costs, in the latter, and that this adjustment process should be expected to take several years (see e.g. Kuus 1997).

The opening of the Estonian economy has been followed by a dramatic reorientation of its trading patterns, especially so far as the trade-partner composition of merchandise transactions is concerned. Comparisons with the pre-August-1991 era of incorporation in the USSR are somewhat strained, because the Estonian economy was then dominated by decisions made in Moscow. But in the late Soviet era more than 90 per cent of cross-border merchandise flows were with the rest of the USSR (UN/ECE 1992). By the first quarter of 1996 Finland had become the main trading partner, accounting for 30.2 per cent of merchandise trade turnover. Russia was second (15.0 per cent), followed by Sweden (10.1 per cent) and Germany (8.0 per cent). (Eesti Pank 1996b, p. 40). Roughly this pattern of partner-composition of trade continued into 1997 (Eesti Pank 1997).

The product-composition has also changed substantially, as Estonia's cross-border flows of merchandise have come to be determined by the market rather than the Moscow plan. The leading export product groups in 1996–97 were food, clothing and footwear, machinery and equipment, timber and paper, and chemicals (the order of importance shifted around even in the 18-month period for which data are available at the time of writing). Together they accounted for just over three-fifths of the total. On the import side, machinery and equipment, foodstuffs, chemicals and clothing and footwear were the leading groups (Eesti Pank 1996b, p. 39; Eesti Pank 1997, statistical appendix).

The appearance of several product groups amongst the leaders on both the import and the export side suggests that intra-industry trade is developing. This seems indeed to be the case. A substantial element in machinery and clothing flows, in particular, is made up of items imported for processing and then re-exported. According to Eesti Pank (1996b, p. 39), around 21 per cent of Estonian exports in 1995–96 were based on imports processed under contract. This element in Estonia's trade has become particularly important with respect to machinery and clothing exports. There are also substantial entrepot trade flows, e.g. of Russian goods, including Russian newsprint and Russian cars, that pass through Estonian ports and warehouses; these are not included in the figures reviewed here (Eesti Pank 1997).

Some of this contract processing for export is linked with FDI, and consists of flows between parent companies and affiliates. But part of it is the result of arms' length contracting to non-affiliates – particularly in the clothing industry. Swedish and Finnish companies, especially, were quick to seize on the fact that Estonian 'light' industry (textiles, clothing and footwear) typically had skilled workforces and, quite often, up-to-date machinery.

The arm's-length contracting is, in Estonia's case, a significant practical alternative, from a Western company's point of view, to direct investment into Estonia. In other words, some of the considerations of business strategy that might prompt FDI into the country may lead, in some industries, to contracting to non-affiliates instead. The Estonian economy stands to gain in this fashion two of the benefits that are derivable from FDI itself: access to export markets and some transfer of managerial and technical know-how.

In June 1995, Estonia signed a 'Europe Agreement' with the European Union. This was in effect an association agreement, putting Estonia (along with the other Baltic states) in the same position as the Visegrad countries and Slovenia with respect to entry to the EU. The free trade agreements between Baltic and Scandinavian countries already give Estonia, with Sweden's accession to the EU, a very close association with the EU. In general, however, the prospect of full EU membership is an important condition of Estonia's continuing to attract foreign investment. This is discussed in the last section of this chapter.

Growth and composition of foreign investment

In the past few years net foreign investment into Estonia has grown substantially. At the same time, as Table 11.1 illustrates, the amount of (net and gross) FDI declined in 1996–97, while that of other forms of foreign investment (FI) rose steeply.

The shift from FDI to other forms of foreign investment reflects two things. First, there is the ending of the main phase of large-scale privatization. Targeted as it was towards foreign strategic investors, Estonian large-scale privatization entailed relatively large FDI inflows while it lasted. From now on, apart from the impending privatization of some utilities, FDI inflows will depend on the creation of new foreign-owned firms or joint enterprises and on new investment in existing private companies. In fact, reinvested profits are already a substantial part of FDI. Second, there is the influence of institution-building and the (closely related) increase in Estonia's integration into world markets. For reasons suggested in the section on institution-building, above, foreign portfolio investment into Estonia was, if not impossible, constrained to extremely low levels before June 1996. Thereafter, what had been a net outflow turned into a much larger net inflow.

The figures in Table 11.1 are for net inflows. These are more interesting for the purposes of macroeconomic analysis than gross inflows, because they show how much, and in what form, foreign financing adds to domestic savings in facilitating the country's investment as a whole. They can also be of interest for meso-economic (sectoral level) analysis and commentary. For example, the net FDI figures for the second quarter of 1997 show the industrial sector accounting for almost three-quarters of net inward FDI, distribu-

Table 11.1   Foreign investment into Estonia, 1994–mid-1997 (net, EEK billion)

	1994	1995	1996	1997 I + II
FDI	2.8	2.3	1.3	1.1
FPI	–0.2	–0.3	1.8	0.8
Other FI	–0.4	0.8	3.5	1.2
Total	2.2	2.8	6.6	3.1

Note: The definitions are explained in the text. Gross inward FDI in the first half of 1997 was EEK 1.6 billion.
Source: Eesti Pank 1997.

tion for almost a third and financial services for just under a quarter; these, plus some lesser sectoral net inflows, are offset by net outflows from construction, real estate and transport and communications. The 'net outflows' may – and probably do – reflect the buying out of non-resident by resident investors, rather than a simple withdrawal of foreign assets, reducing total assets (Eesti Pank 1997). Gross inflow figures have tended to show industry taking a much smaller share of the total; adopting the net FDI perspective enables one to see how the balance of foreign financing assists capital accumulation at sectoral level.

In 1996 net FI of all kinds was equivalent to 8.7 per cent of Estonian GDP (Eesti Pank 1990b). That meant that foreign financing was on balance enhancing Estonia's investment capacity by close to 10 per cent of national income. Such a large net enhancement of domestic investment by foreign investors (large, that is, relative to the overall level of economic activity) is uncommon. To be more precise: it is a situation that has arisen for short periods in the histories of a number of countries when they have begun a process of particularly rapid growth from relatively low levels of per capita GDP. When it occurs, it is generally an indication that investment opportunities in that country are growing fast, and somewhat ahead of its current savings capacity. It also requires that conditions in the country in question are such as to inspire confidence in foreign investors. That seems to sum up the present (late 1990s) situation of Estonia. Meanwhile, household saving is about 10 per cent of disposable income, and the state runs at worst very small budget deficits, so there is a basis for domestic financing of productive investment in the longer run.

At the same time, there are risks in the late 1990s state of Estonia's external finances. The large capital account net inflow, while going chiefly to the private sector, is now composed, to a much greater extent than in 1992–95, of inflows that create future payment burdens (bond issues and syndicated loans, i.e. borrowing), that can easily stop and fairly easily go into reverse (borrowing in general and portfolio investment) and that generally bring with them no transfers of technology and management know-how, and no access to foreign marketing networks (borrowing and FPI again). In short, FDI brings with it little threat to a country's macroeconomic stability, and it provides considerably more than 'mere' investment finance. The other forms of foreign investment do indeed help to finance investment, but they do so in ways that can increase economic volatility and that bring less additional benefits than FDI does.[5] These and other questions of risk will be considered in the final section.

The stock of foreign capital in Estonia, and its contribution to the activities of particular firms and industries stem, of course from gross, not net, inflows. Here it is chiefly foreign direct investment that can be monitored in some detail. The stock of foreign capital of all sorts in Estonia in mid-1997, as reckoned by Eesti Pank from past financial flows (and not from adding up the foreign stake in companies' authorized capital) was EEK 39.21 billion or, at first-half 1997 exchange rates, about $2.9 billion (Eesti Pank 1997). That is equivalent to well over half the annual GDP when the latter is measured at the exchange rate, or rather under a half when GDP is converted to dollars at purchasing power parity. The stock of FDI was reckoned in the same source to be just over a third of this, at EEK 14.78 billion, or $1.1 billion.

The gross inflows have been concentrated in distribution and financial services, with the industrial sector lagging a little behind. In 1996 the broad sectoral breakdown percentage was distribution 36, financial services 27, industry 24 and other (construction, transport, communications, etc.) 13 (Eesti Pank 1997). This picture in one sense plays down the extent of foreign involvement in Estonian industry. Arms-length contract processing, as has already been mentioned, is of some importance in the clothing, engineering and chemicals branches of industry.

A few examples of FDI will give some indication of the variety of foreign firms' interests in industry and utilities in Estonia: cement production by Atlas Nordic Cement at Kunda, manufacture of ski equipment by HTM Sport, manufacture of electric cookers by Electrolux, textile production at Narva by Boras Wafveri, the manufacture of telephones by Elcoteq and Ericsson, stakes in telecommunications belonging to Telecom Finland and Sweden's Telea, and electricity generation by NRGE at Narva.

There appear to be three kinds of business rationale behind existing FDI in Estonia. First, there are major international consumer-brand-name companies that establish a presence in Estonia as a small part of a process of establishing their presence throughout central and eastern Europe: McDonald's and PepsiCo, for instance. Second, there are FDI activities in transport and communications in which Estonia is – or, it is hoped, will become – part of an interconnected Scandinavian-Baltic network: telecommunications, oil-terminal development, electricity generation. Finally, there are investments that can be justified, given the minimum efficient scale of operation, only to the extent that they create sources for supplying a wider market: HTM Sport or Boras Wafveri, for example, in the list given in the previous paragraph.

The size and growth of Estonian demand are not completely irrelevant in such investment decisions, but they are at best of secondary importance. What must matter more is that Estonia is seen as having reasonable location, communications, law enforcement, legislative and tax stability, together with the necessary skills and relatively low wages. More generally, it is thought to have a hospitable business environment.

Scandinavian, particularly Finnish and Swedish, firms have been the main direct investors in Estonia. Danish, Russian and German companies also loom quite large. Various sources give shares by country of origin for gross FDI inflows in particular periods; the ranking tends to shift around over time. The prominence of Scandinavian companies, however, is clear and stable. It fits well with the second and third of the business rationales suggested above. The first of these rationales, to do with brand-name consumer companies, would be consistent with FDI from anywhere in the developed world. It may well account for most of the US investment in Estonia.

Prospects

The prospects for foreign investment in Estonia may be somewhat different in the short and in the long run. In the short run (in this context, in 1998 and 1999) there are a number of adverse factors. In the longer run there are also some possible dangers, but onwards and upwards looks by far the likeliest scenario.

In the short run there are worries about the Estonian economy's capacity to sustain a current account deficit that is large by international standards: close to 10 per cent of GDP in 1997. The turmoil in world financial markets in late 1997, when events in Asia checked the rather over-heated pursuit of emerging-market securities, made Estonia's reliance on external financing look a little more precarious than it had before. As has already been noted, the rise of portfolio investment and private sector lending to Estonia had by then created the conditions for greater volatility than there would have been a year or two earlier – even if the current account deficit had then been equally large. The TALSE index duly fell, as did stock markets in emerging markets around the world. For a very small, open economy like that of Estonia, changes in its international credibility can have large economic results.

These problems are not, however, merely problems of the markets' ever-changing perceptions. Capital inflows in 1996–97 fuelled the growth of the broad money supply, pushing inflation higher than it would otherwise have been. Unusually, there began to be doubts about the sustainability of the EEK/DM exchange rate, despite the automatic-adjustment mechanisms built into the currency-board arrangement and its legislatively entrenched character. Resident holdings of foreign currency increased relatively to kroon 2 million.

On 7 November 1997 a policy memorandum was agreed between the Estonian government and the IMF, covering the 13 months to end-1998. Policies introduced in late 1997 were probably, if not IMF-dictated, at any rate IMF-compatible. They included a tightening of commercial banks' reserves and capital adequacy requirements, which contributed to a rise in interest rates; new controls on commercial-bank lending to municipalities (which, if unchecked, might have affected perceptions of sovereign credit risk, since the extent to which the national government might be ultimately responsible for settling municipal debt was unclear); the conversion of perhaps $50 million of state savings, hitherto held as deposits in commercial banks, into DM-denominated accounts and short-term securities held abroad (the budget surplus planned for 1998 would therefore not expand 2 million kroon, but would raise the savings by end-1998 to about $100 million. There were also two rather longer-term policies launched: a conversion of state pensions to a fully funded basis, to contain future general government deficits, and an acceleration of land reform (see *Eastern Europe Daily Brief*, 17 December 1997).

These measures contributed to a recovery of confidence in the kroon and, no doubt, to the upgrading – at a sticky time in world financial markets – of the Standard & Poor's sovereign credit rating of Estonia to BBB+, already mentioned at the start of this chapter.

GDP growth was expected in late 1997 to remain high in 1998: perhaps 8 per cent. But the current account deficit was expected to be slightly lower, as a percentage of GDP, in 1998 than in 1997. The general government balance, having been –1.8 per cent of GDP in 1996, was planned to be between +1.5 per cent and +2.0 per cent in 1998 (Bank of Finland, 'Russian and Baltic Economies', *The Week in Review*, 14 November 1997). Given that the country's debt levels are extremely low by world standards (external debt equal to about 12 per cent of exports, and domestic state debt tiny), it would take widespread and prolonged turbulence on world markets to set the Estonian economy back significantly in the near term.

In the longer run, there are two main sources of uncertainty: possible political instability in Russia and the negotiations over accession to the European Union. In fact, the two are connected, because EU membership is widely seen as providing some sort of security guarantee. Even Estonian managers, according to a 1995 survey, see the chief gains from EU membership for Estonia to be to do with security rather than the economy (Liuhto 1996).

It is the geopolitical fate of the Baltic states to be vulnerable to upheavals in Russia. The possibility of such upheavals cannot but provide an element of uncertainty in the background for all three of them. However, events in 1995–97 have shown that the Russian military in the late 1990s is exceptionally weak and disorganized, and also that the threat of a presidential election victory by either the communists or right-wing nationalists is less than it had seemed earlier. The settlement of border disputes between Estonia and Russia in 1997 provided additional encouragement.

It would help both the Baltic and the Russian economies if transit agreements on shipments to and from Russia through Baltic ports, and between Kaliningrad and 'mainland' Russia through Baltic states, could regularize and improve commercial cooperation. That, however, is a matter of secondary importance so far as Estonia's long-term growth prospects are concerned.

Entry into the European Union is a matter of negotiation, starting in 1998. It could come as early as 2000, but is highly unlikely to happen before 2003, after the EU has implemented monetary union and, with luck, coped with immediate problems arising from it. Delays over Estonian accession, or any major setback to accession prospects, will depress foreign investment. In the mean time, foreign investment is likely to be based on an assumption that Estonia has a high probability of becoming an EU member somewhere around 2003–05. The attractions, for a foreign investor, of the prospect of EU membership are clear – though perhaps a bit too far in the future to have much influence on FI flows in 1998–99.

It might seem at first sight that Estonian accession should present little difficulty. The country is tiny, and easily swallowed. It is already highly integrated, trade-wise, into the EU. Estonia does about 60 per cent of its merchandise trade with EU partners, and that trade (average of exports and imports) amounted in 1995 to just over 36 per cent of Estonian GDP (Kuus 1997). The currency is already pegged to the Deutschmark, the currency (at present) of the leading EU country and the country that is setting the pace for European Monetary Union (EMU). On some of the Maastricht criteria, at least, Estonia would qualify more comfortably for EMU than any of the present members of the EU. Its government balance/GDP ratio has been –1.8 per cent at worst and is expected to be a surplus (compare the Maastricht criterion of a ceiling of –3 per cent negative balances). Its government debt/GDP ratio is less than 10 per cent, against a Maastricht ceiling of 60 per cent.

The difficulties may be less apparent, but they are substantial. To begin with, Estonia's advantage of small size does not really help. Politically, admission ahead of Poland (about 39 million population), the Czech Republic or Hungary (each around 10 million) is unlikely. EU governments with interests in these Visegrad countries are too influential, compared to Estonia's Scandinavian chämpions. The EU governments, moreover, probably have to agree on reforms of the Common Agricultural Policy (CAP) and the structural funds (subsidies to poorer EU regions) before accession of the 'first-wave' entrants from the east can even be contemplated. That could take a long time.

Monetary union within the EU presents separate problems. On present EU timetables, the euro should become the sole legal tender in 11 EMU countries in mid-2002. Arrangements for the four present EU countries not in the EMU first wave have to be worked out: some form of monetary cooperation, currently labelled EMS (European Monetary System) II. The first-wave entrants from the east would probably come in initially as EMS II countries (non-EMU EU members). What that would entail is at present unclear.

Certainly there are two Maastricht criteria for EMU that would be problematic at present for all the potential members of a first-wave eastern enlargement: the formulae setting ceilings on interest and inflation rates. For reasons discussed above, it is not likely that Estonian inflation rates will quickly descend to levels close to those of Germany and other core EU member states. Some special arrangements might need to be negotiated – another politically contentious issue. If the interest and inflation criteria were not eased for the new would-be EU members, they would have to pursue especially restrictive monetary and fiscal policies to achieve the required levels, and this would be to the detriment, in the medium term, of their growth. (This argument is set out by Toivo Kuus: see Kuus 1997).

EU accession, however, also puts a premium on high growth over the next few years. This is because Estonia, like Poland and the other potential first-wave entrants, but to a greater degree, has per capita GDP levels that are far below the EU average; and, the greater the income gap, the greater the CAP and structural-funds reforms that would probably be needed to make their accession sustainable by the limited EU budget.

For all these reasons, Estonia's prospects of EU membership by any specified date are uncertain. That may not matter very much now so far as foreign investors are concerned, but it could begin to be a source of concern, inhibiting foreign investment, as negotiations proceed – and that refers not only to the formal accession negotiations but to the negotiations about structural reform within the EU.

In an uncertain world, however, future rates of foreign investment in any country are unavoidably subject to some uncertainty. The point of this last section has been to identify what look to be the main sources of uncertainty in this particular case. In general, Estonia's economic prospects in the longer term seemed in late 1997 to be good. The government's Economic Strategy 2002 document envisages GDP growth at an average annual rate of 6 per cent in 1999–2002. If this seems entirely plausible – and it does – that is because of the consistent and purposeful pursuit of reform policies in Estonia, alluded to at the start of this chapter.

Notes

1 The Estonian central bank's position was initially that the country's currency board arrangements, under which the government does not issue treasury bills or, in general, issue debt, made it unnecessary and even undesirable to seek a sovereign credit rating. However, debt issues by municipalities, for which the legal status of central-government ultimate liability was unclear, forced a rethink.

2 Not a fixed ceiling, admittedly, but one that would grow only in line with the growth of the Estonian economy. As it is, both Estonian economic growth and stock of FDI have grown faster than many observers expected. In early 1995 Kari Liuhto hazarded a projection of the stock of FDI in Estonia reaching perhaps EEK 15 billion at the turn of the century (Liuhto 1995). He did not say whether this projection was in current or constant prices, but it would not make a great deal of difference. His end-century 'possible' figure was practically reached by mid-1997,

at a growth rate of 53 per cent year over the three years from mid-1994. In that period, Estonian inflation has been substantial, but the kroon value of the FDI reflects (mostly) amounts denominated in foreign currencies and converted to kroons at the fixed rate of EEK 8 = DM1. Allowing for an average rate of inflation of 3 per cent a year in the main investing countries, the real growth of this FDI stock was about 48.5 per cent a year.

3 See Sepp (1995a) and Kuus (1997). Currency boards have generally been successful devices for restricting inflation. See Hanke and Walters (1992). Hong Kong and Singapore are among the more recent historical examples. Lithuania followed Estonia in adopting a currency board. In 1997, after a financial collapse and a resurgence of inflation, and operating with IMF advice and support, Bulgaria also took this route.

4 Author's calculation, as follows. July market turnover $150 million (Lustsick 1997). First-half GDP from Hagelberg 1997, converted to $ at the average of the first six months' exchange rates (EEK 13.48 = $1) from Eesti Pank 1997 statistical appendix, = $2.2 billion. Estimated 1997 GDP total = $4.5 billion. Twelve months' stock market turnover at $150 million/month = $1.8 billion.

5 To be fair, it should be added that loan finance may be used to import capital goods, and perhaps licences and other 'disembodied' know-how.

Bibliography

Acocella, N. (1995) 'Theoretical Aspects of Mutual Relations Between Foreign Direct Investment and Foreign Trade with Special Reference to Integration Theory', in R. Schiattarella (ed.) *New Challenges for European and International Business*, EIBA Conference, Urbino, vol. 1.

Adjubei, Y. (2000) 'Russia', in P. Artisien-Maksimenko (ed.) *Multinationals in Eastern Europe* (London: Macmillan).

Agarwal, J. (1997) 'European Integration and German FDI: Implications for Domestic Investment and Central European Economies', *National Institute Economic Review*, 2.

Aharoni, Y. and Hirsch, S. (1993) 'Developing the Competitive Potential of Technology – Intensive Industries – A Theoretical Framework and Policy Implications', *Development and International Cooperation*, 7 (16) June, p. 139.

Ahrens, J. and Meyer-Baudeck, A. (1995) 'Special Economic Zones: Shortcut or Roundabout Way Towards Capitalism', *Intereconomics*, March/April.

Alter, R. and Wehrle, F. (1993) 'Foreign Direct Investment in Central and Eastern Europe – An Assessment of the Current Situation', *Intereconomics*, May/June.

Andretsch, D.B. (1992) 'Privatization Plans of Central and Eastern European States', *Journal of Institutional and Theoretical Economics*, 148.

Artisien-Maksimenko, P. (2000) *Multinationals in Eastern Europe* (London: Macmillan).

Artisien-Maksimenko, P. and Adjubei, Y. (1996) *Foreign Investment in Russia and Other Soviet Successor States* (London: Macmillan).

Artisien-Maksimenko, P., Rojec, M. and Svetličič, M. (1993) *Foreign Investment in Central and Eastern Europe* (London: Macmillan).

Arva, L. (1994) 'Direct Foreign Investment: Some Theoretical and Practical Issues', NBH Workshop Series, Magyar Nemzeti Bank (National Bank of Hungary), July.

BBC Summaries of World Broadcasts, Weekly Economic Reports (SU/W0380, 21 April 1995; SU/W0411, 4 November 1995; SU/W0416, 5 January 1996; SU/W0470, 24 January 1997; SU/W0476, 7 March 1997).

Bajt, A. (1992) 'A Property Rights Analysis of the Transition Problems in the East', Economics Institute at the Law Faculty, Ljubljana, mimeo.

Baldwin, R. (1994) *Pan-European Trade Arrangements Beyond the Year 2000* (London: CEPR).

Banerji, K. and Sambharya, R.B. (1994) 'Vertical Keiretsu and International Market Entry: The Case of the Japanese Automobile Ancillary Industry', West Virginia University and Rutgers University (Camden campus), mimeo.

Bank of Slovenia (1994) *Monthly Bulletin*, Ljubljana, February.

Belka, M. *et al.* (1995) 'Enterprise Adjustment in Poland: Evidence from a Survey of 200 Private, Privatized and State-Owned Firms', London School of Economics, Discussion Paper 233, April.

Bellack, C. (1995) 'Austrian Manufacturing Abroad: The Last 100 Years', in R. Schiattarella (ed.) *New Challenges for European and International Business*, EIBA Conference, Urbino, vol. 2.

Best, M. (1990) *The New Competition* (Cambridge, MA: Harvard University Press).

BIKI (13 June 1996).

Black, H.C. (1979) *Black's Law Dictionary* (St Paul, MN: West Publishing).

Blomqvist, H.C. (1995) 'Intraregional Foreign Investment in East Asia', *ASEAN Economic Bulletin*, 11, 3.

Bochniarz, Z., Jermakowicz, W. and Meller, M. (1994) 'Development of Foreign Direct Investment in Poland', mimeo.

Böhm, A. and Korze, U. (1994) *Privatization Through Restructuring* (Ljubljana: Central and Eastern European Privatization Network).

Böhm, A. and Simoneti, M. (1993) *Privatization in Central and Eastern Europe – 1992*, CEEPN Annual Conference Series, 3 (Ljubljana: Central and Eastern European Privatization Network).

Borsos, J. (1995) 'Is Production Relocated from Finland to Neighbouring Transition Economies'? Discussion Paper, Helsinki School of Economics, December.

Brennan, G. and Buchanan, J.M. (1985) *The Power to Tax* (Cambridge: Cambridge University Press).

Buckley, P.J. and Casson, M.C. (1976) *The Future of the Multinational Enterprise* (London: Macmillan).

Buckley, P.J. and Casson, M.C. (1985) *The Economic Theory of the Multinational Enterprise* (London: Macmillan).

Business Central Europe, Automotive Survey, 8 February 1994.

Business Central Europe, various issues.

Business Eastern Europe, various issues.

Business International and Creditanstalt (1993) *1992 East European Investment Survey* (Vienna).

Business Week, various issues.

Buxman, R. (1992) 'Comment on Kirscher's Paper on Privatization in Eastern European States', *Journal of Institutional and Theoretical Economics*, 148.

Cantwell, H.C. (1991) 'A Survey of Theories of International Production', in C. Pitelis and R. Sugden (eds) *The Nature of the Transnational Firm* (London and New York: Routledge).

Caves, R.E. (1982) *Multinational Enterprise and Economic Analysis* (Cambridge: Cambridge University Press).

Central Statistical Office (1995) *National Accounts, Hungary, 1991–3* (Budapest).

Ceska, R., Charap, J. and Stern, R. (1993) *Small Privatization in Central and Eastern Europe* (Ljubljana: Central and Eastern European Privatization Network).

Charap, J. and Zemplinerova, A. (1993) 'Foreign Direct Investment in the Privatization and Restructuring of the Czech Economy', Workshop on Legacies, Linkages and Localities – the Social Embededness of Economic Transformation in Central and Eastern Europe, Berlin, 24–25 September.

Chou, T-C. (1988) 'American and Japanese Direct Foreign Investment in Taiwan: A Comparative Study', *Hitotsubashi Journal of Economics*, 19, pp. 165–79.

Cronin, R.P. (1992) *Japan, the United States and Prospects for the Asia-Pacific Century* (Singapore: Institute of Southeast Asian Studies).

Czinkota, M. (1991) 'The EC '92 and Eastern Europe: Effects of Integration vs. Disintegration', *Columbia Journal of World Business*, 26 (1).

D'Cruz, J.R. and Rugman, A.M. (1993) 'Business Networks, Telecommunications and International Competitiveness', *Development and International Cooperation*, 9 (17) December.

Dahlman, C., Ross-Larson and Westphal, L. (1985) *Managing Technological Development*, World Bank Staff Working Paper 717 (Washington: World Bank).

Deutsche Bundesbank (1995) 'Kapitalverflechtung mit dem Ausland', *Statistische Sonderveröffentlichung*, 10 (Frankfurt).

Dunning, J.H. (1986) 'The Investment-Development Cycle and Third World Multinationals', in Khushi M. Khan (ed.) *Multinationals of the South: New Actors in the International Economy* (London: Unwin Hyman).

Dunning, J.H. (1988) *Explaining International Production* (London: Unwin Hyman).

Dunning, J.H. (1991) 'Governments, Economic Organization and International Competitiveness', in L.G. Mattson and B. Stymne (eds) *Corporate and Industry Strategies for Europe* (Rotterdam: Elsevier Science).

Dunning, J.H. (1992) *The Theory of Transnational Corporations*, United Nations Library on Transnational Corporations, vol. 1 (London: Routledge).

Dunning, J.H. (1993a) *Multinational Enterprises and the Global Economy* (Wokingham, England, and Reading, MA: Addison Wesley).

Dunning, J.H. (1993b) *The Globalization of Business* (London and New York: Routledge).

Dunning, J.H. (1993c) 'The Prospects for Foreign Direct Investment in Eastern Europe', in P. Artisien-Maksimenko, M. Rojec and M. Svetličič (eds) *Foreign Investment in Central and Eastern Europe* (London: Macmillan).

Dunning, J.H. (1994) *Globalization: The Challenge for National Economic Regimes* (Dublin: Economic and Social Research Council).

Dunning, J.H. and Kundu, S. (1994) 'The Internationalization of the Hotel Industry: Some New Findings From a Field Study', Academy of International Business Northeast Regional Meeting, 10 Best Papers Proceedings, June.

Dunning, J.H. and Narula, R. (1994) 'The R&D Activities of Foreign Firms in the U.S.', *International Studies of Management and Organization*

Dunning, J.H. and Rojec, M. (1993) *Foreign Privatization in Central and Eastern Europe* (Ljubljana: Central and Eastern European Privatization Network).

Dynamika Prywatyzacji (1991–1993) Warszaw: Department Delegatur Analiz Prywatyzacji, Ministerstwo Przeksztacen Wlasnosciowych, no. 1–16.

Earl, J. and Estrin, S. (1996) 'Worker Ownership in Transition', in R. Frydman, C. Grey and A. Rapaczynski (eds) *Corporate Governance in Central Europe and Russia* (London: Central European University Press).

Economist, The, various issues.

EBRD (European Bank for Reconstruction and Development) (1993) *Economic Outlook 1993* (London: EBRD).

EBRD (1994) *Transition Report 1994* (London: EBRD).

EBRD (1995) *Transition Report 1995* (London: EBRD).

EBRD (1996) *Transition Report 1996* (London: EBRD).

EBRD (1997) *Transition Report 1997* (London: EBRD).

Economist Intelligence Unit (1994a) *Country Reports*, various countries, London, 3rd quarter.

Economist Intelligence Unit (1994b) *EIU Country Risk Service*, various countries, London, 3rd quarter.

Eesti Pank (1996a) *Eesti Pank Annual Report 1995* (Tallinn: Eesti Pank).

Eesti Pank (1996b) *Eesti Pank Bulletin*, 4 (23), June.

Eesti Pank (1997) *Eesti Pank Bulletin*, 7 (34), December.

Ekonomika i Zhizn' (1993, no. 36; 1994, no. 2; 1995, nos. 22, 44, 49; 1996, nos. 10, 19, 47).

Encarnation, D.J. (1993) 'A Common Evolution? A Comparison of United States and Japanese Transnational Corporations', *Transnational Corporations*, 2.

Enwright, M.J. (1994) 'Regional Clusters and Firm Strategy', Prince Bertil Symposium on The Dynamic Firm: The Role of Regions, Technology, Strategy and Organization, Stockholm, June.

Estrin, S. (1994) *Privatization in Central and Eastern Europe* (Harlow: Longman).

Estrin, S., Hughes, K. and Todd, S. (1996) '11 Case Studies of Direct Foreign Investment in Eastern Europe', CIS-Middle Europe Centre, London Business School.

European Commission (1994) *Trade and Investment*, Brussels: Directorate General for External Economic Relations, Unit for Analysis and Policy Planning, December.

European Information Service (1994) *Dossier Euro-East*, 24 May.

Facts about Hungarian Privatization, 1990 to 1992 (1993), *Privinfo*, 2, State Property Agency, Hungary.

Filatotchev, I. *et al.*, (1996) 'Buyouts in Hungary, Poland and Russia: Governance and Finance Issues', *Economies in Transition*, 4 (1).

Finance Eastern Europe, 21 April 1995.

Financial Times (1994) 'Survey on Poland', 18 March.

Financial Times, 28 November 1994; 9/10 December 1995; 10 February 1997.

Finansovye Izvestiya, 3 August 1995; 5 September 1995; 7 September 1995; 26 October 1995; 7 March 1996; 10 September 1996.

Freeman, N.L. (1994) 'Vietnam and China: Foreign Direct Investment Parallels', *Communist Economies and Economic Transformation*, 6.

Friedman, M. (1993) 'Still Singing Let It Be', *Business Week*, 7 June.

Fry, M.J. (1993) *Foreign Direct Investment in Southeast Asia: Differential Impacts* (Singapore: Institute of Southeast Asian Studies).

Frydman, R., Grey, C. and Rapaczynski, A. (1996) *Corporate Governance in Central Europe and Russia* (London: Central European University Press).

Gatling, R. (1993a) 'Foreign Investment in Eastern Europe', *Business International*.

Gatling, R. (1993b) 'Foreign Investment in Eastern Europe: Corporate Strategies and Experiences', research report written in association with Creditanstalt Bankverein, Economist Intelligence Unit, London.

Gatling, R. and Reed, J. (1992) 'Investing in Eastern Europe Starts with Basic Choice: Privatization or Greenfield?' *Business International*, 8 March.

Gerlach, M. (1992) *Alliance Capitalism* (Oxford and New York: Oxford University Press).

Goldman, M.I. (1994) *Lost Opportunity: Why Economic Reforms in Russia Have Not Worked* (New York: Norton).

Gomes-Casseres, B. (1994) 'Group Versus Group: How Alliance Networks Compete', *Harvard Business Review*, July.

Gomulka, S. and Jasinski, K. (1993) 'Privatization in Poland 1989–1993', London, mimeo.

Grey, C. (1996) 'In Search of Owners: Privatization and Corporate Governance in Transition Economies', *World Bank Research Observer*, 11 (2) August.

Gross, M. (1986) 'Ausländische Direktinvestitionen als Exportmotor – das Beispiel der ASEAN Länder', *Die Weltwirtschaft*.

Gruszecki, T. (1990) *Privatization – Initial Conditions and Analysis of the Government Programme (August 1989–mid-April 1990) (Warsaw: Stefan Batory Foundation)*.

Gugler, P. and Dunning J.H. (1993) 'Technology based Cross-border Alliances', in R. Culpan (ed.) *Multinational Strategic Alliances* (Binghamton, New York: International Business Press).

Guisinger, S.E. *et al.* (1985) *Investment Incentives and Performance Requirements* (New York: Praeger).

Gutman, P. (1993) 'Joint Ventures in Eastern Europe and the Dynamics of Reciprocal Flows in East-West Direct Investments: Some New Perspectives', in P. Artisien-

Maksimenko, M. Rojec and M. Svetličič (eds) *Foreign Investment in Central and Eastern Europe* (London: Macmillan).

Hagedoorn, J. (1993) 'Understanding the Rationale of Strategic Technology Partnering: Inter-Organizational Modes of Cooperation and Sectoral Differences', *Strategic Management Journal*, 14.

Hagelberg, R. (1997), 'Developments and Trends in the Estonian Economy', in Eesti Pank 1997.

Haggard, S. and Webb, S. (1993) 'What Do We Know About the Political Economy of Economic Policy Reform?' *World Bank Research Observer*, 8 (2), July.

Hanson, P. (2000) 'The Baltic States', in P. Artisien-Maksimenko (ed.) *Multinationals in Eastern Europe* (London: Macmillan).

Harrison, B. (1994) *Lean and Mean: The Changing Landscape of Power in the Age of Flexibility* (New York: Basic Books).

Havrylyshyn, O. and McGettigan (1999) 'Privatization in Transition Countries: Lessons of the First Decade', International Monetary Fund, *Economic Issues*, 18.

Helper, S. (1993) 'An Exit-Voice Analysis of Supplier Relationships', in G. Grabler (ed.) *The Embedded Firm* (London and New York: Routledge).

Hennart, J-F. (1991) 'The Transaction Cost Theory of the Multinational Enterprise', in Christos N. Pitelis and Roger Sugden (eds) *The Nature of the Transnational Firm* (London: Routledge).

Hiemenz, U. (1987) *The Competitive Strength of European, Japanese and US Suppliers on ASEAN Markets*, Kieler Studien 211 (Tübingen: Mohr (Siebeck)).

Hill, H. (1990) 'Foreign Investment and East Asian Economic Development', *Asian Pacific Economic Literature*, 4 (2).

Hirschman, A. (1970) *Exit, Voice and Loyalty* (Cambridge, MA: Harvard University Press).

Hood, N. and Young, S. (1993) 'TNCs and Economic Development in Host Countries', in S. Lall (ed.) *Transnational Corporations and Economic Development*, UN Library on Transnational Corporations (London and New York: Routledge).

Hunya, G. and Stankovsky, J. (1996) *Foreign Direct Investment in Central and East European Countries and the Former Soviet Union* (Vienna: Vienna Institute for Comparative Studies).

IMF Survey (1993) 11 January.

IMF, World Bank, OECD and EBRD (1991) *A Study of the Soviet Economy* (Paris: OECD).

International Financial Law Review (1991) International Mergers and Alliances.

International Herald Tribune (1994) 'Foreigners Cool to Seoul', 3 March.

International Monetary Fund (1993) *Balance of Payments Manual*, 5th edn (Washington, DC).

International Monetary Fund (1994) *Direction of Trade Statistics Yearbook* (Washington, DC).

Izvestiya, 3 March 1995; 24 February 1996.

Jackman, R. (1994) 'Economic Policy and Employment in the Transition Economies of Central and Eastern Europe. What Have we Learned?', *International Labour Review*, 133 (3).

Jansson, H. (1993) *Transnational Corporations in Southeast Asia* (Aldershot: E. Elgar).

Jašovic, B. (1993) 'Trade Sales of Enterprises to Strategic Investors – Experiences of the Republic of Slovenia', Agency of the Republic of Slovenia for Restructuring and Privatization, Ljubljana, mimeo.

Jenkins, R. (1991) 'The Impact of Multinational Firms on Less Developed Countries: Cross Section Analysis versus Industry Studies', in P. Buckley and J. Clegg (eds) *Multinational Enterprises in Less Developed Countries* (New York: St Martin's Press).

Jermakowicz, W. (1993) 'Economic Reform and Foreign Investments in Poland', in *Economic Transformation in Eastern Europe: Privatization and Foreign Investments* (Vienna: Bank Austria AG), pp. 103–25.

Jermakowicz, W. and Bochniarz, Z. (1991) 'Direct Investment in Poland 1986–1990', *Development and International Cooperation*, 7 (12), June.

Jermakowicz, W., Jermakowicz, E. and Konska, B. (1993) 'The Management Contract as a Restructuring Tool: The Polish Experience', in M. Simoneti and A. Böhm (eds) *The Industrial Restructuring in Central and Eastern Europe 1991* (Ljubljana: Central and Eastern Europe Privatization Network).

Johanson, J. and Vahlne, J-E. (1977) 'The Internationalization Process of the Firms: A Model of Knowledge Development and Increasing Foreign Market Commitments', *Journal of International Business Studies*, 8 (1).

Katz, B. and Owen, J. (1997) 'Optimal Voucher Privatization Fund Bids When Bidding Affects Firm Performance', *Journal of Comparative Economics*, 24.

Kline, J.M. (1992) 'The Role of Transnational Corporations in Chile's Transition: Beyond Dependency and Bargaining', *Transnational Corporations*, 1 (2), August.

Kobrin, S. (1993) 'Beyond Geography: Inter-firm Networks and the Structural Integration of the Global Economy', Wharton School Working Paper 93–10, William H. Wurston Center for International Management Studies, Philadelphia.

Kogut, B. (1983) 'Foreign Direct Investment as a Sequential Process', in C.P. Kindleberger and D. Andretsch (eds) *The Multinational Corporation in the 1980s* (Cambridge, MA: MIT Press).

Kogut, B. and Kulatihala, N. (1988) 'Multinational Flexibility and the Theory of Foreign Direct Investment', Reginald H. Jones Centre for Management Policy, University of Pennsylvania, Philadelphia, mimeo.

Kojima, K. (1978) *Direct Foreign Investment* (London).

Kojima, K. (1985) 'The Allocation of Japanese Direct Foreign Investment and its Evolution in Asia', *Hitotsubashi Journal of Economics*, 26.

Kojima, K. and Ozawa, T. (1985) 'Micro- and Macro-Economic Models of Direct Foreign Investment: Towards a Synthesis', *Hitotsubashi Journal of Economics*, 25.

Kommersant, 20 June 1995; 23 January 1996; 6 February 1996; 18 March 1997.

Kornai, J. (1980) *Economics of Shortage* (Amsterdam: North Holland).

Korze, U. and Simoneti, M. (1992) 'Privatization of the Tobacco Company Ljubljana', Central Europe Working Paper Series, 1, International Private Enterprise Development Research Center, Kenan Institute of Private Enterprise, University of North Carolina, Chapel Hill.

Kraljic, P. (1990) 'The Economic Gap Separating East and West', *Columbia Journal of World Business*, 25 (4), Winter.

Kubielas, S. (1994) 'The Attractiveness of Poland to Foreign Direct Investors: Trends and Factors in 1989–1993', Polish Policy Research Group, Discussion Paper 28, Warsaw University.

Kubielas, S. (1996) 'Technology Transfer through FDI and Structural Adjustment of the Polish Economy', Department of Economics, University of Warsaw.

Kuus, T. (1997) 'Estonia and EMU Prospects', *Review of Economies in Transition* (Bank of Finland), 7.

Kuznetsov, Andrei (1995) 'The Role of Free Economic Zones in Promoting Foreign Direct Investment in Russia', in Roberto Schiattarella (ed.) *New Challenges for European and International Business*, EIBA Conference, Urbino, vol. 2.

Lall, S. (1991) 'Direct Investment in South-East Asia by the NIEs: Trends and Prospects', *Banca Nazionale del Lavorno Quarterly Review*, 179.

Lall, S. (1993) *Transnational Corporations and Economic Development*, UN Library on Transnational Corporations (London and New York: Routledge).

Lall, S. (1994) 'Industrial Adaptation and Technological Capabilities in Developing Countries', in T. Killick (ed.) *The Nature, Significance and Determinants of Flexibility in National Economies* (London: Routledge).

Lall, S. and Streeten, P. (1977) *Foreign Investment, Transnationals and Developing Countries* (London: Macmillan).

Lane, S.J. (1994) 'The Pattern of Foreign Direct Investment and Joint Ventures in Hungary', *Communist Economies and Economic Transformation*, 6 (3).

Lankes, H. and Venables, A. (1996) 'Foreign Direct Investment in Economic Transition: The Changing Pattern of Investments', *Economics in Transition*, 4.

Lansbury, M., Pain, N. and Smidkova, K. (1996) 'Foreign Direct Investment in Central Europe Since 1990: An Econometric Study', *National Institute Economic Review*, 156 (May).

Lawrence, R.Z. (1992) 'Japan's Low Levels of Inward Investment: the Role of Inhibitions on Acquisitions', *Transnational Corporations*, 1 (3), December.

Lee, C. and Beamish, P. (1995) 'The Characteristics and Performance of Korean Joint-Ventures in LDCs', *Journal of International Business Studies*, 26.

Lee, C.H. (1980) 'United States and Japanese Direct Investment in Korea: A Comparative Study', *Hitotsubashi Journal of Economics*, 20.

Lee, C.H. (1983) 'International Production of the United States and Japan in Korean Manufacturing Industries: A Comparative Study', *Weltwirtschaftliches Archiv*, 119.

Lee, C.H. (1990) 'Direct Foreign Investment, Structural Adjustment, and International Division of Labour: A "Dynamic Macroeconomic Theory of Direct Foreign Investment"', *Hitotsubashi Journal of Economics*, 31 (2).

Lii, S-Y. (1994) 'Japanese Direct Foreign Investment and Trade Flows in the Asia Pacific Region', *Asian Economic Journal*, 8.

Lipsey, R. and Zimmy, Z. (1994) 'The Impact of Transnational Service Corporations on Developing Countries: Competition, Market Structure and the Provision of Unique Services', in K. Sauvant and P. Mallampally (eds) *Transnational Corporations in Services* (London: Routledge).

Liuhto, K. (1995) 'Foreign Investment in Estonia: A Statistical Approach', *Europe-Asia Studies*, 47 (3), May.

Liuhto, K. (1996) 'Estonian Enterprise Managers' Opinions on the Impact of the European Union on Estonia', Turku School of Economics and Business Administration, Institute of East-West Trade, Discussion Paper Series C, 2/96.

Lustsik, O. (1997) 'The Anatomy of the Tallinn Stock Exchange', *Review of Economies in Transition*, 7.

Markusen, J.R. (1991) 'The Theory of Multinational Enterprise: A Common Analytical Framework', in E.D. Ramstetter (ed.) *Direct Foreign Investment in Asia's Developing Economies and Structural Change in the Asia-Pacific Region* (Boulder, CO: Westview).

Marshall, A. (1920) *Principles of Economics* (London: Macmillan).

Marton, K. (1993) 'Foreign Direct Investment in Hungary', *Transnational Corporations*, 2 (1), February.

McMillan, C.H. (1993) 'The Role of Foreign Direct Investment in the Transition from Planned to Market Economies', *Transnational Corporations*, 2.

McMillan, C.H. (1994) 'Learning From Experience with Economic Reform', Annual Meeting of the Association for Comparative Economics and American Economic Association, Boston, January.

Meyer, K.E. (1994) 'Economic Analysis of Direct Foreign Investment: A Review of the Literature', London Business School, mimeo, July.

Meyer, K.E. (1995a) 'Foreign Direct Investment in the Early Years in Economic Transition, A Survey', *Economics of Transition*, 3.

Meyer, K.E. (1995b) 'Business Operations of British and German Companies with the Economies in Transition: First Results of a Questionnaire Survey', Discussion Paper 19, CIS-Middle Europe Centre, London Business School, July.

Miller, R. (1993) 'Determinants of US Manufacturing Abroad', *Finance and Development*, March.

Ministry of Foreign Affairs (1991) *Hungary: Democracy Reborn* (Budapest).

Moskovskiye Novosti, 25 June 1995; 2 July 1995.

Murrel, P. (1992) Clague, C. and Rausser, G.C. (eds) *The Emergence of Market Economies in Eastern Europe* (Oxford: Blackwell).

Naisbitt, J. (1994) *Global Paradox* (New York: William Morrow).

Nuti, M. (1994) 'The Impact of Systemic Transformation on the European Community', in S. Martin (ed.) *The Construction of Europe: A Festschrift in Honour of Emile Noel* (Kluwer Academic: Dordrecht).

Obsor Ekonomiki Rossii (1994) *Osnovniye Tendentsii Razvitiya*, Moscow, no. 2.

OECD (Organization for Economic Cooperation and Development) (1989) *International Investment and Multinational Enterprises – Investment Incentives and Disincentives: Effects on International Direct Investment* (Paris).

OECD (1992) *Foreign Direct Investment in Central and Eastern Europe: Policies and Trends in Fourteen Economies in Transition* (Paris).

OECD (1995) *Assessing Investment Opportunities in Economies in Transition*, study prepared by Arthur Anderson (Paris).

OECD *Globalization and Regionalization: The Challenge for Developing Countries* (Paris).

Okimoto, D.I. and Rohlen, T.P. (1988) *Inside the Japanese System: Readings on Contemporary Society and Political Economy* (Stanford University Press).

Oman, C. (1994) *Globalization and Regionalization: The Challenge for Developing Countries* (Paris: OECD Development Center).

Ozawa, T. (1979a) *Multinationalism Japanese Style* (Princeton, NJ).

Ozawa, T. (1979b) 'International Investment and Industrial Structure: New Theoretical Implications from the Japanese Experience', *Oxford Economic Papers*, 31.

Ozawa, T. (1992a) 'Japanese MNCs as Potential Partners in Eastern Europe's Economic Reconstruction', Working Paper 2/92, Institute of International Economics and Management, Copenhagen.

Ozawa, T. (1992b) 'Foreign Direct Investment and Economic Development', *Transnational Corporations*, 1, February.

Ozawa, T. (2000) 'The Russian Far East: The Role of Japan', in P. Artisien-Maksimenko (ed.) *Multinationals in Eastern Europe* (London: Macmillan).

Pangestu, M. (1987) 'The Pattern of Direct Foreign Investment in ASEAN', *ASEAN Economic Bulletin*, 3.

Panic, M. (1988) *National Management of the International Economy* (London: Macmillan).

Pantelidis, P. and Kyrklisis, D. (1993) *A Model for Foreign Direct Investment Effects on Eastern European Trade*, EADI General Conference, Berlin, 15–18 September.

Peng, M.K. (1993) 'Blurring Boundaries: The Growth of the Firm in Planned Economies in Transition', paper presented to the Academy of International Business.

Perez, C. (1983) 'Structural Change and Assimilation of New Technologies in the Economic and Social Systems', *Futures*, 15 October.

Perez, C. and Freeman, C. (1998) 'Structural Crises of Adjustment, Business Cycles and Investment Behaviour', in G. Dosi, C. Freeman, R. Nelson, G. Silverberg and L. Soete (eds) *Technical Change and Economic Theory* (London: Pinter).

Peteraf, M. (1993) 'The Cornerstones of Competitive Advantage: A Resource Based View', *Strategic Management Journal*, 14.

Piore, M.J. and Sabel, S.F. (1984) *The Second Industrial Divide* (New York: Basic Books).

Pitelis, C. and Sugden, R. (1991) *The Nature of the Transnational Firm* (London and Boston: Routledge).

Porter, M. (1990) *The Competitive Advantage of Nations* (New York: Free Press).

Portes, R. (1994) 'Transformation Traps', *Economic Journal*, 104.

Powell, W. (1990) 'Neither Market Nor Hierarchy', in B.M. Straw and L.M. Cummings (eds) *Research in Organizational Behaviour* (Greenwich, CN: JAI Press).

Primo-Braga, C.A. and Bannister, G. (1994) 'East Asian Investment and Trade: Prospects for Growing Regionalization in the 1990's', *Transnational Corporations*, 3.

Purja, A. (1994) 'Privatization with Vouchers in Estonia', Stockholm Institute of East European Economics, mimeo.

Ramstetter, E.D. (ed.) (1991) *Direct Foreign Investment in Asia's Developing Economies and Structural Change in the Asia-Pacific Region* (Boulder, CO: Westview).

Ribnikar, I. (1993) 'Tuje direktne nalozbe pri nas', *Bancni Vestnik*, 42 (1).

Riedel, J. (1991) 'Intra-Asian Trade and Foreign Direct Investment', *Asian Development Review*, 9.

Rojec, M. (1993) 'Foreign Direct Investment and Development of Slovenia', PhD thesis, Economics Faculty, Ljubljana.

Rojec, M. (1995) *Foreign Direct Investment and Privatization in Central and Eastern Europe* (Ljubljana: ACE Project).

Rojec, M. (2000) 'Slovenia', in P. Artisien-Maksimenko (ed.) *Multinationals in Eastern Europe* (London: Macmillan).

Rojec, M. and Jermakowicz, W.W. (1995) 'Management versus State in Foreign Privatizations in Central European Countries in Transition', in R. Schiattarella (ed.) *New Challenges for European and International Business*, EIBA conference, Urbino, vol. 1.

Rugman, A.M. (1979) *International Diversification and the Multinational Enterprise* (Lexington, MA: Lexington Books).

Rugman, A.M. and Verbeke, A. (1990) 'Corporate Strategy After the Free Trade Agreement and Europe 1992', Ontario Center for International Business Working Paper 27, Toronto.

Sader, F. (1993) *Privatization and Foreign Investment in the Developing World, 1988–92*, WPS 1202, International Economics Department, World Bank, Washington, October.

Safadi, R. and Yeats, A. (1994) 'The Escalation of Asian Trade Barriers', *Asian Economic Journal*, 8.

Schmidt, K. (1996) 'Foreign Direct Investment in Eastern Europe: State of the Art and Prospects', in R. Dobrinsky and M. Landesmann (eds) *Transforming Economies and European Integration* (Aldershot: Edward Elgar).

Schroath, F.W., Hu, M.Y. and Chen, H. (1993) 'Country-of-Origin Effects of Foreign Investments in the People's Republic of China', *Journal of International Business Studies*, 2.

Scott, A.J. (1993) *Technopolis: High Technology Industry and Regional Development in Southern California* (Berkeley and Los Angeles: University of California Press).

Sekiguchi, S. and Krause, L.B. (1980) 'Direct Foreign Investment in ASEAN by Japan and the United States', in R. Garnaut (ed.) *ASEAN in a Changing Pacific and World Economy* (Canberra).

Senjur, M. (1992) 'Viability of Economic Development of Small States Separating From Larger Ones', *Development and International Cooperation*, 8 June/December.

Senjur, M. (1993) 'Transition as a Problem for Development Theory and Policy', *Development and International Cooperation*, 9 June.

Sepp, U. (1995a) 'A Note on Inflation under the Estonia Currency Board', *Review of Economies in Transition*, 95 (5).

Slider, D. (1994) 'Privatization in Russia's Regions', *Post-Soviet Affairs* 4, October–December.

Smith, N. and Rebne, D. (1992) 'Foreign Direct Investment in Poland, The Czech and Slovak Republics and Hungary: The Centrality of the Joint Venture Entry Mode', *Mid-Atlantic Journal of Business*, 28 (3), December.

Sommer, A. and Choroszucha, L. (1993) 'Poland's Top-Down Privatization Programme', *Central European*, October.

Stankiewicz, T. and Jermakowicz, W. (1991) *The Management Contract (the So-Called Business Contract) As Used in the Restructuring Program for Treasury-Owned Joint Stock Companies* (Warsaw: Ministry of Privatization).

Statisticheskii Byulleten (21 June 1995).

Stern, R. (1996) 'Putting Foreign Direct Investment in Eastern Europe into Perspective: Turning a Macroeconomic Failure into a Microeconomic Success Story', in R. Dobrinsky and M. Landesmann (eds) *Transforming Economies and European Integration* (Aldershot: Edward Elgar).

Stiglitz, J. (1989) *The Economic Role of the State* (Oxford: Basil Blackwell).

Supplement to The World Bank Economic Review and the World Bank Research Observer (1991) Proceedings of the World Bank Annual Conference on Development Economics.

Svetličič, M. (1992) *Competitive Position of Slovenia in Attracting FDI* (Ljubljana: Center for International Relations).

Sydow, J. (1992) 'Enterprise Networks and Codetermination: The Case of the Federal Republic of Germany', in ILO (ed.) *Is the Single Firm Vanishing? Inter-Enterprise Networks, Labor and Labor Institutions* (Geneva: ILO).

Szabo, K. (1992) 'Direct Sale and Joint Ventures as a Technique of Privatization', Central and Eastern European Privatization Network Workshop, Budapest.

Szabo, T. (1993) 'The Past Three Years and the Preliminaries of Privatization', *Hungary's Privatization*, 2 (16).

Takeuchi, K. (1990) *Does Japanese DFI Promote Japanese Imports from Developing Countries?* World Bank Working Paper 458.

Taylor, F.W. (1967) *The Principles of Scientific Management* (New York: Norton).

Teece, D.J. (1992) 'Foreign Investment and Technological Development in Silicon Valley', *California Management Review*, Winter.

Teece, D.J. (1994) 'Design Issues for Innovative Firms, Bureaucracy, Incentives and Industrial Structure', Prince Bertil Symposium on The Dynamic Firm: The Role of Regions, Technology, Strategy and Organization, Stockholm, June.

UN (United Nations) (1992) *World Investment Report 1992* (New York: Transnational Corporations and Management Division).

UN (United Nations) (1993) *World Investment Report 1993* (New York and Geneva: UNCTAD).

UN (United Nations) (1994) *World Investment Report: Transnational Corporations, Employment and the Workforce* (New York: United Nations).

UNCTAD (United Nations Conference on Trade and Development) (1994) *World Investment Report: Transnational Corporations, Employment and the Workplace* (Geneva and New York).

UNCTAD (1996) *World Investment Report 1996* (Geneva and New York).

UNECE (United Nations Economic Commission for Europe) (1992) *Economic Survey of Europe in 1991–1992* (New York: UN).

UNECE (1993a) *Statistical Survey of Recent Trends in Foreign Investment in East European Countries*, Trade/R.611, Geneva.

UNECE (1993b) 'Role of Foreign Direct Investment in a Small Country in Transition', Ljubljana, 29–30 November, mimeo.

UNECE (1994) *East-West Investment News*, 1, Spring.

UNECE (1997) *Economic Survey of Europe in 1996–1997* (Geneva and New York).

UNIDO (United Nations Industrial Development Organization) (1991) *Industrial Restructuring in Central and Eastern Europe: Critical Areas of International Cooperation*, September.

UNIDO (1992) *Foreign Direct Investment in Central and Eastern European Countries* (Vienna), June.

Urban, W. (1992) 'Economic Lessons for the East European Countries from Two Newly Industrializing Countries in the Far East?' *Forschungsberichte* 182, Vienna Institute for Comparative Economic Studies, April.

Van Tulder, R. and Junne, G. (1988) *European Multinationals in Core Technologies* (Chichester: John Wiley/IRM).

Wallis, J.J. and North, D.C. (1986) 'Measuring the Transaction Sector in the American Economy 1870–1970', in S.L. Engerman and R.E. Gallman (eds) *Long Term Factors in American Economic Growth* (Chicago: University of Chicago Press).

Walters, A. and Hanke, S. (1992) 'Currency Boards', in *The New Palgrave: A Dictionary of Money and Finance* (London: Macmillan).

Wang, Z. and Swain, N. (1995) 'The Determinants of Foreign Direct Investment in Transforming Economies: Empirical Evidence from Hungary and China', *Weltwirtschaftliches Archiv*, 131 (2).

Welch, B.J. (1993) 'Investing in Eastern Europe: Perspectives of Chief Financial Officers', *International Executive*, 35 (1), January/February.

Wells, L.T., Jr (1993) 'Mobile Exporters: New Foreign Investors in East Asia', in K.A. Froot (ed.) *Foreign Direct Investment Today*, National Bureau for Economic Research (Chicago: University of Chicago Press).

Wendt, H. (1993) *Global Embrace* (New York: Harper Business).

Whitmore, K., Lall, S. and Hyun, J-T. (1989) 'Foreign Direct Investment from the Newly Industrialized Economies', World Bank, Industry and Energy Department Working Paper, Industry Series Paper 22.

Willer, D. (1997) 'Corporate Governance and Shareholder Rights in Russia', *Emerging Markets*, CEP Discussion Paper 343 (April).

Williamson, O.E. (1981) 'The Modern Corporation: Origins, Evolution, Attributes', *Journal of Economic Literature*, 19.

Wilms, W.W. and Zell, D.M. (1994) *Reinventing Organizational Culture Across National Boundaries* (Pittsburgh, PA: Carnegie Bosch Institute), January.

World Bank (1994) *World Development Report 1994* (Washington: Oxford University Press).

Zemplinerova, A. (1995) 'Evolution and Efficiency of Concentration', in J. Svejnar (ed.) *Manufacturing in the Czech Republic and Economic Transition in Eastern Europe*, Academic Press.

Zemplinerova, A. and Benacek, V. (1995) 'Foreign Direct Investment – East and West: The Experience of The Czech Republic', ACE Workshop, Prague, 6–8 April.

Zemplinerova, A., Lastovicka, R. and Marcincin, A. (1995) 'The Restructuring of Czech Manufacturing Enterprises: An Empirical Study', CERGE-EI Working Paper 74, Prague.

Index